SECRETS OF THE SUPER SEARCHERS

Basch, Reva.

SECRETS OF THE SUPER SEARCHERS.

Reva Basch

EIGHT BIT BOOKS
Wilton, CT
1993

July, 1994
Second Printing

To Jerry Shifman, the most tolerant and resilient person in the universe, a wise and funny man, a passable cook (despite his constant, futile lobbying for an earlier dinner hour), and my life partner—for continuing to demonstrate both unflagging faith and unconditional love during the time when I needed it most.

CONTENTS

ACKNOWLEDGMENTS

I want to thank everyone I interviewed for the time you spent with me and for the insights you so generously shared. You provided me with wonderful material, an embarrassment of riches. This is *your* book.

I also want to acknowledge the hundreds of unsung super searchers whom I didn't include in this project. I know you're out there, and I hope you feel that your own wisdom is adequately reflected in these pages.

My special thanks to the following:

• Jeff Pemberton, my publisher, and Nancy Garman, my editor, for their enthusiasm, their encouragement and, as it turned out, their remarkable patience.

• Kathleen Creighton, transcriptionist extraordinaire, not only for the online-lingo-literacy she brought to this job, but for her wry, bracketed asides that often made my editing day.

• Karen McLellan, MFCC, who shares my belief that Miss Manners *does* have all the answers, for helping restore my perspective and reorder my priorities.

• The members of the Association of Independent Information Professionals who frequent Section 0 on the CompuServe Working from Home Forum. A couple of you—you know who you are—went above and beyond in your personal and professional support.

• Finally, the extraordinary online community of The WELL—without whom this book would have been finished either a lot sooner or not at all. I especially want to thank the women of WOW, the members of the Writers Conference, and a small group of dear friends who inhabit one quiet, green and leafy cyberhood. You, in particular, did your best to keep me focused and motivated, and when that failed, gloriously entertained. It goes to show you don't ever know...

Reva Basch
Berkeley, CA
September 1993

dictate which mode we invoke. Experienced searchers may lean more heavily toward one method or the other, but they know when it's appropriate to switch or to modify their primary style, or when to combine the two.

• **Super searchers recognize that offline preparation saves online dollars.** They map out at least their opening gambit, their initial search statement or two, *before* logging on. They look up product codes and keywords. They jot down field tags and make notes about any peculiar database features or anomalies that might play into the search. They spend most of their online time inputting information and waiting for the computer to echo back their results. If they really need to *think*, they log off using a placeholder command, or change to a housekeeping database where the meter isn't running at an horrendous rate, and collect their thoughts.

• **Some disciplines, especially in science and technology, rely more heavily than others on highly indexed databases.** Although super searchers take advantage of these codes and keywords, they're aware that indexers are only human, that terms may have been inappropriately assigned and may mask relevant references rather than highlight them. It's rare to find a single, perfect, uniformly-applied keyword that will retrieve every article germane to a subject. A savvy searcher may start by looking up keywords in a print thesaurus. But often the next step is to add some free-text vocabulary, which turns up new records that suggest some additional indexing terms, add *those* terms to their search strategy, and retrieve still more information.

• There's a reason why so many former English majors have become online searchers. **It helps to have an extensive vocabulary.** Especially in free-text and full-text searching, you can never have too many synonyms, antonyms, alternate word-endings, or related concepts. Most searchers are interested in language and how it's used. They're aware of industry jargon, specialized terms, and ambiguous and multiple meanings.

• **Despite the proliferation of full-text sources online, many searchers still approach full text with caution.** They may start with a bibliographic database, not just because of its superior indexing, but because there are fewer searchable words per database record, which means more control over vocabulary and a greater chance of relevant retrieval. Some plunge right into full-text searching, but others will go that route only if the bibliographic search doesn't yield good results, or for selective document retrieval.

• **The standard recommended techniques for searching full-text files, though helpful, are imperfect.** Using proximity operators instead of AND, starting with unique search terms rather than common ones, restricting terms to the lead paragraph, and so on doesn't always work. Even super searchers end up browsing titles and keywords in context, judging relevance on an item-by-item basis (or having their clients do so), then printing records selectively. It's not elegant, and it's often tedious, but it's better to screen in advance than to download, sight unseen, hundreds of full-text records, many of which are probably off-target.

• **"Browse before buying" is good advice, even in bibliographic databases.** It's seldom prudent, especially when ordering offline prints, to close your eyes and push the "print" key. You may have mistyped a product code, failed to eliminate a major source of false drops, or inadvertently applied your print command to the wrong answer set or in the wrong database. Always look at a representative sample in a free or low-cost format, before committing to printing or downloading a lot of records.

• **Multifile searching and duplicate removal are powerful features, and super-searchers use them judiciously.** They know that applying a single search strategy to a collection of

TRENDS AND THEMES

Collectively, these two dozen searchers (for convenience, I'll count myself among them) stressed several important themes:

• Although they might have degrees in library science, and/or formal training in online information retrieval, **most didn't become truly proficient searchers until they had some on-the-job experience.** Nothing hones one's skills like accountability—knowing that one's professional credibility, and perhaps departmental budget, are on the line.

• **Veteran searchers don't believe that online is the One True Path.** To the contrary, one of the hallmarks of a super searcher is knowing when *not* to go online. Many questions can be answered far more easily and cheaply by checking a printed reference source or picking up the telephone.

• **When it comes to selecting online services, everyone plays favorites.** Most searchers have a "home" system, usually the one they learned first. They tend to prefer that one wherever it's appropriate, even if a cheaper alternative exists, because they know they can search more cost-effectively on a system they're comfortable with. They migrate to competing services for two reasons: (1) Content: They'll use a system they detest, or consider overpriced, if it's the only source for a certain publication or type of information; (2) Features and Functionality: Does one system allow them to do something that they need to do and that they can't do on other systems? Economic considerations figure in as well, but pricing is generally a background factor, not a major decision point.

• **Some searches are generic, but the more interesting ones tend to be iterative, modular and dynamic.** The pros approach these searches in stages, perhaps from various directions, adding and subtracting individual components along the way. Since experienced searchers try to avoid dumping hundreds of questionable citations on a client, the requester is usually an integral part of this process. Especially when working in unfamiliar territory, searchers present the surest results first, suggest possible next steps, and modify their strategy based on the feedback they get. Often, the result of a complex search is not a single answer set, but several groups of database records arrayed along a gradient of relevance, or encompassing different aspects of the subject. Sometimes, the answer is the sum of those individual sets; sometimes, it's not an answer *per se*, but a pointer to where the answer, or answers, might be found.

• **Real searchers don't over-qualify at the outset.** Databases are too unpredictable in both structure and content to yield the perfect response upon presentation of a single, exquisitely-crafted search statement. Some searchers prefer to cast their nets broadly at first, then draw in. Others like to see how close they can get on the first pass, knowing that they might have to loosen up and try again, once, twice or three times more. Veteran searchers are always prepared for surprises; they have alternative terms and strategies in mind. They multitask, they maintain a "what if" mindset, and they "go with the flow." Online searching is inherently interactive; if it weren't, we might as well be back in the batch-processing era, the Stone Age of electronic information retrieval.

• **Barbara Quint's "ant" versus "grasshopper" metaphor has caught on as a useful bit of shorthand for two different approaches to online searching, the meticulous versus the intuitive.** Although it's convenient to typecast searchers by style, the truth is that the nature of the search itself, and the circumstances surrounding the request, often trunk, while to another, it's all tail, or ears, or tusk. For that reason, I attempted to select as representative a group of informants as I could. The 23 men and women I interviewed work in corporate information centers, government agencies, law firms, public libraries, academia, or as proprietors of their own independent research companies. Most are professional searchers, although a couple represent that elusive species, informed end-users. Some are generalists, willing to tackle projects in almost any subject field, while others have carved out niches in areas like business and finance, journalism, law, the humanities, telecommunications, patents, chemistry and medicine. I tried for an international perspective as well, insofar as language and logistical considerations allowed, talking with searchers in the United States, Canada and the United Kingdom.

I started each interview with a few basic questions about the searcher's background, training and experience. Then, as the situation warranted, I asked each of them to tell me how they dealt with clients, kept track of research projects, formulated their search strategies and tactics, and delivered the results. Each interview lasted for an hour or more, and ended with an invitation to muse, in an unstructured way, on what I called the "zen" of online searching. What does it feel like to be fully engaged in the search process? What makes a good search and a good searcher?

Several years ago, I said that writing about online information retrieval was like trying to change a tire on a moving car. That's even more true now, given the tremendous acceleration in both technological change and corporate restructuring that the information industry has undergone in the last year or two. These interviews were conducted in mid-to-late 1992, and reflect the sources, systems, features and functionality that were in place at that time. In the course of editing, I found that some statements had been superseded, or might be modified, in light of subsequent developments. DIALOG had not yet introduced its RANK command, for instance, and NEXIS had not unveiled its streamlined method for searching multiple occurrences of a term within a document. VU/TEXT was still a free-standing online service; Data-Star and DIALOG were competitors, not sister companies. By the time this appears, there will undoubtedly have been more such changes; that's the nature of the information business. Rather than pepper the text with editorial addenda, I decided to emphasize the universals, the principles that apply across files and online services. Since the book focuses on the essence of the search process itself, my hope is that its worth won't be materially affected by the ongoing evolution in system features, database structure and content.

Within the loose framework of questions and answers, I encouraged all the interviewees to talk about what was important to them. They, not I, determined the form and direction of our conversation. All of them gave me much more valuable material than I could possibly use. In most cases, I had to boil down the raw transcripts to less than half their original length, and that meant cutting not only what was clearly extraneous (or delicious but unpublishable), but also some interesting diversions and background explanations. As I went on, the act of editing became a delicate three-way balance among avoiding repetition, reiterating key points that others had made from their own perspectives, and emphasizing unique and important information.

In the course of doing and reviewing these interviews, I discovered that everyone *was*, in fact, looking at the same elephant. True, an intellectual property specialist has a different perspective on the critter than does a high school librarian; likewise, certain components loom larger for a journalist than for a business searcher. But there seems to be fundamental agreement on the nature of the beast.

SECRETS OF THE SUPER SEARCHERS:

AN INTRODUCTION

The word "intermediary," as it's used by information professionals, has always struck me as unduly self-deprecating. It implies a passivity, an "I am merely the vessel" mentality that has never been part of my online searching experience, or that of most of my colleagues. Searching does involve, perhaps, an element of channeling. But if so, it's a robust and interactive kind of channeling in which the medium talks back to the ghost in the machine. ("Channeling?" I can hear some of my colleagues say, "It's more like pro wrestling!")

The point is that good online searchers are more than just bridges or brokers. They're also more than gatekeepers, another widely-used and equally inaccurate metaphor. They do know how to gain access to the treasure vault, but nobody's handed them a set of keys on a heavy iron ring. They have to pick the lock whenever they want to get in, and the tumblers turn differently every time.

What bothers me most about the gatekeeper image is its aura of exclusivity and exclusion: "We're members of the Priesthood of the Sacred Modem, and you're not." In truth, people who love to search are anything but proprietary about their hard-earned knowledge. They'll talk your ear off; just ask. That's what I did, and that's what *they* did. As these interviews illustrate, the experts are eager to share their wisdom. If there *is* a mystique, a veil of mystery, surrounding their abilities, they didn't create it, and they don't want to perpetuate it, either. Searchers are like model railroad enthusiasts dragging you down to their basements to show off their new layouts, or Deadheads making copies for you of their favorite tapes. They want to turn you on.

I conceived this book as a series of personal insights into the realities of online searching. It's not intended as a textbook or a "how to" guide, but as a collection of informal case studies, portraits of working searchers *in situ*. The accumulated wisdom of these experts and their individual hints about effective searching and search management should interest both experienced and aspiring online searchers. Information professionals who have mastered the mechanics of searching can learn how the experts—or *other* experts—conceive, build and execute a competent, even inspired, online search.

I've also tried to convey enough of the "gestalt" of searching—what it feels like to go online—to satisfy the casually curious, the readers who may have read about "info-surfing" in computer magazines, business journals or the general press. These interviews should either whet their appetites or douse their aspirations with a big wave of ice-cold reality. Yes, there *is* a world of information available online, and it is, in a manner of speaking, literally at your fingertips. But there's quite a bit more to it than that. Online searching may not be rocket science, but it does take a little more knowledge and intellectual effort than bungee jumping. Sometimes, come to think of it, it feels like a combination of the two.

THE INTERVIEW PROCESS: FINDING THE ELEPHANT

Going into this project, I anticipated finding an electronic version of the parable of the Blind Men and the Elephant—discovering that, to one person, online searching is all dissimilar file types can produce unexpected, misleading, or just plain useless results. They reserve mega-global searching for needle-in-the-haystack projects, or for the times they find themselves on foreign soil, subject-wise, and really don't know where to begin.

• **Seasoned searchers are cost-conscious as well as cost-effective.** Even when they don't have a per-search budget to adhere to, they maintain a sense of scale about the level of effort that's appropriate to each project. They've developed a feeling for when to pull out all the stops, and when a "quick-and-dirty" search will do. If in doubt, they know to ask the client if he wants to leave no stone unturned, or whether a couple of key articles will do.

• **Cost estimating is an art.** It can never be entirely quantified. You can't tell until you go online how much there's going to be or how long it will take you to find it. As long as connect-time-based pricing remains the dominant model, an experienced searcher will quote a range or a not-to-exceed figure, or suggest a phased "Let's see what's out there" approach.

• **A useful tactic for search planning and estimating is to ask the client how much he expects to find.** If he says "very little" and thousands of references turn up, he may have neglected to supply a crucial qualifier. If he anticipates a lot of information and little or nothing appears, there's obviously something else going on. Stay in touch with the client; don't presume that he is wrong or that you are infallible.

• **Only rarely do experienced searchers take "no results" for an answer.** Zero hits, or very few, might mean that they or the requester have misspelled a search term, that they've searched the wrong databases, used too restrictive a connector or qualifier, or made some other faulty assumption about how, where and when the concept should appear. Especially in a research environment, recent work may not show up in a bibliographic database for several months. Never be 100 percent confident about negative results; always explain what you did, and be open to exploring new approaches. Of course, slim pickings is sometimes just what the client is hoping for. It may mean a green light for patentability, a dissertation topic or a journalistic scoop.

The opposite situation, a search that retrieves too much information, can be handled in several ways. There are logical limiters like language, date and country of publication. Adding an indexing term or code to a free-text search usually helps refine results. But it may just be that there *is* a lot of material on the subject, no matter how you slice it. It's better to discuss "next steps" with the client before imposing arbitrary and perhaps inappropriate qualifiers.

• **Most searches are "finished" when you reach a point of diminishing returns, not when you're out of money or have found the perfect answer.** You start to see the same citations, or information based on the same citations, over and over again. Experienced searchers have "dead horse" sense; they know when to call it quits. At the same time, they have to fight the temptation to get carried away by the excitement of the game itself and the urge to track down every last reference. Most customers are happy knowing that they've probably gotten 80 percent of what's available, especially if tracking down the remaining 20 percent would blow away their budgets. Often, all they want to see are the proverbial "few good articles."

• **Everyone post-processes.** Now searchers have the ability to turn online output into presentation-quality documents, and they take advantage of it, even though it's more time-consuming than the old "rip and ship" approach. Post-processing can range from simply deleting irrelevant references and inserting page breaks, to stripping unneeded codes and bolding key portions of records, to downloading into a spreadsheet, to preparing bound, analytical reports based on the information retrieved online.

CHAPTER 1

SUSANNE BJØRNER: SEARCHING AS A PARTNERSHIP

Susanne Bjørner is principal and senior information specialist with Bjørner & Associates in Woodbury, Connecticut. She writes the OUTPUT OPTIONS column for *ONLINE* magazine, and is the compiler and editor of *Newspapers Online*, a guide to full-text newspapers published by BiblioData.

Did you learn to search in library school, or was it strictly on-the-job?

When I was going to library school, we didn't have computers. We certainly didn't have online searching. For the most part, I spent my library career in very small libraries, at small institutions, with a staff of one person, or at most two or three. To a great extent, the online searching revolution of the 1970s literally passed me by. It wasn't until 1980, when I took a job in a start-up library serving people throughout the state of Massachusetts, that I started to use microcomputers. It was either that or type catalog cards.

I found out about searching in the course of figuring out how to load the ERIC database tape on our minicomputer, a PDP-11. We wanted to be able to do ERIC searches for educators all over the state. In the midst of that process, sometime in March or April of 1981, one of our users told us about this thing called a modem. We started to investigate online services, and I discovered BRS. It was the first system I learned, in order to make ERIC available to my primary user group. As it turned out, of course, BRS had a lot of other databases that were attractive to educators as well.

I spent about another year in that job. That's where I was first exposed to online searching, and where I learned how to do it. Generally, the people I did searches for were geographically dispersed. They usually relayed requests by phone, and they often didn't realize that we had this new capability. So they weren't asking for searches, they were asking for *information*. Sometimes I told them I was going to do an online search, and sometimes I didn't.

From that library, I went on to a job as an automation consultant for the Massachusetts state library agency. At that point, I became more involved in promoting the *use* of online searching rather than actually *doing* online searching. I had to be a very strong advocate, because the main goal of the organization at that time was the implementation of automated resource-sharing systems. This essentially meant putting library catalogs on computers. I wanted to make sure that people could dial *outside* the library to reach other resources, as well as from my work is writing and teaching about the online field in general. Besides, I don't have any particular expertise, subject-wise. I majored in philosophy and religion.

Part of the reason I've been able to make a go of it as a generalist is that I started in 1984, before there were as many people wanting to be information brokers. Those of us who were there early learned how to operate in that kind of broad-based environment. It's addictive to be able to research "everything," and it's hard to give that up.

What do you ask in your reference interview?

I tend not to ask anything at first. I try to just listen for awhile. I try to keep the client talking. There *are* a couple of things that I'm listening for, but I hope it comes from the client without my having to ask for it. I'm trying to find out how they're going to use the information. I'm trying to find out how far along they are in the project, what they've already done and where they've looked. I'm praying, all this time, that they're not expecting the project to go out right now, except for one key fact they need me to find. I hate it when they say, "We've looked everywhere and we've gotten everything we need on this. We're just missing this single bit of information we need you to find, and we need it tomorrow."

Suppose they say, for instance, "I've already searched DIALOG."

Then I ask them *what* they searched on DIALOG. You can usually tell whether they know what they're talking about, whether they can tell you what files and whether it makes sense to have searched those files. At this point, you sometimes have to do a little bit of education. The problem is that there's such a wide range of levels of understanding out there, not only in what they know, but in what they *want* to know.

Do you talk about the inherent limitations of the online process and the fact that databases don't always have everything even if they're supposed to be full text? Do you suggest that some information just isn't available online, or that there's always a chance you might miss something?

I tend to do that when an alarm bell goes off in my head that the client is expecting me to perform miracles. You begin to sense, after awhile, when they are expecting that. I do take care to stress the limitations when I'm doing patent searches in particular. Still, I do sometimes get a nagging feeling that a person really doesn't have an understanding of what's available and what the search process is about, and that bothers me.

The most important part of the reference interview, I think, is not to fall into that pattern of thinking, "Oh I've done this search before." You have to keep listening actively to what the client is telling you.

How do you negotiate a budget?

I try to ask people how much they expect to spend. I let them suggest a fee. You know, you can say, "We could do it for $500, or we could do it for $5,000. Which comes closer to what you were thinking of?" I figure that I can afford to put a quarter or a third of the total budget into online time, and the rest covers my labor and overhead and miscellaneous expenses.

Is there a formula for judging whether the overall budget is realistic? Can you say a typical search will take two hours of my time plus x dollars?

I seldom do a search that takes less than two hours of my time. When I do, it's for a new client who's very cautious and just wants a taste of what I can do for them, or it's a follow-up on something I've already done. A lot of time goes into the administrative part of dealing with the client, and you have to account for that. I don't literally start the meter running at the beginning of the reference interview, but I am aware of whether I spent 15 minutes, a half-hour or an hour, and that gets factored in. I do keep track of the post-processing time, which can be significant.

It sure can. It seems that now we're capable of making searches look pretty when they go out, we're all doing it. But it does take a lot more time. When we ordered hardcopy prints, we didn't have to worry about them until they came in. We had a couple of days to go ahead with other work, and when the prints came in, we'd just highlight the best ones, cross out the obvious false drops and send them off to the client.

I never got into the habit of ordering offline. At MIT, people came in thinking they were going to save a bundle if they ordered offline prints. That was during the period that rates were changing drastically. I had to tell them that there wasn't really that much difference. Not only that, since we were on the East Coast, it would take longer than a couple of days to get them.

I use DIALMAIL for print delivery now. It makes the most sense, especially since prices have been equalized. Instead of charging a higher rate for offline prints, and less for downloads, the cost is now the same for most files. Since it is the same, it's obvious that if you download prints in DIALMAIL the next morning at $24 an hour, it's cheaper than downloading 50 or 100 records in a file that costs $100 or $200 an hour. Of course, there are still some files where it doesn't make that much difference, like MEDLINE or ERIC.

Needless to say, there are some cases where you don't have the luxury of waiting until the next morning. I wish it were possible to always do searches as soon as I get them, so they're ready for downloading the next morning. I wish it were possible to predict that I'd have *time* the next morning to do the download and send the search out the door.

Let's move on to searching *per se*. What kinds of topics are you typically asked to search?

I've researched the status of women in the Philippines, non-traditional career choices, the color desktop scanner market, and all sorts of diseases. I've done a lot of occupational safety and liability issues—photocopy machines, cherry picker accidents, and that sort of thing. I do a lot of technology—engineering, computers and software. I am trying to focus a bit more on technical topics. I don't do financial searches, especially really important financial projects. I would never bill myself as a business searcher.

It's hard to remember what I've worked on. I have a poor memory for search topics. I used to think it was because I did so many, and it was all a blur. I've come to believe that it has to do with the process itself: Someone comes in. You do the search. You concentrate very heavily on it. They want to leave at the end of an hour and a half with the search in hand, or to have it in hand the next day, and usually they do. After you've done that three times in a row, you don't remember the first one, unless it was a particularly strange request or you had a problem with it.

I've had the same experience. Somebody asks me what I worked on today, and my mind is a complete blank. I was so focused "in the moment" for every one of those searches that I didn't consciously tally them.

I'm so glad to hear that. Not remembering what you worked on helps with the confidentiality problem, right?

It sure does. Now, I gather that you use DIALOG pretty heavily. What other systems do you use?

I use DIALOG 90 percent of the time, although I am using Data-Star more and more. I like it. It's so familiar; it feels like going home to me, because it's so much like BRS. I'm delighted now that it has such a good range of files.

Cost isn't much of a factor for me. It's certainly not reason enough to switch to a different system. I am more facile with DIALOG so I am going to save money using DIALOG, simply because I know it better. But if a file is on Data-Star, it'll be a Data-Star search. Right now, since I'm trying to move in that direction, it's going to be a Data-Star search if it can be done on Data-Star, and if I'm relaxed and unpressured enough to make sure that I'm doing everything right. If I'm busy and it has to get out the door, I search in a system that's rote to me.

I don't worry too much about specialized systems because I tend to search generalist topics for generalist people. I use DataTimes when I need one of the newspapers it carries. I've been known to actually go to the library and get a story on microfilm. It's cheaper, and if I can combine the trip with other work I have to do there anyway, why not? So much of the information that I'm looking for is product-related—I have to find advertisements, for instance—and I'm not going to find them online anyway.

I don't use very many systems, and I am acutely aware of that. But I'm already working with two different computer operating systems, the Mac and the PC, which is essential because of my OUTPUT OPTIONS column. So I've already doubled the complexity of everything I do. I had two jobs for awhile and commuted between two different cities. I speak two languages, English and Danish. One of those is primary, but I can handle the other. I don't think I could handle a third, at least not fluently. This is my own personal efficiency level. There's only so much I can keep in my head.

That's an interesting parallel. Does that apply to databases as well, or do you go further afield when it comes to file selection?

I definitely have favorites. I love ABI/INFORM, Predicasts and INSPEC.

Those are all very highly structured databases that have really good indexing, codes as well as controlled vocabulary terms—various ways of getting at things.

I don't always use those access points, though. You can miss things. Indexers are only human, and who can tell for sure how they may have classified something? I do tend to take advantage of indexing in the files I mentioned, and in MEDLINE, too. I also do a lot of patent searching, and I almost never use the patent classification system. If somebody has figured that a patent goes into this classification or that one, that's fine, but it's also a place to hide something. If you're doing a patentability search, it's much more effective to use free-text, natural language in all its possible ramifications, and then scan titles. Certainly it's safer. You scan thousands of titles sometimes, but most of the attorneys I deal with seem to feel that it's worth it, just to be sure. In fact, they worry if they *don't* get a lot of stuff to look at.

I find that I tend to wing it a lot more these days. I like to go in and see what codes, terms and so on are actually assigned to the records, instead of trying to anticipate everything beforehand by consulting printed search aids. I like to be able to react to what I find and to be interactive. You could say that I'm searching in a less-structured, but more alert, environment than I used to. I suppose that's largely a function of experience. I *hope* that's the reason.

What about the overall search strategy? Do you do any advance planning or make any notes on paper?

I don't plan everything out. I think about the first three or four "actions," and I write down some keywords. You can get lazy with DIALOGLINK because that's what you do there. You build your line-by-line search strategy, and it releases a line at a time. So you don't have to do it on paper.

What about date and language limits, basic things that you want to remember to do?

Date limits, yes, but I seldom limit by language. If the client requests it, I will, but I wouldn't normally think to limit by language first. That's definitely a function of my experience at MIT, where people would say, "I'll take anything in English or German or Japanese or Ukrainian..." Then I had to explain that it was going to take longer to limit by those languages than to just take everything, and run the slight risk of having to deal with citations in Romanian or Bulgarian, too.

You run much more risk of losing information when you limit by language. Often in technical areas, there's a lot of international research being done. In some fields, all the important work is being done overseas. It eventually shows up in English-language journals, but sometimes not for awhile.

But you do have to keep language in mind, as a parameter, whether you use it or not. It's amazing how much foreign-language stuff shows up in databases like PAIS, for instance. I often forget to limit there, and by the time I realize it, it's too late; I've already retrieved all that stuff.

How do you build a search? When do you know when you should start broad, versus being extremely focused right from the beginning?

I never put in all the possible qualifiers to begin with, or all the possible synonyms. I can tell pretty quickly that it is either a specific search or a broad search. Once I've figured that out, I know how to proceed. If it's really specific, I think constantly about synonyms and jargon; I focus on the exact object of the search. It's different if the purpose of the search is to learn about the literature of something, to learn *if* there's a technology, if it's been written about, or how *much* it's been written about. Then I don't overqualify until I see how much we're getting or if we're getting anything at all.

Often language itself is a problem, not just different national languages, but technical versus non-technical language. At MIT, there was always the factor of not knowing whether someone was using a technical term or not. Someone's experience of a term can be very well-defined, and very narrow, for them. It can mean something entirely different to someone else. My favorite example is when a client wanted a search on something to do with "stress." I couldn't figure out for the life of me what kind of stress we were talking about. Psychological stress? Stress loads on bridges? The requester couldn't help me; it was like, "There's only one kind of stress here."

Another favorite was when I was talking to someone and we really couldn't understand each other's national languages. I asked him to write down what he was looking for, and I couldn't read his writing. The labs at MIT are named in such a way that I couldn't even tell what discipline he was working in. Finally I asked, "When you're talking with someone outside your department, how do you describe what you *do*?" He looked at me and said, "I never talk with anyone outside my department."

I did the search, finally. That brings up an important point: Sometimes the best thing to do, instead of spending more time getting nowhere, is to sit down and try the search. If somebody's giving you a strategy that you know won't work, that you know will produce 25,000 hits, and they won't accept that, go on and do the search. Do it. Illustrate your point. Don't print everything out, for heaven's sake, but show them *why* it won't work. It's faster and cheaper in the long run, and it's definitely easier on your blood pressure.

That's one of the great uses of fax. You can say, "Wait a minute, let me fax you this and you'll see the problem." Then I fax the strategy, along with the number of hits for each of their keywords, and circle the offending number. In DIALOG, I just do DS for DISPLAY SETS, capture it to disk and print it out.

You've written the book, so to speak, on newspapers online. Let's talk a little bit about how you search full-text files like that with shallow-to-no indexing, or no useful indexing.

Positional operators are probably the most important thing to remember in this kind of searching. By that I mean "within" or "near" connectors that require that a word or a group of words appear within five or ten words, in the same paragraph, or in the same sentence as the corresponding group of words. A variation is using repetitive terminology, looking for "apple" within so many words of "apple" within so many words of "apple" again, to make sure that the article focuses on Apple Computer. Or, perhaps, the article is all about apples. The point is that the word isn't just mentioned once, in passing, or used in a figurative sense.

Techniques like that help, but you still have to be prepared to print a lot of titles, along with the biggest KWIC window you can, and judge each item individually. If you can't use KWIC, use Format 8 on DIALOG, or an equivalent format that shows the indexing along with the title.

You have to be prepared to laugh, too, because you're going to get some weird stuff. You always do with full text. It's not so funny, I guess, if you're paying for it. You do have to watch out. Some of the short formats that used to be free aren't, anymore. I like the way Data-Star lets you type "free" as the format name, to get whatever they're going to give you for no charge.

Do you do a lot of multifile searching and duplicate removal?

I do, and I like deduping on DIALOG. I think it works very well, although it's not perfect, of course. It doesn't work in the PAPERS file, unfortunately, because all newspapers don't give the same headline to a wire story or to a syndicated feature. Whenever you have a title that the database producer has augmented to make the meaning clearer, it screws up duplicate detection. However, I'd much rather have that augmented title, even though you risk picking it up multiple times. I don't worry too much about not deduping something that ought to be duped out. I worry more about losing something that I don't want to miss.

I never dedupe on a patent search. I tend to be cautious in the technical files, too. A conference paper may later become a journal article, or sometimes vice-versa. They often carry the same title, and one may be more complete, or the database record may be more complete, than the other. One is often a couple of years more current, too. If that turns out to be one of the duplicate records that's been removed, you never know there was something more recent in the literature than the reference you got.

Another thing to watch out for is multipart articles. If the part numbers don't make it into the title field, you're going to eliminate all but the first one in the series. Actually, you'll usually drop all but the last article, since most files are loaded in reverse chronological order. At least if you get Part 4, you can figure out that Parts 1, 2 and 3 exist.

As far as multifile searching is concerned, I usually determine file order by cost. I do a lot of searches in MEDLINE, EMBASE and BIOSIS, in that order. You can also think about whether you're going to get abstracts or whose abstracts you prefer. When you try to combine two of those factors—say cost and quality of an abstract—that gets to be a hard decision for me.

I used to dedupe routinely in PsycINFO and Sociological Abstracts, but I had an interesting revelation, thanks to a client who took an interest in the process. It was a search in the area of organizational behavior and corporate culture, and it really was cross-disciplinary. I told him that I was planning to search both files and remove duplicates. He pointed out that sociologists look at the subject from a totally different perspective than psychologists. He wanted both sets of abstracts, duplicates or not, because they'd probably pick up different points from the articles.

How do you know when you're done with a search?

I'm either out of time or money, usually time. It's easier for me to know when I'm out of money than it is to know when I'm out of time. I get so involved that the time just seems to disappear. Often it depends on what my clients want. We may not be out of time or money yet, but I know they don't want a lot of stuff. So whether or not we're done is up to the client. There are some projects for which it's just not appropriate to turn over every stone, and others for which that is essential.

How quickly do you turn projects around?

Two days is typical. I can do it faster, but two days allows for ordering prints via DIALMAIL. Sometimes I deliver search results electronically, too, although that can be a pain in the neck. When you deliver on disk, which I also do, you have a few basic questions: Apple or IBM? What size disk? ASCII or a certain word processor format? With online delivery, there are many more things that can go wrong.

Delivery options have provided several learning opportunities for me. Systems like CompuServe and DIALMAIL have length limitations, so if you have a lot of material, you have to chop the message into several parts. Uploading takes time. I love being able to copy something in my mailbox on DIALMAIL to somebody else's mailbox, but that doesn't allow you to eliminate false drops. That's not wonderful for your credibility. In effect, you're distancing yourself from the search, from the completeness of the answer, when you do that. I like it better when I have the opportunity to really get involved with the searches I'm doing. I feel I have more control. I *want* the results to come to me. I want to spend some time with them.

Let's talk about post-processing, since that's one of your areas of expertise. Do you typically use a standard format for printing or downloading?

I tend to print in the fullest format possible, sometimes eliminating the descriptors. In a citation-only database, I usually leave the descriptors in, because it gives the client more to go on. I don't clean up individual records to the extent of stripping out CODENs and ISSNs and that sort of thing, unless someone has specifically told me that they don't want to see that stuff.

I have to keep reminding myself that most people don't know anything about database records. They don't know how to read them. If it says AU, they don't understand that it means author, even if it's obviously a name. They don't know that TI means title. I used to assume that people would understand a bibliographic citation. They wouldn't necessarily call it that, but they'd know what they were looking at. We tend to get trapped in librarian jargon, or at least in the assumptions that go with it.

When you do print out search results, what does the final product look like? Do you present a bound report?

The trouble with binding is that what I present is usually very extensive. Finding a way of binding it and keeping it together isn't easy. I try to make it readable. It's laser-printed, page-numbered, and divided into sections as appropriate. Each page has a header with the client's name, the search title and the date the search was done, so that each page means something. There's a footer with "Prepared by..." and my name, with my telephone and fax numbers.

That's a little low-key marketing right there. But it's also important, especially if it's an interim set of results, just titles or citations, to have the contact information right on the page, because they'll need to get back to you. Also, clients pass these things around their organizations, and you want someone down the line to know how to get in touch with you, too. You want to leave your footprint.

Speaking of footprints, do you document for your clients the files you searched, the strategy, keywords and so on?

I list the files on a cover sheet. I do that to remind myself, as much as anything else, of what I've done for them. As far as showing the strategy, it depends on the client. I usually explain my basic approach. Depending on their expertise and how interested they are, I may show the individual steps I went through, but I don't show the strategy as a matter of course.

What's your most frustrating search experience?

Where shall I start? The most frustrating *type* of search experience for me is when something happens that shouldn't and is completely unexpected. You know I don't mean "unexpected" in a positive sense. It's frustrating when I go in thinking that this *should* be really, really easy. I go in by the seat of my pants without much advance planning and without looking anything up in the documentation. Maybe it's the end of the day, and I just want to do this one little search—quickly, because I've done it a million times before. Then I get on and something has changed—or *not* changed. Sometimes I've built a script offline for a file that's supposed to have been reloaded, but the reload hasn't happened and the search doesn't work.

Whatever it is, all of a sudden I'm just sitting there facing an absurd number of citations or an error message. In the worst case, I'm facing a big expense, no answer, and my own anger at myself because I didn't prepare adequately. It's the combination of the unexpected and feeling responsible for it that frustrates me the most.

It can happen under a variety of circumstances. It might be a technical thing. It may be that I'm doing everything right. I have terrible telephone problems here; line quality is very poor. Sometimes I'm knocked offline in the middle of a long search by line noise, and then find the search is gone when I log back on. Sometimes I can't get on at all, and have to dial four or five times to get connected. By then I've forgotten what I was going to do when I got on.

There are other just stupid things that you do when you're tired, distracted or under stress. You might do a logoff hold and forget to change files when you log back on, and end up running the search in the wrong file. Or worse, you might issue another BEGIN command because you've forgotten you're already in the file, wiping out the search results you wanted to save. They are stupid, silly things. I really hate wasting money like that.

I'm sitting here cringing, because so much of what you're describing is familiar to me! We all know theoretically how we should operate, yet many of us don't put it into practice, at least not consistently.

That's what scares me. There's such a small difference between learning from your experience and being trapped by your experience. You never know when you've crossed that line.

I've done substitute searching for several different organizations. Generally, what happens in a situation like that is that you're on your toes. You know you're in a foreign environment and you're really paying attention. You want to fit in and to do it the way they and their clients expect you to do it. Almost invariably, I see practices that I don't like, and I say to myself, "*I* would never do that." Later, yes, I *do* do that; maybe not that particular thing, but something similar. We all sink into our own little habits, and develop a false sense of security. We get a bit lazy.

That's the down side of being an experienced searcher. What about the up side?

It's so adventurous. You can find anything. I mean, I know there are things you *can't* find online, but you can *look*. You can find something that is either related or interesting. I don't understand people who say you can't browse online. It's a fantastic browsing mechanism. You can find all sorts of serendipitous stuff there. It's a whole world.

Very, very seldom am I bored when I'm online, even considering that some of the topics I search are completely incomprehensible to me. I've been handed some awful terminology that the client can't really explain. All I know is that it has something to do with biology, electronics or physics. But, even if you don't know anything about it, there's almost always something interesting about the process. Something happens that engages you.

And it does add to my store of knowledge, superficial as it may be, about the subject. I wish I could know more about everything I work on. Don't you run into this constantly? Everywhere you go, somebody mentions a term and you remember, "Oh, yeah, I worked on that." But you can't really put any context around it.

It's the librarians' disease. We know the questions to ask. We know what we need to learn to structure the research project, but we certainly couldn't design the circuit, or whatever it is.

Right. I don't really *want* to design the circuit, either, but it is nice to be able to respond to somebody who is designing one, and understand what they're talking about. Somebody said to me once, "Oh, it must be wonderful to know what you know; you must be so great at a cocktail party." Well, I'm *not* great at a cocktail party. I can't come up with all these exciting stories about what I know. I can *respond* to people, if they come up with a topic I recognize. I have enough context to be a good listener. I know what questions to ask.

SUPER SEARCH SECRETS

On communications software...

DIALOGLINK is much better than any Mac communications software I've used in terms of its ability to upload a search line-by-line. I find that especially important when I'm doing output searching—simply ordering the full text or complete citations of items that I've browsed, using a series of record numbers or accession numbers.

On the search process...

I view the search process as a very important partnership agreement. One person comes to the equation with the subject knowledge, and the other person comes with the online systems knowledge.

On the reference interview...

I try to just listen for awhile. I try to keep the client talking. There *are* a couple of things that I'm listening for...to find out how they're going to use the information...to find out how far along they are in the project, what they've already done and where they've looked.

On cost estimating and budgeting...

I figure that I can afford to put a quarter or a third of the total budget into online time, and the rest covers my labor and overhead and miscellaneous expenses.

On delivery of prints...

I use DIALMAIL for print delivery now....it's obvious that if you download prints in DIALMAIL the next morning at $24 an hour, it's cheaper than downloading 50 or 100 records in a file that costs $100 or $200 an hour.

On patent searching...

I also do a lot of patent searching, and I almost never use the patent classification system....If you're doing a patentability search, it's much more effective to use free-text, natural language in all its possible ramifications, and then scan titles. Certainly it's safer.

On limits...

Date limits, yes, but I seldom limit by language....You run much more risk of losing information when you limit by language.

On searching full text...

Positional operators are probably the most important thing to remember in this kind of searching. By that I mean "within" or "near" connectors that require that a word or a group of words appear within five or ten words, in the same paragraph, or in the same sentence as the corresponding group of words. A variation is using repetitive terminology, looking for "apple" within so many words of "apple" within so many words of "apple" again, to make sure that the article focuses on Apple Computer. Or, perhaps, the article is all about apples. The point is that the word isn't just mentioned once, in passing, or used in a figurative sense.

CHAPTER 2

KAREN BLAKEMAN: MAKING A DIFFERENCE

Karen Blakeman runs a U.K.-based research and consulting firm, RBA Information Services. She specializes in business-oriented information related primarily to the pharmaceutical, telecommunications and information technology industries.

Are you a librarian by training?

No, I'm not a librarian at all. I started off as a scientist; my first degree is in microbiology. After I graduated, I worked in a laboratory for about a year, which was not really to my liking. Then I met someone who told me about their job, which sounded like exactly the sort of thing that I like doing. They were called an information researcher, and they worked on some unusual and interesting projects. Eventually, I got a job working for Wellcome Plc in research and development information.

At that time, which was 1978, we didn't really have an online industry in the U.K. We would buy magnetic tapes from people like Chemical Abstracts and load them on the mainframe. My first go at searching databases was on the in-house mainframe. It wasn't until I was at another pharmaceutical company about four years later that I actually started using real online. It was before PCs were an everyday thing. We used an ancient teletype terminal, but we thought this was very impressive. They had been using *Index Medicus* in hardcopy, but suddenly to be able to access MEDLINE online and to do searches for several concepts at once was fantastic. About two years later we got our first PC and started playing around with different communications packages and getting really sophisticated. That introduced me to computers and was the start of a long interest in telecommunications as well.

What communications software do you use?

I do most of my searching at 9600bps using PROCOMM Plus, which I find very useful because it has a usage log. From my dialing directory, it will record the time that I go into a database or host system and the time I log off, so I automatically get a tally of how long I've been online. I can check that against the telecommunications billing when it comes. The log feature is in a file called PCPLUS.FON; in the setup you have to make sure that you switch that on. A lot of people don't realize it's there.

I also use a software package called As-Easy-As, which is a Lotus 1-2-3-compatible spreadsheet. I have entered the prices of individual databases, so I can put in my estimate of how long a search is going to take, how many records or lines of text I'm likely to pull off, and then it will calculate for me how much the search is likely to cost. Once you've set up the basic spreadsheet, all you have to do is keep up-to-date with the main hosts you use, and make sure that you put in any changes to the connect-time and display rates. I put the system newsletters into my tray and make sure that that gets done. There's a field for currency exchange rates as well, and the formulae in the cells use that figure to calculate the final cost. It takes a while to actually set it up, and then to maintain the price changes, but it's definitely worth the effort.

I use the spreadsheet routinely when estimating projects. Someone will ask, "Can you do this search for me, and how much is it likely to cost?" I can easily say, "Okay, if we do *this* search in this database and get so many records, it's likely to cost you *this* much." I feel I can give a much more reliable cost estimate. Sometimes when I'm online, and the results look as though they're going to be different from what I anticipated, I use the DOS shell facility on ProComm to come out and do a quick spreadsheet check of the cost.

How did you come to operate your own business?

In 1988, after my work in the pharmaceutical industry, I joined a management consultancy firm in London. We did a lot of strategic, long-term consulting, which really concentrated my mind on business information. Then, at the end of 1989 or beginning of 1990, I started my own business. Most of my business is gotten by word of mouth. Some are small to medium-size firms that tend to be within my local geographical area. But I do have some clients in the city of London who ask me to do company profiles on competitors, or merger-and-acquisition searches. For reasons of confidentiality, they don't want to use their own in-house information people.

I work mostly on telecommunications and pharmaceutical industry projects, although I do take on inquiries outside my general field, providing they're fairly straightforward. Not long ago I had someone ask for a year's worth of competitor intelligence on conveyor belt manufacturers. They just wanted a simple Predicasts and Infomat search and a few newspaper clippings. But there are some subjects I loathe, such as financial services. I'm totally out of my depth, and I won't take on the sort of thing where I'm not comfortable with the jargon and not familiar with the industry. I don't think it's fair to the client to take on something about which you are not knowledgeable and therefore can't evaluate the data that you're getting. Of course, if they find that there's a problem with the information you're supplying, it doesn't do your reputation any good. I think you should know enough to at least suspect faulty data, even if you couldn't prepare a deeply analytical report based on it.

How do you proceed when a potential client calls and wants to have research done?

It depends on the way they present it, and that can differ widely. Some people are quite vague, and you have to sit down and talk to them about exactly what they're looking for. If I don't know the company or the organization, I try to get as much background on them as possible, and on their department, to try and put their research needs into context.

Sometimes I find that the marketing people aren't very familiar with what's available, so you have to give them examples of the kinds of information you can get: Would you be interested in seeing the accounts of the company for the last five years, or newspaper articles, trade magazines, and directory listings? You have to guide them along the way, tell them what sort of information they can get from those sources, and how that can be used to present a fuller picture of what's going on.

The other extreme is someone who thinks they know exactly what they want, and they ask you a very, very precise question. That always rings alarm bells for me, because so many times in the past that question was not really the one that they wanted the answer to. I had a beautiful example of that recently. A client said that they wanted a general search on the microwave cookware industry in Europe and were interested in certain companies and what products were available. In our discussion I said, "We might get an indication of some of the patents that have been taken out." He immediately said, "Oh, can you find out about trademarks?" I told him that I could, and he said "Ah, right, well, if you can find out if Company X owns this particular trademark, we'd be very grateful because then we won't need the rest of it. We're only interested in this company because we've been told that they have this trademark." That was the only thing he really needed. I suppose I should have kept quiet because there wasn't as much money involved! Since he thought it was going to be too difficult to find out about trademarks, he didn't even think to ask.

It doesn't matter whether it's a very vague question or a very precise one, I still like to get a feel for the context, to try to find out what they would like to do with the information. That can affect how you approach the entire project.

Do you keep a search log or project file?

Yes, I do. Bits are produced on the computer, but I keep most of it in a paper file. I find it far easier to pull out a folder or a file box if someone phones me. Then I can and say, "Okay, this is what we did." I use a search request form, more as a tracking list for myself than anything else. Also, should anything go wrong, I've got something right there that documents exactly what I did and why.

What items do you have on that form?

The date the inquiry came in, how it was received—by letter, phone or fax—and notes on the initial search interview and how we decided to proceed. I include a page of notes on how the search was conducted, any hardcopy sources that we used, databases, search strategies, and any problems. I also track any other telephone conversations subsequent to or during the research period, what was discussed, any decisions made. It's almost like a diary, really. I think it's wise to have a very complete form. Sometimes you find that someone has left a company and that another person has taken over the project. If it's a long-term project, you need to be able to bring the new person up-to-date on what's been going on, what's happened and why.

Do you work within a budget for each project?

Half and half. Sometimes I say, "I can do this for x number of pounds or if you want a little bit more we can perhaps go up so much." Sometimes people are very cost-conscious, "Oh no, no, no, can't afford that. All I've got to spend is £50." Then we sit down and try to work out what is the most essential information that they're going to need. That's where the spreadsheet-estimating program comes in handy.

On the mergers and acquisitions side, though, it's really anything and everything, no limits. They need the information regardless, and you just go ahead and keep them posted on the costs. They usually want the information as soon as possible, because they're doing a presentation in three days. Once someone said, "I'm doing this matrix chart for an overhead for tomorrow morning's meeting, and we've got three gaps in it. Would you please fill them?"

Is that typical? How quickly do you usually turn projects around?

It depends on what else I've got going at the time. I try to clear at least the first stage as soon as possible, hopefully within 24 hours, certainly within 48 hours. That's using online. If I feel that hardcopy sources are going to be more appropriate, it depends on when I'm going to be able to get to the library. Again, I can usually do that within 48 hours. Some people will call and say, "I really need this desperately this afternoon or tomorrow morning." If I can't do it, I tell them, "I can't manage that, but I know someone who might be able to help you." Sometimes I contract out some basic library work, straightforward things like looking up details from directories, or getting photocopies of articles.

Do you have favorite databases that you go to repeatedly for certain kinds of questions?

Predicasts' PROMT used to be my favorite, but not so much now. They used to have a wonderful little analytical abstract that told you so much; you knew straightaway how relevant the full text was going to be. Now they tend to have much longer, waffly paragraphs that they take from the articles themselves. They call them "extracts," and I've found them much less informative. But I still use Predicasts, or a combination of Predicasts and Infomat, mainly because of the coding. Now that Infomat is using the Predicasts' coding, searching the two together is very useful for getting some good market information. I also use Chemical Business NewsBase a lot, for the chemical and pharmaceutical industries.

If the same file is up on more than one host, what determines where you search it?

Familiarity, generally; I usually use Data-Star for that reason. If I go onto a less familiar host, I have to spend a lot more time thinking about the search language, "Can I do this that way on this system?" But sometimes the format of the data that I require determines which host I use. DIALOG has a very nice REPORT feature. If someone wants data on a U.K. company, say just the name of the company, number of employees, a couple of financial ratios and so on that they can put into a spreadsheet eventually, I'd use DIALOG so I could get the table format, instead of Data-Star where I can only get the preformatted record. And if someone wants a list of companies in a particular area to do a mailing, I would have to go to a system that could produce sticky labels that are ready to go onto the envelope.

One lovely feature on Data-Star is a ..KEEP command. If you do a search and the client says, "I want to look at the titles first and decide which ones I want," you can pull off the titles and do a ..KEEP. It will keep that set of documents separate for you. Now you can send that list off to your client to pick the ones he wants, and when he doesn't get back to you for a week or two, you don't have to worry about the fact that the database has been updated and the record numbers have all shifted. You can go back to your original set of KEPT documents and just put in the numbers of the ones he wants. It's a vital feature, especially with files now going up that are updated four, five, six times a day. Without it, you have to put in the accession numbers to pull the records, and if you have to select about 50 documents out of 150, that's a pain.

Do you do a lot of multifile searching and deduplication?

Yes, especially for cross-file searches on MEDLINE, Excerpta Medica and BIOSIS. You have to be careful, though; it works very well as long as you're using files that are similar in structure. Data-Star is nice in that respect, in that you can choose to carry out exactly the same search on all the files, or you can change it as you go along, using a different descriptor or a code that only exists in certain files. But you can still combine the results at the end and then dedupe them. I find DIALOG's approach to cross-file searching is too generic. You can't really get specific enough on some of the files, or you have to put in one strategy at the beginning to account for all the variations among files. It's just more awkward.

One of the problems I find with deduplication in general is that it works great as long as they keep the original title of the article. As soon as they start enhancing titles, or rewriting the same article under different titles, you're in trouble. But overall I think it does work, and you do save a significant amount of money.

Having said that, though, it's interesting to see how little overlap there is between files like MEDLINE and Excerpta Medica. It's very surprising; there's probably no more than 30 percent duplication there.

Do you plan your search strategy extensively before you go online?

I jot down some ideas for terms that I want to use. First, I identify the main concepts. If it's the market for a product in a particular country, I make a note of what the product is, what the countries are, whether there is a timespan that needs to be covered. If the database has coding—I don't use all the manuals but the Predicasts one I do use a lot—I check the manuals for the codes. I also look at the database documentation, the data sheets, to remind myself which fields are searchable and which ones you can limit. Sometimes I find myself in the middle of a search, not getting any hits, and I wonder why and then realize, of course, that one of the fields isn't present in that database. So I double-check on that sort of thing.

When you build a search, how do you know when to start broad and when to take a more focused approach?

If it's something like getting a set of company financial accounts, where I know that that's exactly what they're looking for, I take the focused approach. I use the company name indexing or some other very specific access point. I tend to start broader when I'm looking for general industry news or market information. Often, the terminology is unsettled, especially if it's a new product or concept. A colleague once had a search where someone wanted the market for sunbeds—you call them tanning beds or tanning salons—in Korea. In a case like that, you have to broaden your search terms beyond what the client supplied, or you're likely to get zero hits at the first level. If you do a broad search and still get zero hits, there's something wrong. You might have gotten the wrong terminology or the wrong spelling or the wrong codes, or the wrong database entirely. Or it could be too new a development to be in the literature.

The only way to really check that you're getting anything that's relevant is to browse some of the titles or free formats. I do a lot of title browsing first, and going back and selecting, or having my client select, the ones that sound particularly good. That's also a good way to double-check the search process, especially if you're using numbered codes.

I still remember a search we did, a few years ago, on a whole series of topics in the broadcasting area. I was sitting with the analyst who wanted the information, and we'd been searching Predicasts and getting this fantastic material. It was really precise, exactly what we wanted. We would go in, browse the titles, pull off the full records, and so on. We got to about the fifth one and said the hell with it, we won't bother browsing the rest, we'll just pull off everything. Well, it was all wonderful stuff, but it wasn't about broadcasting, it was about the U.K. ball-bearing market. I had transposed two digits in one of the product codes I'd used. So that's a reminder to always check in a free format and look at a few scattered records at least. Do it just to make sure. It's worth the connect time to make sure that you have gotten the right company or the right product before you end up paying a lot of money for useless information.

Do you do a lot of full-text searching?

I use FT Profiles, for one. I used to use NEXIS a lot, which I like because you can search everything at once if you need to. It's not often that you need to do that, but when you do it's a godsend. Most of the full-text files I use have fairly rudimentary indexing. It's often too broad to use alone, so I look for words and synonyms within a sentence, within a paragraph or within a number of words of each other to make sure that they're linked. Then when I look at the results, I use keyword-in-context displays around the term. None of this is foolproof, but we don't have too many options.

Full text can be invaluable when you're searching for a piece of information that you just can't find anywhere else. I had to do a search on some value-added telephone network services and the client wanted to know how many subscribers a particular company had. We couldn't find the information in any of the articles that focused on the company itself, or in the corporate directories or financial filings. So we did a broad free-text search in a full-text database, looking for the company's name together with terms like "subscribers," "users" or "customers" within the same paragraph, and we found the number in a throw-away line in a profile of a competing company. It just said, "Company X has so many subscribers. Its nearest competitor, Company Z, has this many…," and that was the figure we wanted.

That reminds me of one that a colleague told me about. She was also working for a major telecommunications firm who wanted to know how other companies, regardless of industry, had celebrated signing up their millionth customer. She tried all kinds of generalized search terms, "milestone," "corporate growth," and so on, until it occurred to her to just put in the word "millionth," and the results were right on target.

We have to get away from thinking, "What is the term or descriptor for this?" and think instead, "How would a journalist write it?" Sometimes journalists get the spelling of companies wrong, too, and you have to take that into account.

What happens when you do a search and you don't get anything?

First, I check that I'm actually typing it in correctly. Sometimes I just type it in again, because there might be noise on the telecom line that doesn't always appear on the screen. If I really do get zero results and I think there must be *something* out there, I check the spelling, check whether I am searching the right fields, check whether I've selected the right database. I ask myself whether I should be using a broader term or a different term. If I can't work out any of the obvious solutions, I phone the help desk and see what they say. There might be something else at fault, like a technical problem with the database.

It may also be that the client doesn't expect, or want, anything, and they haven't told you that little piece of information. They may want to do some original research. They may be looking at some possible patenting and they haven't trusted you enough to tell you that's what they're doing, or they might have some other reason not to have divulged it. So I usually go back to the client and say, "This is what's happened, is it reasonable or not?" If it isn't reasonable, we start again, thinking of some alternative strategies.

What about the opposite situation, when you find an overwhelming amount of information? What if the client has told you "If you find two dozen articles I'll be surprised," and there turn out to be several hundred?

When that happens, either we don't know the subject area very well, or we're putting in the wrong terms. In that case I might pull off some titles and ask "Does this sort of thing look right?" Then we take it from there. It may be that we have to refine the search strategy a bit, especially if they haven't been able to articulate exactly what it is that they want, and they've given me just the broadest terms.

In files that are keyword-indexed, especially on Data-Star, where the free format usually shows you the indexing terms, I pull those off as well. I explain that we can search by descriptor, and ask them to tell me which are the most relevant. Often they'll say, "Oh well, that one's irrelevant. I forgot to tell you I don't want that particular aspect." Or they'll say, "There's more there than I anticipated. Just give me the most recent 20."

How do you decide when a search is done?

It depends again on the type of inquiry. It could be that we've reached the ceiling on the amount they want to spend—that is often the case. On something like a mergers and acquisitions project, you tend to come up with exactly the same sort of data very quickly, so you know that you've got most of the relevant facts and it's not worth going any further.

Do you have any other specific search advice or money-saving tips that we haven't covered?

Use free formats as much as possible to make sure that what you're pulling off and paying money for is really what you want. Learn to use your favorite host really well and get to know all of the commands on it. For instance, if I want to pause for a couple of minutes during a search on Data-Star and ask myself, "Now, where am I going wrong?" I know to use the ..PARK command, which cuts down on the charges while you're thinking, and the ..GO command to start searching again.

Make use of the free time that the hosts give you. Even if you don't have a search to run in that database that day, it's good practice just to get to know the database, the different commands you can use and what the file looks like, to get a feel for the information that's in there. If you're not sure of a search strategy, try running it in a training file to see whether the logic works.

Moving on to output, I'm curious whether you generally print online, order offline prints, or use electronic mail for print delivery?

The only time I use offline prints is for things like mailing labels, because it makes sense to do that instead of downloading all the information and putting it on sticky labels, or giving it to the client to input again. If they know they want sticky labels, great, I do that offline. But offline prints are often not fast enough for some of my clients, and I don't like the paper copy because I usually want to do a bit of editing to make it easier to read, or to edit out false drops. (You know, I always feel a little bit happier if there are one or two false drops, because then I feel that I haven't missed anything. If everything is exactly what I want, I wonder, "If I had done a broader search, might I have gotten a little bit *more* that was relevant?")

I tend to download most of my information to disk. Often, if I want to send headlines, for example, to a client, I might either e-mail them or, more frequently, request that the e-mail message be delivered as a fax on the other end. Very few people I do business with have e-mail. It drives me up the wall sometimes that they don't, because I'm so used to using it. I usually follow up by sending print copies, in any case.

Do you go through the records themselves and bold or highlight the key points?

Yes, although some clients want a descriptive report as the end product, so they may not ever see the original records. But sometimes they do want the references. If they're interested in recent developments and what's going on in the field, I may prepare a cover sheet explaining what I feel are the main points to look at. If it's in the telecommunications or pharmaceutical area, I may bring my own contacts into play, mention rumors that are circulating within the industry, and so forth, to help put the information into context. For that sort of thing, I prepare a presentation-quality report with a binding and a title page. Usually I'm charging them dearly for it, because I'm using my expertise and knowledge of the industry to interpret the information.

But if it's a field that I don't know very well, then whatever write-up I prepare is based directly on the records I've found online. Generally, I just leave it to the client to read and draw their own conclusions. What I always do, though, is explain what I've done, not necessarily with the search strategy with all the Boolean logic— usually I just say that I looked for *these* words, in *this* country, or I used the code for *this* product in *this* particular database. I always list the databases I used, the host system, and the date on which the search was done.

Have you encountered problems with database quality that affect your ability to get accurate information for your clients?

One tends to have particular grouses against particular databases, but they're usually the ones you know very well; you know the shortcomings through experience. I try to follow up on errors that I find, because I want to know if the data is eventually corrected or updated. It's only when you know an industry really well that you can spot when something's wrong with a particular piece of information. If you're working in an industry or using a database that you don't know well, you don't always recognize that something's wrong. Things like missing issues are insidious. If you don't know that the database has missed one or two issues of a journal that it normally covers comprehensively, the mistake is just invisible.

As far as specific databases are concerned, I have colleagues in the U.K. who've done product searches on KOMPASS, the company directory database. In some areas, the coding is not very accurate. I've had people tell me they've had 30 to 40 percent false drops. They've had clients who refused to pay the bill because of it. I'm not sure that it's altogether the database producer's fault. I think it could be the companies that fill in the forms. They don't understand the coding, or they check off all the boxes even though they don't make all the products on the list.

You have to make the situation clear to people beforehand—what you can and cannot do, and the charges involved, and that the data has to be paid for even though it may not be exactly what they wanted or expected. I'll do my utmost to ensure that we don't get irrelevant information, but if it's downright wrong, this is something we have to take up with the database producer.

SUPER SEARCH SECRETS

On communications software...

I do most of my searching at 9600bps using PROCOMM Plus, which I find very useful because it has a usage log....it will record the time that I go into a database or host system and the time I log off...The log feature is in a file called PCPLUS.FON; in the setup you have to make sure that you switch that on.

On cost estimating...

I also use a software package called As-Easy-As, which is a Lotus 1-2-3-compatible spreadsheet. I have entered the prices of individual databases, so I can put in my estimate of how long a search is going to take, how many records or lines of text I'm likely to pull off, and then it will calculate for me how much the search is likely to cost....There's a field for currency exchange rates as well, and the formulae in the cells use that figure to calculate the final cost. It takes a while to actually set it up, and then to maintain the price changes, but it's definitely worth the effort.

On favorite databases...

Predicasts' PROMT used to be my favorite...I still use Predicasts, or a combination of Predicasts and Infomat, mainly because of the coding. Now that Infomat is using the Predicasts' coding, searching the two together is very useful for getting some good market information. I also use Chemical Business News Base a lot...

On useful system features...

One lovely feature on Data-Star is a ..KEEP command. If you do a search and the client says, "I want to look at the titles first and decide which ones I want," you can pull off the titles and do a ..KEEP. It will keep that set of documents separate for you....You can go back to your original set of KEPT documents and just put in the numbers of the ones he wants.

On multifile searching...

...especially for cross-file searches on MEDLINE, Excerpta Medica and BIOSIS. You have to be careful, though; it works very well as long as you're using files that are similar in structure.

On getting zero hits...

First, I check that I'm actually typing it in correctly....there might be noise on the telecom line that doesn't always appear on the screen....I check the spelling, check whether I am searching the right fields, check whether I've selected the right database.

Other search tips...

Use free formats as much as possible...Learn to use your favorite host really well...Make use of the free time that the hosts give you....If you're not sure of a search strategy, try running it in a training file to see whether the logic works.

CHAPTER 3

STEVE COFFMAN: MINING FOR GOLD

Steve Coffman is Director of FYI, a fee-based research and document delivery service of the Los Angeles County Public Library.

What is FYI's mission, and how are you involved?

The primary mission of FYI is to provide a one-stop research and document delivery service for business and professional communities all over the country and, to some extent, the world. It's the equivalent of a full-scale information brokerage operating from inside a public library. My major job responsibilities are the actual running, development and overall direction of the FYI unit. I also do searching myself and consult with staff members on search strategy on a day-to-day basis.

Are you a librarian by training?

Yes, I graduated from UCLA in 1985 and went to work directly for the county library after that. I spent several years behind the reference desk, and when the county librarian decided to start a fee-based service, I was picked to develop it. I spent a year doing the development work, and then was fool enough to take the responsibility of *directing* it! We started in 1988, the development period was a year, we opened for business in 1989 and have been going strong since then.

How large is your staff now?

There are six and a half of us, including myself, four of whom are professionals. We operate in an office that is about the equivalent of 600 square feet. It's very cramped. But we get a lot of work out of this small space. We don't need to walk around much. We just hand stuff around. The reason we've been able to delay a network is that we're all within an arm's reach of each other.

Who are your clients?

It's a really broad spectrum. In terms of numbers, only about 50 percent are businesses, small as well as large. Probably another 35 percent are professionals of various types—lawyers, doctors, engineers, journalists, writers and so forth. Then there is a small component of individuals who simply need research done.

One service we offer is a people-locator service based on the PhoneDisc CD-ROM. The library has 90 branches all around Los Angeles County, and I make sure that everybody in those branches knows about this particular product. When Joe Blow comes up to the desk looking for Ann Blow, they send him to us. In a normal research environment, you could not deal in that kind of service. We can also turn to Information America, and we have a number of other options for locating people.

What determines when a question comes to FYI, as opposed to being handled by the regular county library reference services?

A basic philosophy underlies that division. It's right on the front of our brochure. It says that the next time you need information, you've got two choices. You can get it yourself—and it shows some poor guy slogging away—or you can call FYI and have it delivered. Reference is committed to preserving access to information by *helping* people locate that information. But if you want to have everything done *for* you from the word "go," that's what FYI is for.

People come to us: 1) if they want to have the entire project done for them; 2) if they need certain online services that are not available to the regular reference desk; or 3) if they contact their regular reference desk and specifically request an online search. If they ask a subject-related question that just happens to require a bit of online searching in conjunction with the rest of the reference process, then it's handled through the regular reference desk.

Is most of FYI's business walk-in?

Actually, about 90 percent of initial requests are phoned in. We have an 800 number that works nationwide. Once people get to know us, they often start faxing. But most people still want to talk over a project a little bit with a live human being, not just drop it to you in a fax. They want to know who they're dealing with, and to just generally fill you in. There are occasional walk-in customers who just happen to be in the library, or who want to see the actual search done. They may come in to do some work themselves, and then drop in here and we'll finish it up for them.

What's the first thing that happens when you get a request?

The phone is usually answered by a staff member, not a researcher, who informs the caller of our general operating requirements, our rates, and the fact that it *is* a fee-based service, which some people are not aware of. Having someone give that spiel weeds out the calls that aren't going to be worth our while to follow up on. If they're interested in pursuing a project, we take down the contact information and the basic nature of what they're looking for, and have a professional searcher get back to them, normally within four hours, or sooner if it's a rush situation.

We operate that way because we found that it was difficult for the professional searchers to switch gears every thirty seconds, to quote on new projects in the midst of working on other things. This way, they can give a little thought to the request before they call the customer. When they do call back, they may be able to provide an estimate right then, or get back in touch with them later in the day after they've had a chance to work up a realistic quote. Doing an estimate often involves discussion with other searchers to figure out the best approach. We sometimes look at DIALINDEX to see how well the databases cover the subject area.

One area where we always do a little preliminary work before quoting prices is in business lists, which are a significant component of our work. I'm talking about going into the Dun & Bradstreet or American Business Information directory files, for instance, and looking for companies in a certain area or a certain SIC or whatever, with so much in annual sales or so many employees. What makes business list projects unique is that you can't even begin to get an idea of the potential cost unless you get a record count. There's a hell of a big difference between getting 100 records and getting 10,000 records. The search itself is going to be straightforward, because there's no question of what parameters you have to use. That's one of the few kinds of searches where you *can* get an exact estimate. So we will get the total count and tell the patron before going ahead with the project.

We do have to draw a line, though, in terms of how much time we'll spend on a project before we actually launch into it. We have to be careful how far we go, because otherwise you could spend your whole day estimating projects and not get a damn bit of actual paying work done. But it's a fine line that you have to learn to walk; the patron has a right to know, or at least have some general idea, how much that information is going to cost.

Do you charge on a labor-plus-expenses basis?

Yes. $65 an hour—$65.47 an hour, actually, plus direct expenses. We also have some flat-fee products, like trademark searches, that we have costed out on an average basis. We did that by taking a very close look at how we were actually searching both Trademarkscan and the common law. We came up with a limit, a specific number of records that we would print in certain formats. Then we looked at the various ways of getting down to that limit. One way is to use class codes. Another is to print exact matches in full format, and then use the REPORT format to list just the mark and perhaps a class code for close matches. Then the customer could decide whether to go after the second tier, or just take the exact hits. What we did was analyze the entire search process and to come up with some logical limits that would make sense. At the same time it would give the patron more complete information, and more options to follow up on if they wished.

So far, it's worked pretty effectively. In fact, we're planning to bundle the trademark search package with a Nolo Press book on trademarks for the layperson, because most people who come in here for a trademark search don't really know the implications of what they're asking for.

FYI sounds like a pretty high-volume operation. How do you keep track of projects?

We have a paper system and an automated system that work hand-in-hand. First, we have a log book where we enter every project that we're actually going to work on. It's assigned a sequential invoice number, and then we record the patron's name, basic contact information and the date. New customers are also assigned a customer code. We use the log as a payment register, too; when they pay, it's marked off there.

At that point, projects are also entered into our automated billing and accounting system, which is on a program called Timeslips. It's very, very effective, and I highly recommend it. We've used it for about four years with many thousands of customers, and we're really pleased with it. Timeslips has the capability to track the time that an individual researcher puts in on a project. It can also track time in progress, if you want it to. In practice, because we're normally working within an estimate, we only keep approximate track of the amount of time we're spending on a project. The important thing is to deliver it within the time and the dollar amount we've quoted, or at least a realistic approximation. We're not sticklers down to the sixth of an hour. But if you have the time and the inclination, you can use Timeslips to find out how close you are coming to your estimate. You could record the actual time you spent, but still charge the patron whatever you agreed to charge. Then at the end you would say, "My God, I spent *six* hours on that and I only quoted *two*!" It could be a great management tool.

What do you ask in your reference interview?

Most important is *why* they want the information. Another approach that we frequently use is to ask, "If you could have exactly what you wanted in this particular situation, what would that look like? Describe it to us." That will frequently get them fantasizing. But it gives us something to go on. Then, of course, we have the standard questions like how far back they want to go in the literature, do they want English only, and so on. The most important thing is to get them to tell us what they want it for, why they want it, and to get them to give us a picture of what their ideal package would look like.

Since you're in a public library setting, your search topics must range all over the map. Typically, though, what kinds of things are you asked for?

You're right; they do range all over the map. Company information is a fairly large component of what we do. In fact, it's so common that we're looking at developing some kind of basic company profile package, like the trademark package. We also do a lot with industry and market information; some drug companies, for instance, use us heavily in that area. Then there are the business lists we talked about, which is another large component.

After that, it begins to break down into thousands of different subject areas. I just finished a project on aneutronic fusion, which is not something you normally think of a public library getting involved in. Even where you're dealing with scientific work, in medicine or chemistry or some related field, there often is a kind of pragmatic approach to it. We also do quite a bit in demographics, and in various kinds of management information. I'm doing a project right now for a city here in Southern California about the success of flex-time schedules in other public sectors. We really cover an incredible spectrum. We tell people that if it's published or publicly available we can deal with it.

What online systems do you use?

We use something like 25 different systems. I'm actually cutting out a few this year that we haven't used on a regular basis, because there are other ways to access them, or alternative ways of getting the same kind of information. The top system we use is DIALOG, followed by LEXIS/NEXIS, and then by Dow Jones. The fourth system that we use quite heavily is Dun's Direct Access, which is Dun & Bradstreet's own version of the Market Identifiers database. Direct Access is much less expensive than going to File 516 on DIALOG, and it has a beautiful software interface. It's $45 a year plus $2 per count if you're going to do a search, and 88¢ per company look-up. If you want the Dun's enhanced record, which is a more extensive record than the File 516 record on DIALOG, it's $1.13.

We use Dun's Direct Access for our company profiles and business list projects. Frequently, the only information available on small private companies is likely to be Dun & Bradstreet. We have the Dun & Bradstreet account identification service which is useful to locate a Dun's number. With that number, you can go online and quickly find something in File 516. Dun & Bradstreet is now making that service available on CD-ROM. It works work hand-in-hand with Dun's Direct Access (DDA), so once you find the company on the CD-ROM it asks, "Would you like to look at something on DDA?" If you say "yes," it logs you on automatically, pulls the profile and downloads it. It's a beautiful system. That's the reason Dun's Direct Access is number four.

Beyond those top four systems we use all different kinds of systems as necessary. We use Information America occasionally, for state coverage of corporate filings that you can't get on LEXIS, for instance. We also have Damar, a real estate data service that provides tax assessors' data for all counties in California. You could use that for locating people, assuming they own a house. We also use it for people who are interested in moving and want to find out what houses are selling for in a particular neighborhood. Or you can find properties in Ventura County that are selling in a certain price range. If a person is interested in a specific property, they can find out what it last sold for, who owns it and many other details; it's a great negotiating tool. A good real estate agent will provide you with that kind of information, but if you're just beginning to get interested and don't want to start messing around with real estate agents yet, this is a good place to start.

Down the road, we're looking at putting together some kind of neighborhood profile package. The idea would be that you could select a zip code or census tract or whatever, and do the demographics on that area and show people what houses have been selling for. With National Planning Data Corporation, I can give the crime risk in that area. I can tell them the credit card debt. There are a number of different components that we can put together into a nice little package that will be available for a flat fee.

As far as searching is concerned, do you have favorite files that you keep going back to for certain types of questions?

We use the newspaper databases when we're looking for an elusive bit of data. It might be information on a person or on a company. There's such a wealth of material in newspapers; if you're going to find a lead *anywhere*, you're likely to be able to pick it up in the full-text newspaper files. They're the haystack when the search topic is a needle.

If the same database is up on more than one system, what determines where you search it? Is it cost? Convenience? Your familiarity with the system? System features?

All of the above. All things being equal, it's cost. But the problem frequently is that all other things are *not* equal. There often are limitations. The first question is, can we do this search in that file as it's mounted on that system? And if we *can* do it, then the next question is, is this the cheapest source for it? There's a third element that comes into play, too: familiarity. We tend to use the more familiar systems, even if a file is slightly more expensive, simply because we don't want to have to look things up.

Cost really is very significant, especially as more and more things become available in a variety of different formats. You do have choices. We consciously try to ferret out deals like Dun's Direct Access. Another example that we just finished researching is American Business Information. They have two business list databases, Files 531 and 532 on DIALOG, and they have a CD-ROM disc that contains basically the same information, but with more limited search capabilities. You can also get direct online access to their database in Omaha, Nebraska. They're in the bulk mailing list business, too, where you just order labels; that's a *lot* cheaper, like $60 a thousand, which is just 6¢ a record.

We're doing so many of these lists that I called American Business Information and said, "I know that this stuff is available in a thousand different guises all over the U.S., and I know that it's available for much less than what we're paying online." They said, "Well, you're right. And since you're such good snoops, we're going to give you the wholesale rate." Not only did they give us the wholesale rate, but we don't even have to mess with the search. I just call and tell them what we need in terms of SIC number, geographic area and whatever other criteria we're looking at. They call back with a count and a quote, and if the patron decides to go ahead with it, they do the work, print the labels and ship it directly to us. The rate, for a basic name and address list, is 2.5¢ a record. That's the wholesale rate. There's a $75 minimum, so if you're doing a small list, online is still a better option.

The point is that it's important for us to be aware of the fairly narrow context in which we're operating. Frequently, we library-based people are *not* really conscious of that. We don't look outside and say, "By God, there must be other people who need this sort of information; where do *they* go for this kind of service?" You *know* they aren't going online for it. The image I have is of a horse with blinders on. We know what the basic information providers that we deal with have chosen to tell us. But it's important, and often imperative, to get out and look at how other industries are solving the same kinds of problems. They're frequently solving them far less expensively than we are.

So, if the real estate people are using something cheaper than LEXIS, find out what they're doing and see if you can get access to the same thing. You'll sometimes discover a better product as well. In fact, just about every time we've made the effort to really explore a particular area, we've found that there are companies with better solutions than the familiar ones that we know.

That's a very useful perspective, Steve. Let's talk a little about the nitty-gritty of actually running a search. Do you make notes before you go online, or do you wing it?

In certain unusual situations, we will do some extensive planning. I'm talking about using a database like PharmaProjects, where a single record costs $60. But in normal circumstances, if it's a subject-related search, our standard technique is to wing it. We'll probably start in DIALOG because it has broad coverage of many different areas. We'll often start with a DIALINDEX search to find out where the meat is. Then we'll make some decisions about what files we want to search. Whenever possible, we'll do a OneSearch as well, since even though you may lose a little bit of control, you gain a lot in time. When you begin to factor time in as a cost element, it makes a lot of sense. You give up some things, like precision, to save time.

So you do a quick-and-dirty search, rather than an elegant one, to get the most information in the shortest time?

Right. One of the real problems with online is that you lose the ability to browse like you can in print. You can open a printed periodical index and cover thousands of articles very quickly, which you can't do very easily online. We try to approximate that broad coverage for certain kinds of subject searches. We do it by doing a relatively general search, printing out a hell of a lot of titles, and then going back and selecting from the best of those. We sometimes print in Format 8 in DIALOG, which gives you keywords and some additional clues about the article or whatever, without a lot of additional expense.

Do you use the preset OneSearch categories or make up your own file groups?

We almost never use DIALOG's own OneSearch categories. When we start with DIALINDEX, we normally combine a broad number of categories. Then we add some selected files that ought to be in there, if they're not already included as part of a standard category. Next, we rank the results to find out where the hits are. We review the outcome to see if it makes sense or if we've overlooked anything obvious. Then we make a decision about what files should be included in the OneSearch, and in what order. All other things being equal, we'll put the cheapest file on top.

Do you prefer to search full-text databases if they're available?

It depends on a number of things. If the budget is relatively small, and especially if it's a quick turnaround, full-text files are an important element. We know that the patron wants *some* information, not necessarily a lot, and doesn't care if it's selective—which it is. Usually, when you get to full text, it's whatever the producers happen to load into the database, and that's not necessarily everything. If they want just a few good references, and want them fast on a limited budget, it's frequently cheaper for us to get the stuff full-text online, than to photocopy it out of a collection. So that's what we do.

Often the patron wants a broader, more comprehensive search. That might mean that we first provide a list of titles, they make the selections, and we go back in and get abstracts or bibliographic citations or the full text of the document. We use the two-step approach if the patron has some time and wants to exert a little more control over the process. We cast a broad net, and then we go back and get the little fishies we like.

What determines the conclusion of a project? Is it usually budget, or diminishing returns, or some sixth sense that tells you that it's not worth going any further?

That's a very difficult thing to learn. Many of us research types tend to want to follow everything down to the bitter end. The problem is that you can spend a lot of time and money, normally your own, trying to do that. Ideally, it's nice when you can see that you've come to the end and the project terminates naturally. That happens when you start to pull up the same information you've already gotten, but from different sources. You just develop the feeling that you've covered the ground adequately.

Another type of conclusion, of course, is when you find exactly the information you're looking for. Sometimes it's very simple. You do a Dun's Direct profile on a company, you find it, that's the end of the project. When the question is, "What is the market share of such-of-such a company?" and you find the article that gives the information, that's it. You don't have to go any further.

Both are nice ways to terminate a project; you're happy when it ends like that. What happens more commonly is that you come to a point where you feel that you've done what you can within the patron's budget. You try to exhaust at least the standard sources, and hopefully you turned up some information—perhaps not the full answer, but some information appropriate to that budget level. Then you're able to go back to the patron and say, "Here's what we were able to find within your budget. Based on our searching, here are some initial suggestions that you might want to follow up. This is how you can do it yourself, or we'd be happy to handle it for you." That's the more typical outcome, unfortunately, because there are time and cost restraints. The perfect, comprehensive answer might be available if you wanted to spend $10,000 getting it, but it's not usually worth that much to the customer.

You might spend $9900 trying to get the remaining 10 percent worth of information.

That's right. In fact, we express it in terms of the 80/20 rule. We figure we've probably got 80 percent of the relevant material with what we've done so far. To get the remaining 20 percent, you're going to have to pay through the nose. Most patrons accept our judgment on that.

What would you like to share in the way of search tips?

Remember that your computer can do a hell of a lot for you, and you should take advantage of that wherever you can. I'm talking about things like storing login scripts, macros for searches that you run habitually, and uploading search strategies that you prepare offline. We don't do a lot of "live" searching online. We use Pro-Search and type in what we're looking for, logon, run the search, and get off. It's like guerrilla searching; you go in and do a quick hit, pull down the stuff, take a look at it at your leisure, get back on and do some more. As modem speeds increase, that type of searching behavior is likely to become much more common. You're going to want to take full advantage of 9600bps; you're not going to want your fingers to get in the way.

How much cleaning up and post-processing do you do?

Not as much as I think we should, but we do quite a bit. Most of the search session is saved to disk, and we pull it into WordPerfect to clean it up before we print it out. We knock out all the search strategy and the cost figures. We format it and put it in a nice font, something other than Courier 10, and put page breaks in the appropriate places. We review the results as we go along; we don't just drop them raw into the client's lap. We strip out false hits, and we highlight items that are particularly germane. We use little red stick-on arrows for that.

All searches go out with a cover letter that explains what we've done, what we've found and what remains to be done. Depending on the project, we may also list the databases and the strategy we used; we do that for trademark searches, for instance. If the patron is from an academic or a research environment, or has expressed an interest in the research process—if they *think* of it as a "literature search"—we list the databases and the strategy.

The average business customer doesn't really give a damn what the strategy was or what databases you used. All they're concerned about is getting the information; they don't care where it came from. In fact, frequently our packages are a portmanteau of various sources. They include the search itself, maybe several different searches, photocopies of articles and pages from various texts, perhaps even written reports of interviews we have done.

What goes out is more than just a search printout. It goes out in a nice envelope, too. We have a folder with the name of the service foil-stamped on it, and a place for the researcher's business card. It makes a nice little presentation package. In fact, at one point, we even had little medallion-type stickers to seal the folder, but it was a little gaudy so we backed away from it. This is not exactly the Magna Carta we're delivering.

What do you love about searching, and what do you find most frustrating?

What I really love is the kind of reach that you have with online. I see a serious problem with the migration in many libraries to CD-ROM; I'm afraid we're going to lose the immediate access to what Barbara Quint is fond of calling "universal human knowledge." We're not going to have that at our fingertips any more if we break it into all its little fragments, which is what CD-ROM does. A primary strength of online is a sense of integration, both on a single service and among services, too. In the same search buffer you can have DIALOG and Dow Jones or NewsNet or DataTimes or any of the rest. You can integrate everything right there on your computer and do it relatively conveniently. To me that was and is one of the very, very important elements of online, and something that's not duplicated anywhere else.

What about those moments of glory when you're actually running a search?

Most of the time, there's a lot of slogging and continuous decision-making to do as you work your way through a search. You are trying for the closest approximation you can, and considering yourself lucky to get that. There are occasions—rare ones, but they do happen—when you go online and find the exact little thing that perfectly matches what you're looking for. It answers every last question. And you thought it was going to take six hours to do it, but, by God, you pull it off in 15 minutes. When that happens here, you always know it. Someone jumps out of their chair, slams their hand down on one of the partitions or a computer or something, and says, "By God, I've found it!" That only happens about once a week, but everybody shares in the glory. Everybody knows what happened. No, it's not a stroke or an orgasm, it's a best-case search!

I always think of online like mining. We've "gotta go down in the mines," and it's just like it was in 1849. We're the ones who are slogging it out. We're the ones with the low salaries, too. But we're in there looking for nuggets and it's up to us to separate the dross from the gold, or whatever. What's been happening is that the online services put the raw material out there, the ore, and give us a few tools to manipulate it and to locate things. We've got the picks and shovels, by God, and we're still doing that, picking and shoveling. But it seems to me that there are many, many things that could be done to make the information available in a form that people can use.

I'm talking about things like trademark searching. We have a package, a strategy and a whole set of tools to allow us to pull that stuff from the raw material that DIALOG and Thomson & Thomson have made available to us. DIALOG could have done the same thing. They could have taken basic strategies and built a whole package around that particular information need instead of just dumping the raw material. That's only one example. There are millions of information needs like that. If an online service can define some of them, it's got a huge potential market.

A good example of this kind of thinking is Dun's Direct Access. The system is designed for people who are not searchers. It's designed for businesses, for people who actually use the information. The software itself has the SIC codes built into it. It takes you through the whole process of constructing a business list. There are so many areas where an online service could say, "Look, here's the information we've got; what do people really want from this? Let's design something that gives them the information they need instead of just dumping a ton of stuff into their laps to sort through."

People are constantly reinventing all these wheels. If DIALOG's not going to do anything about it, maybe we should. I think that's where the most progress could be made in making online a better, more effective tool. Other things like quality, indexing, presentation, lag times, and what's there and what's not are all important, but they are subsidiary to the more basic issue—making information available in a form that people really need and can use.

SUPER SEARCH SECRETS

On logging search requests...

We have a paper system and an automated system that work hand-in-hand. First, we have a log book where we enter every project....It's assigned a sequential invoice number, and then we record the patron's name, basic contact information and the date. New customers are also assigned a customer code. We use the log as a payment register, too; when they pay, it's marked off there....projects are also entered into our automated billing and accounting system, which is on a program called Timeslips. It's very, very effective, and I highly recommend it.

On the reference interview...

Most important is *why* they want the information....ask, "If you could have exactly what you wanted in this particular situation, what would that look like? Describe it to us." That will frequently get them to fantasizing....The most important thing is to get them to tell us what they want it for, why they want it, and to get them to give us a picture of what their ideal package would look like.

On searching newspaper databases...

We use the newspaper databases when we're looking for an elusive bit of data....There's such a wealth of material in newspapers....They're the haystack when the search topic is a needle.

On browsing online...

We try to approximate that broad coverage for certain kinds of subject searches. We do it by doing a relatively general search, printing out a hell of a lot of titles, and then going back and selecting from the best of those. We sometimes print in Format 8 in DIALOG, which gives you keywords and some additional clues about the article or whatever, without a lot of additional expense.

On guerrilla searching...

We use Pro-Search and type in what we're looking for, logon, run the search, and get off. It's like guerrilla searching; you go in and do a quick hit, pull down the stuff, take a look at it at your leisure, get back on and do some more.

On cleaning up search results...

Most of the search session is saved to disk, and we pull it into WordPerfect to clean it up...knock out all the search strategy and the cost figures. We format it and put it in a nice font, something other than Courier 10, and put page breaks in the appropriate places....we highlight items that are particularly germane. We use little red stick-on arrows for that.

On online...

A primary strength of online is a sense of integration, both on a single service and among services, too. In the same search buffer you can have DIALOG and Dow Jones or NewsNet or DataTimes or any of the rest. You can integrate everything right there on your computer and do it relatively conveniently. To me that was and is one of the very, very important elements of online...not duplicated anywhere else.

On the perfect search...

There are occasions—rare ones, but they do happen—when you go online and find the exact little thing....It answers every last question. And you thought it was going to take six hours to do it, but, by God, you pull it off in 15 minutes. When that happens here, you always know it. Someone jumps out of their chair, slams their hand down on one of the partitions or a computer or something, and says, "By God, I've found it!"....No, it's not a stroke or an orgasm, it's a best-case search!

CHAPTER 4

LUCINDA CONGER: CONSUMMATE GENERALIST

At the time of this interview, Lucinda Conger was Acting Chief of the Reader Services Branch of the U.S. Department of State Library. Her permanent position is that of Principal Reference Librarian and Coordinator of Information Services.

How and when did you get started in online?

I've been a professional librarian since 1964, so that makes me a real old-timer. I learned to search in 1975, when DIALOG was still in its infancy. At that time, I was a data archives librarian in the social science library at Yale. Yale was hoping to get involved in this new online business, but I had a feeling, even then, that it was going to be difficult in a college environment because of the costs. So I started then to cast my eye about for other places to try to break into the online business and get involved in what was going on. I knew this was something important; I could sort of see it coming down the pike.

I was very fortunate to get a job at the State Department, because what they wanted to do was to go online in a big way. They had been online with the New York Times Information Bank since 1974. I was hired to bring additional online services into the State Department Library. When I came here, there were four full-time reference librarians. We were all trained on DIALOG at the same time. Then we were all trained on ORBIT, and in December of 1976 we were all trained on BRS when it came up.

The only way I stayed sane during this period was that I discovered that there was a District of Columbia online users group. It was one of the first in the country, and quite active. We exchanged ideas and shared stories and experiences. Gradually, to keep track of what was going on with all the different online services, I prepared a command chart for my staff, and I shared it with the other members of the online users group. When *ONLINE* magazine started, I contributed the chart in its then-current form, and it was first published there. It's been greatly expanded since then, of course. It's an excellent reference tool. The committee that put together the international Common Command Language asked me for advice about how to think about certain commands, and which would be the most useful. They used that chart as the backbone of their entire effort.

My *modus operandi*, both as a reference librarian and as a searcher, is that I like to have a lot of control. I'm very organized, and I like to have guides to help me find my way through the thicket; otherwise it's overwhelming.

How many systems do you currently search?

We have access, on paper at least, to about 25 different systems, but we probably don't search more than about ten regularly. We use DIALOG, LEXIS/NEXIS, Dow Jones and LEGI-SLATE. We use Juris, which is a Justice Department service that's not available to the public currently. We use EPIC, and will probably be using it more heavily in the future. We've used VU/TEXT, although only for one particular patron. We use USA Today Decisionline to prepare a daily briefing summary that goes to the top offices in the department. We use BRS primarily for downloading articles from the Comprehensive Core Medical Library.

I'm surprised that you get into the medical area. Obviously I have misconceptions about the range of questions you get at the State Department.

The variety is one of the reasons I've stayed here. A lot of people might think, "You've had so much experience, why are you still at the State Department?" In fact, this is a wonderfully general, full-scope reference-requirements kind of place. We aren't narrowly focused on foreign policy. It's an enormous range. We do business research. We have procurement people who are trying to find out how stable a company is, so we have to do company investigations, or at least credit reports. For that we use DunsPrint, primarily. Our Inspector General's office investigates legal matters related to companies with which the department does a lot of business. We get involved there, too. Of course, we get requests for information about foreign companies as well.

On the medical side, we have a large medical services division that's responsible for the health of all of our employees overseas. It also oversees people who return from abroad with strange diseases, and people who are going overseas and have normal health problems that they need to have addressed. So we have a whole battery of doctors to serve the needs of people in the State Department, and several doctors who regularly peruse the literature. We run some SDIs for doctors. We have some people who are involved in environmental health as well, and we get a full range of requests for articles and books dealing with mental health.

We have a whole legal services division, too. There's a Legal Advisor's Office, which is primarily involved with international law and making treaties. We get a lot of requests for treaty information, and about the specific language used in treaties.

The department is constructed so there's a geographic division of labor, with country desks, and a subject division of labor, with functional bureaus. There is some overlap, of course. One of the more challenging questions I got recently was from a woman in the Office of Oceans and Environmental Affairs who wanted to keep track of joint ventures or joint scientific endeavors between the former Soviet Union and the United States. Someone recommended that she try Science Citation Index, which does identify people in these former Soviet republics who are writing scientific articles. But that's only part of the puzzle. It does not tell where their funding comes from, or whether a corporation or another type of institution is putting up the money. Even if you could identify the academic cooperative efforts, how can you get at the ones that are being funded by Ford, let's say, or Hewlett-Packard? This is a work in progress. Every time I see a database that I think might be helpful, I go at it. There are some newsletters in the area, but they're not comprehensive or cumulative. They're awkward to use on a current-awareness basis.

Ever since they discontinued the Soviet Science and Technology database, I don't really know where to go for that kind of information.

It sounds like someone should take up the gap. What other kinds of research do you get into?

We do a lot of document delivery. We go online for document delivery for things that we don't have in our own collection, like the IRS cumulative bulletins that we can get from LEXIS. When something is missing from the shelf, or when we're out of paper in our microfilm reader, we just go online and get it.

I mentioned that I really like being in control of things. Besides the common command chart, one of my other major investments of time and effort has been in creating a database of our periodical collection. The reference staff has always been responsible for maintaining some sort of indexed access to our periodicals. In 1984, we got our first personal computers, and I started to create an online index of periodicals. It records whether we have a periodical, its call number, whether we bind it, and how far back it goes, plus whether it's available online and if so, where, and how far back.

What's your search environment like in terms of hardware and software?

We started going online using SMARTCOM II, and we have not budged from that particular standard. I looked at SMARTCOM III and I didn't like it. SMARTCOM II does most everything that we need. We also use an earlier version of ProComm. We don't use DIALOGLINK. We do use LEXIS 2000. Juris has its own dedicated software. But primarily we use SMARTCOM II. Since we have so many different telephone numbers and passwords to access all our different systems, we use two copies of SMARTCOM II to allow room for logon scripts for everything.

We are running a network of 24 workstations in the library, four of which are end-user workstations. We are running one optical server at the moment, and 24 compact disc drives with about 22 different CD-ROM titles. We are planning to add another optical server and about a dozen more titles. These are all accessible on the public workstations.

How do most of your search requests come in?

They walk in the door. Occasionally, someone phones in. We're hoping to get onto a worldwide Department network so we can handle requests electronically from around the world. Now, people mostly just come in and say they want information on something. At that point, we decide whether it can be answered quickly online or by a judicious use of the collection.

The first step is to decide whether the request is a candidate for an online search. We have a search request form that has been evolving since we first went online in the mid-1970s. At this point, I think it's a pretty good form. A couple of years ago, we added a message at the top that says that searching commercial online information services involves the expenditure of government funds, and that searches are therefore done by trained library personnel and only for work-related questions or for training supported by the Department. That covers us in case we're ever investigated by our Inspector General for waste, fraud and abuse, in case we're accused of doing research at government expense for people who are taking courses that the Department doesn't pay for, or for their kids, or for subjects that they're interested in that have nothing to do with their employment.

The search forms are very useful because they get a requester to formulate their request in such a way that they can write it down. Often people have an amorphous idea of what they need, but when they write it down, it crystallizes. They fill the form out, and then we use it as a talking point. The first section is used to describe the subject. Some people know about keywords and jot them down, although we certainly don't insist on it. In fact, I really am not too fond of people second-guessing how we're going to conduct their research for them. I'd rather just have them put down a couple of sentences, and then I can extract words that I think would be useful. Sometimes when they say, "Here are the keywords," those aren't the keywords at all. Giving me a list of terms isn't nearly as useful as, "Tell me what you need, tell me what you want." It's vital to know what they need the information for. We used to ask requesters to tell us what information is *not* needed, in other words, what they had already looked at, but that confused them, so we eliminated it from the form. It's really up to the librarian to determine what they've already looked at. That's part of the reference interview.

Do you log search requests in some systematic way?

Each searcher keeps track of the searches he or she has done. We don't file the request forms in a centralized place. Of course, I've read the literature, and was involved in many of the discussions of how to keep track of these kinds of things. We've been in business for a very long time, and we've let a lot of that record-keeping go by the boards. We used to keep statistics that we reported weekly, but people would inflate their statistics to make it look like they were doing a lot more work.

Now we require that everybody report on the interesting topics they have researched during the past week. We prepare a weekly report that indicates what offices asked for a particular kind of information, and where we found it. This is especially valuable, because at the end of the year you have some record of the kinds of questions you've answered. You have something to give your supervisor on which they can base an evaluation. The weekly summary goes up the line to management, so senior managers can say, "Gee, the library did a search on such-and-such last week." That's much more useful than saying, "The library did 25 searches last week," because they can see directly where we have input. An Assistant Secretary might be sitting in a meeting with other Assistant Secretaries and say, "Oh, I see the library did a search for you last week." This may be news to the others, but it shows them how useful the library is. I think that's a wonderful way of maintaining a connection between the work we actually do and the people for whom it is done.

That kind of reporting takes a lot less time than keeping statistics. You don't have to remember to log in every request that you've done, or which databases you searched and how many hits you got. You don't have to itemize any of that, which is pretty meaningless, anyway. You can just say, "I had to search in five databases until I found one that actually did the trick." It's a snapshot of the work we're doing.

With all the systems you search, are individual staff members responsible for keeping up-to-date on particular systems, or is everyone pretty much of a generalist?

Everybody's a generalist. We don't have a big enough staff for specialization to make sense. Sometimes if people indicate that they have a particular interest in doing certain kinds of searches, then I try to redirect projects to them as they come in. Currently, we have two part-time and two full-time professional reference librarians in addition to myself. We all do online searching at various levels of expertise. One person besides myself has been searching for a considerable period of time. Two are recent library school graduates, so they're building their skills, and another has a fair level of expertise. In terms of preferences, one person has a lot of legal experience, which doesn't necessarily mean she likes doing that kind of work, but I tend to send legal stuff her way. Another really likes doing medical searches, so I send a lot of that sort of thing her way, but I like doing medical searches too.

I gather that you're not in a charge-back situation as far as search costs are concerned. Do you still find yourself going through mental equations about how much time and effort to spend on some requests relative to others?

Yes. The library as a whole tracks how much money is spent on each online service. I get reports from time to time saying that we're spending too much on such-and-such a service. I go back to the staff and I tell them that we've got to pull back on our use of such-and-such; we can't do a lot of printouts, we can't do a lot of full-text searching. That's the point at which we pull back. What it means is that people have to be on their toes about how they deal with the requester at the point when the request is made. When someone comes in and says, "I want the full text of all these articles," you have to negotiate. You might say, "Well, we don't have enough money to do that," and they understand, because *their* funds are being cut, too.

What we generally do when we go online is print out the search results in a short bibliographic format. If we're on Mead, we use the Cite format. We give the bibliographic records to the requester and, if the full text is available, we ask them to make a selection. We try to ask them to be as judicious as possible. Then we'll print out what they ask for. But it is negotiated all the way along.

Do you find yourself using certain sources repeatedly for certain kinds of questions?

We go to NEXIS a lot, and to other full-text databases, for nitty-gritty kinds of questions, where we can get the actual information online. We're getting more comfortable with the PAPERS file on DIALOG. I am trying to redirect some of our searching from NEXIS into other full-text sources, because NEXIS is a bit more expensive than others. The PAPERS file takes longer to search than it does to search CURRNT or even the News file on NEXIS. On the other hand, I like the way it outputs the information, listing all the articles from each paper in chronological order.

In practice, if we have a choice of where to go for the same information, each searcher decides where to look for it. The decision is based on how far back they have to go and how familiar they are with searching the system. Generally, when the same database is available on two services, I go to the one that I feel most comfortable with.

The other consideration is whether I will have to use another database on the same system to do more searching on the same subject. If, for instance, I'm going to have to look in the Washington Post and perhaps Public Affairs Information Service and perhaps ABI/INFORM, too, I may decide to do the whole thing on DIALOG, even though someone else may go to NEXIS for the Washington Post and then into DIALOG for the other two files.

The first step is to decide whether the question should, in fact, be answered online. The next is to choose the most logical database. I start broad when I don't think there will be much online about a subject; I cast my net as widely as possible. I start narrow when I'm afraid I'm going to be overwhelmed with hits. I try to get the requester to be as specific as possible. I restrict by general parameters like date or geographic area or language. Generally speaking—and this may surprise you—most of our users, although they may speak another language or maybe even several, want their research in English and don't want their research results in some other language.

I mentioned that I search full text for nitty-gritty information: events, statements, names, and new terminology. We had a request recently from a guy in our economic bureau for a search on "command basis GNP." I advised my staff member to go to the theoretical economic literature in Economic Literature Abstracts. She did, and she couldn't find a thing. Then I thought, maybe "command basis" is a new term, and the only way you're going to find it is to go into some big, broad, huge pool of free-text, full-text data—in other words, to take the needle-in-a-haystack approach. I advised her to go to CURRNT, the current file on NEXIS. She got ten hits there. They were all in the *Survey of Current Business* and, as it turns out, the term is used *only* by the *Survey of Current Business*. That was okay, that's what the requester wanted to know.

Usually my choice of systems or databases is topic-driven. I go into the index files because of the special nature of what they cover, whether it's chemistry, paper products or coffee. I often search abstract files for chronologies. We have a group of historians in the Department, and they often want to track an event, like all the summit conferences, back through time. The same thing is true for biographical information, and for geographic background data for people who are going overseas and who want to know what the political situation has been in the last six months.

Business International has been a lifesaver for that kind of search. I got a rush request from someone at 3:30 in the afternoon who needed—by close of business that day—everything that had been published in the last six months on the oil industry in Azerbaijan. I went into the Business International database and found that not only could you limit the search by USSR, but you could limit it by Azerbaijan. I got everything she could possibly want. Because she was in such a hurry, I determined what articles to print out in full text. I also got her one of the Business International snapshot profiles of Azerbaijan with the economic, political and demographic information, and then a whole bunch of articles on the Azerbaijan oil industry. She could write her paper and get it done in plenty of time. That's a good example, I think, of intelligent use of full text. Without that particular database, I would have been all over the map, so to speak.

When you're running a search, do you normally process it straight through, or is it iterative, where you check back with your client at various stages along the way?

Oh, very iterative. If I don't get the results I expect on the first pass, I generally feel there's something wrong. I get back to the requester to tell them that I didn't get the results they expected, or to ask them to define exactly what it is they want. This is where intuition comes in, as well as a good deal of experience. If you selected a database that you think ought to have information on the subject, and you don't find what you expect, or the number of hits you expect, then there's something wrong somewhere.

When I find too little information, I look for a file that might give me more. Or I redo the search using a different operator or a more distant proximity operator. Often I think searchers make the mistake of using an operator that is too specific. They use adjacency or a single phrase, when they would get better results by rotating the terms or using a NEAR operator. You can't always predict the order of terms in index files, abstract files, and especially in full-text files.

Usually when I search, I don't do a lot of preparatory work. If I'm using an indexed database, I go in with a free-text term, to see whether there is a keyword or descriptor I can use. In DIALOG I look at Format 8, which shows descriptor terms. I display maybe five or six records if they look relevant. Sometimes I display the abstract, too, to see whether the terms are coming up in the right context, or what other terminology is being used to describe the same subject. Then I'll play around with the terms.

I got a search once on "Buy America." That was the way the search came to me. I thought to myself that the term didn't sound quite right. So, just intuitively, I truncated on "America." That turned out to be smart, because almost all of the articles that I got were on "Buy American." Both phrases are right, both are used, but I would have missed a lot if I'd just gone in with "Buy America." That was instinct. I don't know how you can teach people to account for possibilities like that. There are cases where it would be safest to truncate, and cases where you shouldn't because it's going to set you up for a lot of false drops.

Truncation is tricky. When I am mapping out a big search that requires a lot of different terms I set up the different parts of the search in columns, put the synonymic terms together, and then decide which to truncate. For instance, I did a search on money laundering on offshore islands, like the Caribbean and other places. I had one column for money laundering, one column for "offshore" concepts, and one column for "place" concepts, the geographic parameter. Seeing the terms lined up that way makes it easier to decide which ones to truncate.

Of course, some words you should never truncate. "Policy" is one. You have to put in "policy or policies," or you get "police," and that sort of thing. That reminds me of a pet peeve I have about NEXIS—I don't understand why they don't yet have an option to turn off the automatic pluralization feature. Many times we need to search on AID, the Agency for International Development. That can't easily be done, because you're going to pull up entirely too much about AIDS. *(Now NEXIS has this feature. —RB, September 1993)* So, there are considerations about which database to select based on system features, and what kind of difficulties you might encounter on one system or another.

Again, that's where training comes in, plus familiarity with how a particular system works. No matter how much training you've had, if you don't have a lot of experience on top of the training, you're not going to have the knowledge to make that sort of judgment.

How quickly, typically, do you turn searches around?
Usually the same day. It depends on the time of day that the request comes in, of course. If someone tells us that they need it by the close of business, we try to accommodate them. We have a sort of triage approach. Okay, this person said that they needed it today; now can we call the other guy and say, "We just got a rush request, if we can't finish yours until tomorrow, do you mind?"

Just how anguished did that fellow sound? Or is this the guy who always "needs it today" and then lets it sit on his desk?
That's right. We get very, very unhappy when we've made a special effort to get something done in record time, and then the person doesn't pick it up. In fact, they may *never* pick it up, because it turns out they needed it to answer a question right then, and they hadn't told us that they needed it *that* quickly.

What about output? Given your turnaround time, I assume you print everything online or download to disk and then print it out.

We discovered that no printer can keep up with 2400bps, so we invariably download. We do a certain amount of post-processing and cleaning up, especially if we're going to fax the results and we need to get it down to a manageable number of pages.

Do your requesters care about where the information came from? Do you list the databases and document the strategy you used?

Sometimes people will come in and say "I want a NEXIS search." If NEXIS is not the appropriate place to get the information, we'll generally tell them. Most people don't care. Some users do like to see what the search strategy was, but those are mostly people who are somewhat sophisticated about how searching is done; perhaps they've done it themselves. They might want to replicate it at some point, or want us to do an update for them.

What haven't we touched on, in the area of search skills, that you'd like to mention?

I think a lot of searchers don't understand enough about what the computer is actually doing when it's "searching." It's not just a matter of understanding what an inverted index is, it's understanding that each term is assigned a number, a unique address. The computer isn't really looking at the word you think it's looking at. Just because *you* can see two words adjacent on the screen doesn't mean that the computer is seeing them that way, and indeed it's not.

When I became chairperson of our local online user group, back from 1981 to 1983, I invited the pre-eminent trainers from each of the major online services to come and talk about how their computers were actually looking at the information. Anne Caputo did a series of wonderful sessions on how the DIALOG system works; people from BRS talked about how they throw all the terms together in a single pool. Someone from ORBIT talked about how they did it, and someone from NEXIS described how their system works. Hearing all four perspectives gave us a feeling for the reality that these are all totally different systems.

This goes way beyond what you get in the standard training session, because the trainers just tell you how to do it. They don't tell you what the computer is looking at. You grasp the fact that even commands that superficially appear to be doing the same thing are based on totally different ways of loading the data, totally different kinds of indexes. Obviously, none the speakers gave us proprietary information, and they didn't try to teach us programming. But the simple explanation of how their computers do it was extremely useful. We don't have enough of that kind of training. Fortunately, I got it at a time when I needed it. It's now part of my background and the way I approach a search, but it's not how new searchers are taught to think.

I also find, and this may be true of all of us who started searching way back, that I still use some of the old DIALOG commands, such as COMBINE. Also, on DIALOG you have to remember—and this goes back to what I was saying about how the system works—that if you put in two words with a space between them, it only searches in the descriptor field. This is an anachronism in this day and age, when most systems search for terms in proximity when they are entered that way.

Another thing that I feel is critical is that searchers are not given enough information about each new file that's loaded to make an intelligent decision about whether or not it's going to be useful. DIALOG's *CHRONOLOG*, for instance, announced that TEXTLINE had come online, and that all the English-language periodicals would be in full text. But they didn't provide a list of what those periodicals are. How useful is that? Until you go online there's no way of determining which ones are going to be available in full text.

Of course, I also know that "full text" doesn't really mean "full text." TEXTLINE is a business database, so it's bound to be selective. It's the same kind of "full text" as in Business Dateline and ABI/INFORM. Even when you know it's selective, you don't know *how* selective, or by what criteria. Not enough information is given about the database. In a sense, it's a little bit dishonest. It's certainly not fair to the searchers, because we'll say to someone, "This journal is full-text on ABI/INFORM now." But when you go online, where is the article?

What other problems do you encounter in terms of quality and completeness?

I constantly remind searchers on my staff to do an EXPAND on names of authors and companies, and even of subjects if the database allows. There is just no way we can second-guess how a name is going to be entered. Anytime there are alternative ways that information might be entered, I do an EXPAND instead of going in with a straight SELECT statement. I just think it's safer.

What kind of search do you enjoy the most?

My favorite searches are the ones that allow me to explore either a new area, or a database that has just come up or that I have not had a chance to use before. The Azerbaijan search I described gave me a wonderful opportunity to use the Business International database. I also probably could have used the new NEXIS geographic group file; I like the idea of grouping search resources geographically. I also like the challenge of figuring out the most effective technique to get the answer I need.

What do you think makes a good searcher?

I think that a good searcher cannot be distinguished from a good reference librarian; they're one and the same. This was made clear to me by one of my former colleagues who was not comfortable with online searching. In his case, the discomfort with online searching made visible his lack of intuition about the reference process altogether. The process really is very much the same. You have to decide what sources you're going to look at. You have to be familiar with your collection, or with the resources that are available to you. You have to be familiar with the contents of those resources, the format and the indexes.

With online searching you also have to know the command language, sure. But mastery of a command language and facility with the use of computers and so on are just techniques. Technical expertise helps you get more out of an online product, but it's not as important as being aware of what the resources are in the first place. Database selection, the selection of the appropriate reference tool, is the most important thing. Building up a databank, in your head, of appropriate and useful resources is what makes a good professional librarian and a good searcher.

Database selection is the one thing that the end-user is not good at; it is very, very difficult for an end-user to be aware of the full extent and range of databases available. But if you're going to be answering different kinds of questions in different kinds of databases the way we do here, you really need to spend all your time learning what's available and becoming acquainted with it and using it.

How much of a role does creativity play in deciding how to approach a problem, or how to choose search terms?

We don't spend a lot of pre-game time, as it were, looking up vocabulary terms; we don't make a special point of collecting all the thesauri. If you're not familiar with a subject, use a dictionary or an encyclopedia that will give you some terminology. Do a little research on your own to familiarize yourself with the subject area. It's nice to be able to get some idea of what it is you're searching before you go online. Say you're not familiar with the term "nephritis." It helps to have a general idea that this is about kidneys. Or that hepatitis B is a liver disease. It helps to have some background information, no matter how minimal.

My mind happens to be a trash heap of bits and pieces of information. I don't know whether you'd call this "creativity" or not—I have little hooks all over my head, and they have all sorts of little connections on them. I have a bit of experience in a lot of different areas, and very few subjects come in that are completely new. I read widely. Before I came to the State Department, I was a reference librarian in academic libraries, and you get the full range of questions there. I have an honors degree in general studies. General studies, what a wonderful degree for a reference librarian! You have to be acquainted with many things but a master of none. I've often thought it was a mistake for reference librarians to have to get an advanced degree. An advanced degree in *what*? You don't need to know more than the average undergraduate knows in any one subject area. You need to know *something* about a wide *range* of subjects.

It's useful to know, when you're doing free-text searching—and this is something that they bring up in NEXIS training—what the European terms are. It helps to have a good vocabulary. If you're looking for articles on wealth in the United States, then it might behoove you to look at articles on poverty, too. It's very useful to try to draw on as much as you know about a subject. I did a search for someone on small businesses in Japan. He had specific terminology relating to small businesses that he wanted to use. He sat with me while we did the search. First, I put in the term he wanted; we weren't finding anything. I said, "Let's just *try* these other terms." By Jove, we found everything we wanted.

You have to be flexible in your thinking, and not ruled by your preconceptions. You try one way, and if it doesn't work, you try another. Whatever you do, you have to be prepared for all the different angles.

SUPER SEARCH SECRETS

On document delivery online...

We go online for document delivery for things that we don't have in our own collection, like the IRS cumulative bulletins that we can get from LEXIS.

On search software...

SMARTCOM II does most everything that we need....Since we have so many different telephone numbers and passwords to access all our different systems, we use two copies of SMARTCOM II to allow room for logon scripts for everything.

On search request forms...

The search forms are very useful because they get a requester to formulate their request in such a way that they can write it down. Often people have an amorphous idea of what they need, but when they write it down, it crystallizes. They fill the form out, and then we use it as a talking point.

On keeping search logs...

Each searcher keeps track of the searches he or she has done. We don't file the request forms in a centralized place....we require that everybody report on the interesting topics they have researched during the past week. We prepare a weekly report that indicates what offices asked for a particular kind of information, and where we found it. This is especially valuable, because at the end of the year you have some record of the kinds of questions you've answered.

On favorite sources...

We go to NEXIS a lot, and to other full-text databases, for nitty-gritty kinds of questions, where we can get the actual information online. We're getting more comfortable with the PAPERS file on DIALOG.

On selecting an system...

...if we have a choice of where to go for the same information, each searcher decides where to look for it. The decision is based on how far back they have to go and how familiar they are with searching the system. Generally, when the same database is available on two services, I go to the one that I feel most comfortable with.

On decision points in the search process...

The first step is to decide whether the question should, in fact, be answered online. The next is to choose the most logical database.

On truncation...

Truncation is tricky. When I am mapping out a big search that requires a lot of different terms I set up the different parts of the search in columns, put the synonymic terms together, and then decide which to truncate....Seeing the terms lined up that way makes it easier to decide which ones to truncate....Of course, some words that you should never truncate. "Policy" is one. You have to put in "policy or policies," or you get "police..."

On using EXPAND...

I constantly remind searchers on my staff to do an EXPAND on names of authors and companies, and even of subjects if the database allows. There is just no way we can second-guess how a name is going to be entered.

On free-text searching...

It's useful to know, when you're doing free-text searching—and this is something that they bring up in NEXIS training—what the European terms are. It helps to have a good vocabulary.

CHAPTER 5

LINDA COOPER: CLIENT-CENTERED ENTREPRENEUR

Linda Cooper is President of Cooper Heller Research, Inc., an independent research firm in Philadelphia.

How did you get started in the online world?

I graduated from Drexel University with a master's in library science in 1977. Database searching hadn't really become a part of the library school curriculum, though we discussed some of the concepts. I was hired at ISI, the Institute for Scientific Information, as an indexer and a manual researcher. I worked with Eugene Garfield there for about five years. I pretty much started my own business on his recommendation. He told me that if I could fulfill his research needs, I could probably fulfill anyone's. He was quite an inspiration to me.

It was at ISI that I learned to search, but in kind of a roundabout way. When we needed online searching, we'd have to request it from another department. I had to go say, "Gene Garfield wants to find out how many times so-and-so has been cited." So this fellow would sit down at his Silent 700 terminal and rip out a SciSearch for me. One day, when I asked for a search he said, "Well, I'm just about sick of this, so you're going to learn to do it. Stand here and *watch*." So I did, for the next half dozen or so searches.

This was back when people were still using pluses, minuses and asterisks in their DIALOG searches instead of ANDs and ORs. It was really hard for me to follow. But he'd occasionally reach over with a pen and scribble something on the printout, and say, "this means OR." I'd say, "Sure, okay." Then I took the printout back to my office and said, "What *is* this? What are these people *talking* about?" But I started doing searches myself on his Silent 700. Eventually he got a more powerful machine and gave the Silent 700 to my department. DIALOG grew, and I grew as a searcher. I never went to DIALOG training. I learned everything hands-on.

Tell me what your physical search environment is like now.

We started out with IBMs, and we've gradually switched to Macs. We're completely networked now. I finally bought a PowerBook, and now I do almost everything on it, even in the office. We use SMARTCOM for searching on both the IBM and the Mac.

One of the things I find fascinating is how little I really know about computers and software. This is despite the fact that I spend ten or eleven hours a day working with computers and software. It's not that I'm proud of it; it's just a fact. To me, computers are just a tool to reach another machine that can help solve my client's problems. I don't know how many other people feel that way, but I can't stand fussing around with the software. I have absolutely no interest in it.

What do you view as Cooper Heller's market niche? Who are your clients, generically speaking?

My clientele is mainly people who write for a living. That means people in public relations, communications, marketing and sometimes journalism. Often, it's people who need to write or evaluate marketing plans. Sometimes, they just want to justify what they already know damn well they want to say. They call me for the statistics, background and so forth.

We also talk to a lot of consumers, people who have never heard of database searching. But they need it for one reason or another, and don't even really know what they're asking for. That can be quite a challenge. One of my researchers had a funny conversation with a woman from Texas who wanted an article from the *Houston Post*. We explained that it would probably take about ten or 15 minutes to do the search and explained the costs. Our time would be $18.75 based on our $75 an hour rate, plus database costs of x amount, which would probably add up to $25 or $30 for this article. She listened to the whole spiel, and then she said, "So you mean to tell me I have to pay $30 for an old newspaper?"

Granted, that sounds like an awful lot of money for a photocopy, which I'm sure is what she was thinking. We're not really set up to do document delivery, anyway. We do a lot of referrals to document delivery firms and to the library. But we also talk to *bona fide* new clients, business people, who are almost in the same position as the off-the-street consumer. They don't know what this is all about or what they're really asking for. We spend a lot of time with clients like that.

This year we began running DIALOG's DialSearch, a telephone search service that provides expert searching of all of DIALOG's databases. I ran a similar service for years for VU/TEXT, a sister company of DIALOG that's based here in Philadelphia, providing searches for clients who were not VU/TEXT subscribers. Many people call the online services asking for literature searches. They either can't or don't want to do it themselves, and DIALOG isn't set up to do it for them, so those calls are referred to us. If what they need can be covered by a DIALOG search, we handle it. We turn more than half these projects around within 24 hours. DialSearch actually has two parts, the search service itself, and a referral service. If a client needs information that goes beyond what DialSearch can fulfill, we refer them to members of the Association of Independent Information Professionals who have registered with DialSearch.

How do most of your projects come in?

Ninety percent of our business is by phone. We try to encourage people to fax the details. We occasionally get a direct fax request from a client who already knows us, knows how to use us, and doesn't need that voice contact. It's about the same with e-mail; we might get one project a week that way.

What's the first thing you do when a client calls with a search?

The phone rings. I say, "I'm not getting it." Usually people ask to talk to Linda Cooper, which can be a pain in the neck. If your name is connected with the company, you're the one they want to talk to.

Once they've identified themselves, we make an *ad hoc* distinction: Class I and Class II. We field about 200 calls a month, so we really have to divide them into categories. Class I consists of current clients, people you've worked with before, and Class II is people off the street. We emphasize custom research, so when a *bona fide* client calls, we want to jump right on it. We try to listen hard and not make them talk any longer than they need to. We really focus on that phone call.

Class II calls are also divided into categories. One is, this person finally found us and they *need* to be here. The other is, "Get rid of this person as efficiently, politely and quickly as you can in a way that will be helpful to them and not detrimental to us or our clients." A lot of the skill in fielding calls breaks down into knowing, within the first minute, what category the person you're talking to fits in.

Next we reach for a job sheet. We have two kinds. The more detailed one is for what we call quick-and-dirty searches, the off-the-street clients that might use us once, maybe, for a $30 newspaper article. We try not to spend more than ten minutes on the phone with them, but we have to get a lot more information than we do with repeat clients. We need their exact address, phone, fax, Fedex number, credit card or credit approval information, time, date, deadline, rush or no rush, and ballpark and not-to-exceed estimates. All the details are clearly spelled out.

The other kind of job sheet is for long-standing, good clients. It's basically a lot of blank space where we jot down whatever they say. They're telling their story, basically, and that's the way I direct the conversation. The reference interview section on the quick-and-dirty form is about two and a half inches high, and the same space on the long-standing clients form is half a page. We really invest a lot more listening time in the reference interview for our ongoing clients.

After a job comes in, do you keep any kind of project log?

We have an erasable wall chart where we log in each job as it gets sold. It lists the job number, subject, client name and company, budget and due date. We erase each project when it's invoiced. There's also a rolling file, a cart with hanging file folders that we make up in advance with job numbers. So when job 1030 is sold, you go over, put the search form in the file marked 1030, and mark it on the board. So you've got a search form, a file folder and a board. Then everyone can figure out what the job number is, where the paperwork is living until the project is finished, when it's due, and how much they can bill for it.

Let's focus on the reference interview itself. How do you get at what they really want?

The first few minutes I like to be open-ended and just listen to them ramble. After that, I have a series of questions that help us zero in on some factors we need to know. I usually start by saying something like, "It would help if you could tell us a little bit about what you're going to be using this information for. If you can't, that's okay." Some people are sensitive about confidentiality, but they usually understand that we're not asking them to divulge everything, we're just trying to get some context. We *will* sign a nondisclosure agreement if it makes them feel more comfortable. If it's an old client, of course, we just say, "What are you using this for, pal?" With new clients we're really careful about asking that question, because it *is* so important.

We always give a ballpark estimate on the first call. We do that in one of two ways. We might say, "Sounds like a $600 search," or we'll ask, "Do you have a budget in mind?" We usually wind up setting a not-to-exceed price, which is generally a figure that I toss out. How we approach it depends on the client. Some clients just want to know, "Am I talking $150 or am I talking $3000?" Other clients are always sort of hesitant; they've been "told they can have $300." They couldn't care less how that breaks down in terms of labor versus online costs. Ninety-five percent of them don't care what I'm doing with the money. They just want to know the total that they'll be billed. Our standard line is that it'll be within 25 percent either way.

How do you calculate what a project is going to cost?

I have two basic methods. One is for the type of project with which you're very familiar. "I need articles from major business publications on the Bendix Corporation between the years of this and that." If you're generally familiar with what is going on in the business world, and you know that there wasn't an explosion in the literature about that company during that period, then you count on an average amount of coverage. You divide the project into one of three categories.

I basically think in terms of A, B and C projects. There's a minimum-but-adequate effort, a medium effort, and a no-holds-barred. The numbers that correspond to those, generally speaking, start with $150, which is more or less our minimum, although it's actually getting to be too low. That covers about an hour of research and related database charges. That's usually appropriate for a small client with a limited budget, when I know that they will be very happy with a $200 project, and I think I can do a good job for them for that price. Then there's the $300-$500 project, which is average-size, average-complexity, for clients with a decent but not very large budget. Finally, there's the $700-$1200 project, which is usually for large companies for whom money is not that big an issue, but I know that I'll really have to work hard for them. Those are the three categories that I can pull out of the hat. I give the client a ballpark figure and ask them to set a not-to-exceed, and they'll say, "Do not go over $650."

That approach works when you have a general sense of what you're getting into. Another category is when they ask for a mailing list, or everything that's been printed in local newspapers about, say, Imelda Marcos. You have no idea how much material you're going to find. In cases like that, I tell them I'll get back to them that day or the next with an estimate. If I think it's a likely sale, I do a quick preliminary search to get the counts. If I don't think it's a likely sale, I just think about it and give them a figure based on my past experience, an educated hunch. Maybe 20 to 25 percent of our searches involve doing some preliminary work to nail down the price. I may use DIALINDEX for that, or go directly into the databases, whatever seems appropriate.

I have a big clock in front of my desk. I also have a clock radio that I can click on, and it runs for an hour playing music and then goes off. We also use kitchen timers, for estimates in particular. I'll set the timer for 15 minutes. When that bell goes off, I don't do another thing except maybe quickly come up with a final price. If you're a good, curious searcher, you can get so involved in your estimate that you don't come out until you've solved the whole search problem. After the client has agreed to pay for the time, even if the searcher has spent too much time on it, it's going to be okay as long as the search is going somewhere. But before the thing is sold, we sometimes have to pull ourselves back to reality and remember that no one is paying for this yet.

When I get back to the client with an estimate, I can tell by their voice if the figure I'm quoting is close to what they were expecting. If I sense that it isn't, I tell them that if the estimate I'm giving them is not appropriate to their concept of the project, they should give me some idea of what they were expecting. Almost always, I can figure out pretty quickly what, if anything, I can do for that amount. I may come back to a client and say, "I think we're looking at $350 here," and I can tell from their reaction that it's much more than they were expecting. So I'll ask, "What *did* you have in mind?" and they say "$150." Then I can reply, "For that, we can do the following..." It works out pretty well that way, because they're getting *something*, but they know they're not getting what I would really like to do for them.

I do tell them explicitly what they're *not* getting because they can't afford it. We generally call what we're doing for them a preliminary search. When I send it out, I say, "Enclosed are the results of our preliminary search on your topic of ABC. The total charges so far are $178.27. If we were to continue, we would need you to increase the budget to $500, as we discussed on the telephone. If you would like us to do anything further, please call me to discuss it." Sometimes I give them an indication of the kinds of things we might be able to do for them, given a budget increase. About half the time, they do come back. They take what I've given them to their Powers-That-Be, and they say, "If you give me $300 dollars more for this, I can get what we *really* need."

What are some typical projects? What are you working on now?

Here's a client who has developed a new kind of toothbrush for children. She asked for a complete overview of the dental care market for children. She wanted everything from statistics on how often kids go to the dentist, to case studies of how parents teach their children to brush their teeth and what problems are associated with that training, to profiles of other companies that are making childrens' toothbrushes, to a list of competing products. Getting all this information involved searching ten or so different databases.

We're working on phase two of that project now. The client called yesterday and told us, "I've got a major corporation in personal care products biting on my proposal. Tell me *everything* about them for the last six months to a year. Get their annual report. Get their financial statistics, their press releases, their management changes, their new product lines, their advertising and their marketing plans. Get everything that's been written about them in the local newspapers." She's going to use all this material to make herself smart about this company. We do a lot of similar projects, although not all of them are this extensive.

We also have clients who are doing benchmarking in areas like corporate communications, public relations or quality. They want us to find companies "just like them," in cities across the country, that have gotten press for doing something innovative. A lot of managers have gotten the quality bee in their bonnet, and they tell their people, "Get out there, make site visits and find out how Federal Express won the Baldrige Quality Award." My client isn't going to pick up the phone and call Federal Express and say, "Can you tell us how you won this award?" So we survey the management literature for them, find out who's doing well and getting recognition in these areas. Then we call the companies and try to get the names and phone numbers of the people responsible for administering the program they're interested in, so our clients can call them directly if they want.

What databases do you use the most?

I always start in one of three places. PROMT is the first place I go, usually, for an industry overview. If the client doesn't have enough money for PROMT, I go to Trade & Industry Index. If it's clear from the outset that this is a very local company, or if the client says, "I heard about a new competitor. It's a tiny company located in Salt Lake City, and I want to know if they've ever been in the newspaper before," then I go straight to the newspaper databases. Often it's stupid to try PROMT for these tiny companies, although I do find myself trying it anyway, just in case. Part of me always thinks the company will show up there. For one-stop shopping, I go to PROMT.

How do you figure out your search strategy? Do you block it all out ahead of time, or just start with an idea in your head?

In certain rare cases, I begin by making notes on paper, but I do that less and less as the years go by. When I do make notes, it's usually after I've done a preliminary search. That might sound a little backward, but what a preliminary search does is tell me whether I'm in the right universe. Am I using the database I need to be using? Will I be able to actually produce an answer? I mostly do that by printing titles. Sometimes I start with CROS in Data-Star or DIALINDEX in DIALOG, to help with file selection.

If I'm going into PROMT, I routinely look up product codes first. I know the event codes by heart, so I'll slap in an event code with a good product code, and limit it to the last year or so. I get 65 hits or whatever, print out the first ten titles, tell the system to hang onto my search, logoff and look at what I've got. Then I start putting pen to paper and figuring out what I'm doing. The titles are usually enough to tell me if I'm headed in the right direction, and if this is going to be a hard one or an easy one.

This might sound strange, but if I don't start in PROMT, I often start with *Business Periodicals Index*. We subscribe to the print publication, and we keep it very close to our desks. You can do things like find out how to spell Bhopal. You can find out if this large corporation that you've been asked to search on has in fact made a lot of news, or if it's what we call a quiet corporation, one that wants to stay *out* of the news. If you get a subject search in an unfamiliar area, you can get some of the lingo from *BPI*; you can use it like a dictionary. What is "benchmarking," anyway? You can get that from context even if you're just looking at cites. Has the term even appeared in *BPI* yet? If it hasn't, that means we'll probably have to do some free-text searching. I don't use *BPI* the way it was meant to be used, to gather citations. I know they're going to come up, anyway, when I go online. I use it as a tool to show the paths that I'm going to have to follow to do the search.

This leads into my next question. What kinds of documentation do you look at before you go online? What references do you keep near the search terminal?

The most important guide is the Predicasts code manual. Next is *Business Periodicals Index*, then the database documentation, the bluesheets and so on, for the online systems we use the most. We use *Fulltext Sources Online* a lot, and we've ordered the other BiblioData publication, *Newspapers Online*. We also keep a rolling file of newsletters, tip sheets and things that we get in the mail from the online services and the database producers. There's a file folder for each online system, and for each of our "fave" files and file families, like Predicasts and IAC. It's sort of an extension of an in-box. We just shove the material in the folder. Then when we're stumped, we say, "Well, what *have* these people been sending me all these months?

Maybe I'd better read it." We clean it out three or four times a year to make sure that the information is current.

How do you approach a search? Obviously, it varies by project, but what are the various ways you look at it?

I try to be as specific as possible, starting with a Predicasts product code, for instance, combined with an event code or a free-text term like "market share." If hits come spilling out on that, you're golden. If they don't, I generally don't muck around; I shoot way out to the broadest possible approach. I put in, say "toothbrush," just to see what comes out this time. I'll pull titles, look at some descriptors, and do a couple of KWICs, to find out where the hell we are. It's not rare to find myself changing direction or calling a halt in midstream. "Well, that approach wasn't productive, now let's go broad and see what the possibilities are. Maybe a different product code will pop out." It makes sense, economically, to do all that in one session. When I sit down, I've got to be prepared to go both narrow and broad. I have sort of a mental backup going on, like, "If this one doesn't work, I'll try this other area."

I used to spend a lot of time looking up controlled vocabulary ahead of time. I don't anymore. Instead, I pretty much do it live online. I try to find an on-target article right off the bat, and use it to get to the indexing terms. Or I EXPAND in an online thesaurus to see what terms are available. Then I do a logoff hold on DIALOG, or FILE into a cheap file, so I can go back to my search after I've thought about it. I find that much more efficient than purchasing a bunch of print thesauri and keeping them up to date, and having to paw through the pages. There are a couple of exceptions, like the ERIC thesaurus. That is kind of a false economy, I guess, because the ERIC database itself is so cheap, but the thesaurus is well thought out. The other is Predicasts, which I mentioned I look at constantly.

Do you tend to go for full text whenever it's available, or do you sometimes go into a citation file first?

It depends on the client, but I seldom search or print full text from the get-go. I usually start with a bibliographic file like Newspaper & Periodical Abstracts, because it pulls together a lot of sources, including the *Wall Street Journal* and the *New York Times*. You can get a sense of what's out there, and then decide whether you're going to go into NEXIS, Dow Jones or some other full-text database. I either send the cites to the client or make a decision myself. In general, I try to hold off on the full text because I don't want to overwhelm my clients with a lot of stuff.

I do print full text when I know it's really good, but I do it selectively. I write down the record numbers with my eyes on the screen. Then I just say, "Type 3/9/42..." or whatever, and pull the ones I'm sure of. I don't even logoff to look at the titles. I use the buffer on my Mac, which is pretty large, and while the system is downloading titles or whatever, I can page down at my speed. Generally, by the time it finishes scrolling, I'm on the last page. I'm just a few seconds behind it, so it isn't costing any more in connect charges, and I just shoot right in to the TYPE command.

Do you do a lot of multifile searching?

I do. I do a broad multifile search when I'm trying to get a handle on a subject and I have no idea where to start. For instance, we were asked to find out who's using lasers to clean things. Figuring out the search strategy for something like that is kind of complex, because the applications could be anywhere, and the technology is fairly new. So I threw it into the ALL category in DIALINDEX, because, you know, why bother to think? It will tell you the ten files out of 300 that you should be looking in.

Next, I transfer the search itself into those files, and run the same broad strategy I used in DIALINDEX. I learned the hard way not to refine too much before going into a OneSearch, because you lose a lot. Then when I get the OneSearch results, I always type the first couple of hits FROM EACH database in the title format. Using the FROM EACH command is important, because it shows you a cross-section of what you're getting. If you start directly with a OneSearch with a group like the Predicasts files, it helps to know whether your 40 hits are all from PROMT. If they are, that means a lot of them are probably going to be older than if each file had several hits.

When I get my results, I might go back into an individual file and refine my search. If "laser" and "cleaning" or whatever I started with turns up a perfect record in Predicasts with a product code that might be useful, then I look up that product code in the thesaurus. I see what it's related to, read the citation itself more carefully, maybe pull out some other terms, and generally get a little smarter on the issue before I go back online.

Do you use the deduplication feature where you can to eliminate duplicate citations?

I use it on DIALOG a lot. I always put my favorite file, PROMT, in first, so if there are duplicates, I'm sure to get the records from PROMT. If it's more of a management than a marketing-type project, I may put ABI/INFORM in first. Usually, though, I do a DIALINDEX search first. Then as the system posts the number of hits for each file, I scan the columns and jot down the files with the most hits, the ones that have 90 hits when all the others have 3 or 4. I screen out the ones where I know that the high postings must be false drops, like a Japanese company database where I'm sure one of my terms just happens to occur in the wrong context. Then I throw the most fruitful-seeming ones into my OneSearch.

What do you do to refine results when you've gotten too many hits? How do you narrow it down?

If I can, the first thing I usually do is limit by date, to the last year or year and a half. I play with the vocabulary a lot. I take a key term that I might have entered as a synonym in an OR statement, that seems to be used in most of the really relevant articles. I'll AND it back in so it appears in everything. Or I restrict my key terms to the title, descriptor or lead paragraph. I might take out a word, if it seems to be bringing in a lot of marginal stuff. Maybe I included it because I thought I'd need it, in case I got too little. I might put in an odd combination of words, something that it wouldn't normally occur to you to try.

Here's an example of that. The other day I was searching in an subject area called geotextiles, for a kind of fabric called non-woven fabric. "Non-woven geotextiles" was the exact term I used. I ran it through DIALINDEX, and I almost fainted when I saw how much came up; there was a ton of stuff. So I called the client and asked what she was trying to do. She said, "I'm trying to prove that non-woven geotextiles are better than woven." So I went back online and put in "geotextiles" and "non-woven" AND "woven," meaning that the articles I get have to talk about both kinds. That really narrowed it down.

There's another way to approach that, which I sometimes use. That's to include terms like "cost-benefit," "better," "superior." I use the word "success" and "successful" a lot, because writers like to use that word. If something was successful and your client wants success stories, it works. I've fallen back on that many times, with very happy and successful results.

Here's another example. A client wanted some information for a speech on why it's more cost-effective for a business to conduct itself ethically. I did a search in the management literature, and kept getting stories about how Nestle mishandled infant formulas in the Third World, and about the Exxon oil spill, the Bhopal refinery disaster and so on. What the client wanted was general articles about ethical behavior in business, and all I was getting were stories about specific incidents. I finally just took them all— Nestle, Arco, Bhopal, and a couple of others I'd found—and I said that they *all* had to appear. That worked, because what I found then were case studies that were referred to in the course of a more general discussion.

What about the opposite kind of situation, when you've gotten too little information?

First of all, a seasoned searcher usually has that alarm bell go off during the reference interview, the one that says, "Oh no, this sounds like it could be a tough one." In that case, I tell the client right away that there may not be very much out there. "How about if I spend half an hour and then I'll call you back?" That gives me enough time to find out if my instinct is correct. I may have to go back to the client and say, "We can't find anything about this particular aspect of plastics recycling that you're talking about. Would something of a more general nature be helpful to you?" Sometimes it is. That makes it easy because you already know where to look and how to approach getting the more general stuff.

I did a project on the designer sunglasses market where we didn't find very much on designer sunglasses *per se*. But I was able to combine the sunglasses market, in general, with a couple of consumer behavior articles about the appeal of designer labels. That gave the client all the information she needed.

Exactly. I always make sure they get *something* for their money. If there truly is nothing available, I often write a detailed memo about what I've searched, what those sources cover, how far back, the words I used and the whole routine. I may include database descriptions that I paste in from the online blue sheets. I have a couple of them stored on disk, for the databases I use heavily, and I just pull them into my word-processing document.

How do you know when a search is done?

I think the best way to decide you're finished is when you start seeing the same material again in different databases. Unless there's something fundamentally wrong with the way you're thinking, you've probably done a thorough job. Of course, we usually stop because we run out of budget. Another stopping point is when there just aren't any more options; there's nowhere else to look.

At some point, we may realize that this is not an online project, this is a interview project, or whatever. It's the job of the database searcher to know the difference, either before the search is started, or once they get in there and look around a little. We can get seduced by this online stuff. We've got to stop sometimes and pull back and say, "No, this isn't going to work. We can answer this one in a phone call or two instead of spending $150 online."

How fast do you turn projects around?

I ask the clients what their time frame is. They almost always start by saying, "As soon as possible." I try to pin them down, because "as soon as possible" for one client might mean today, and for another it might mean a week. Most people either really do need it the same day, or else they're perfectly happy with a one-week turnaround. If I've got that week, though, I want to use it. Not only because I'm busy, but because I can do better work for them. I tell them that when we're negotiating the delivery time.

If it's not a rush project, I make a mental note of what's going on around here in terms of workload, and then suggest a date. I try not to suggest one that's more than a week in the future, unless the size of the project makes it necessary. Usually, I say, "Okay, this is Tuesday, how about this time next Tuesday?" Sometimes they freak out, and then I know that we have to talk about *this* week. Sometimes they say, "That would be great! My meeting isn't until May 15." When I hear that I jot it down. If I get in a jam, I can call the client and say, "I know that we discussed getting this to information to you by Tuesday. Would it make a great deal of difference to you if you don't receive it until Thursday?" We phrase it carefully, and they go over their schedule in their mind. Quite often they say, "Fine, I'm really not going to have a chance to look at it until Thursday, anyway." That works out really well, and they don't feel slighted.

Do you do a lot of post-processing?

I make it look really good, yes. I put page breaks between records, unless they're only citations. Even then we put in logical page breaks, so we don't break in the middle of a cite. Whether I strip out CODENs and ISSNs and so on depends on two things. If I need to analyze the search, to really go through it closely myself, I might as well clean it up while I'm scrolling down my screen. It doesn't cost anybody anything extra to do that. It also depends on the client. If they're going to pass my work along to someone else, I don't want them to have to clean it up. I do it for them out of goodwill.

Are we talking mostly print output here, or do your clients take electronic delivery, too?

We're about half and half at this point. We do ten to fifteen percent e-mail delivery, which is my favorite. We also do tons of what I call e-mail fax, through AT&T Mail and MCI Mail. My PowerBook has a fax modem. Print delivery is next, and disk is after that. People occasionally do ask for search results on disk, and since we have both Mac and IBM, that's no problem. I suspect our pattern isn't typical, that most people would do more print delivery, but it probably has something to do with our turnaround time. We work with a lot of large companies that live on fax. If it's 25 pages or more, I can usually convince them to let me Federal Express it. If it's less than 25 pages, they want it by fax. They don't have to know anything about e-mail. They receive it as a fax, and they like it, because it's really clear and crisp, much more so than a fax that starts out on paper. We don't have to pay for paper, or stand there and shove sheets into a fax machine. So that's just about become our default method for what I would call "short search" delivery.

We try to estimate what it's going to be like on the client's end, to be sure that they're not going to be on the receiving end of a 300-page fax. We specify 10-point type, and then use a command called Repaginate, which counts the pages and tells us within five percent how many pages it's going to be on the client's end. That also tells us how many pages to charge them for transmitting.

Do you document for your clients what databases you searched and what strategy or keywords you used?

I only do that when asked, or under special circumstances. I find it time-consuming to put together a summary like that, especially on rush projects. It also tends to encourage some clients, who think they're very smart about databases and really aren't, to second-guess me on strategy, file selection and so forth. I have a few clients who are very good database searchers themselves, or have been in former lives, and I do tell them what I've done. But most of my clients couldn't care less.

There are two exceptions. One is the null set search, when we've been asked to look for something and can't find it. It may be a trademark search, or something in the open literature. Often, the client wants to prove that it doesn't exist. So we tell them exactly where we went, what systems and databases we searched, and we include the database descriptions, like I described earlier.

The other exception is anything that's litigation-related. Then we spend an additional hour preparing a cover memo, explaining what we did and why we did it, what we got and where else we might look. In effect, we give them sort of a deposition on our research efforts. I do charge for the time it takes to write that up, and it makes me feel as if we're covered on our end, too.

Do you make a follow-up call after you've shipped a project out?

It depends on how busy we are and on the client. With big clients and big jobs, meaning $1000 or over, I always call. "Did you get it? Did you like it? Do you like me?" With really big jobs, I try to hand-deliver it. I always include in the cover memo a line saying, "Please call me after you've had a chance to review this material." Some do and some don't, but if anything's wrong or unclear or they want more work done, they call. I give them an open invitation to discuss it.

With old clients, I pretty much know if I'm going to have to discuss the results. I do try to call new clients the first time I send something out to them. I kind of hold my breath for the first ten seconds of the call, because I don't know what the person's going to say. It could go either way. I find that fascinating. You never know how someone is going to use information, or whether they even understand what it is you've done for them. If you're a designer, you have a lot more confidence, knowing that if a client thinks that what you did was worthless, it really wasn't. It's just a matter of personal taste. In the information business, we don't have that kind of luxury. I've been doing this for ten years and I still go through that ten-second period where my heart stops until they say, "This is exactly what I wanted."

I love it when you don't think you've done a particularly good search, and you send it out sort of apologetically, saying, "Well, we really tried." You document all the approaches you tried, and the client says, "It was fabulous! I know you didn't find *much*, but this one article answered all our questions."

About half the searches we do for new clients go out with a cover memo specifying that it was a preliminary search. It explains that so far we've used up no more than half their budget, and that I'd like them to look it over and call me. There are two reasons for doing that. One, I want to be sure I'm doing what they expect. Two, it gives me another day or two. You can do *half* a search pretty quickly. That technique works out well for us, and the clients like it. It saves them money, and they feel as if they're participating in the research process. After a few searches, I've learned a lot about how they expect information to be presented, not to mention about the way their business operates and their information needs in general. I tell new clients, right at the beginning, that we will not be doing business this way after a half a dozen projects, but that it's best for both of us to do it this way now. Of course, at the same time, I'm planting the idea of having us *do* half a dozen projects for them.

Sometimes, frankly, they're either too wealthy, too lacking in time, or they just don't care to participate in the research process. Sometimes, they've already made the time-versus-money calculation, and they just tell us, "No, I trust you; you're the expert in your field." But at least I've covered myself, and they know I'm being responsible on their behalf.

What do you like most about searching, and what do you dislike?

The thing that surprises me most about my line of work is how different every single project is. You'd think that after a number of years you'd just be able to whack these things out, but each one is always a little bit different. That's why I think it's funny when online services get all huffy about information brokers "reselling" search results. In ten years, I've had perhaps ten opportunities to resell something, and even then it wouldn't have worked because it was out of date. Every project has its own particular spin and takes a certain amount of creative skill.

What you do get good at after ten years is pricing. I can do it off the top of my head now. I spent my first five years as a database searcher trying to figure out how to estimate search fees. It's still a challenge to keep up-to-date on database features. I think our systems have to develop something beyond DIALINDEX to help us with file selection. They have to be more evaluative. These are their wares they're hawking. When you walk into a candy store, the candies that the store is pushing are displayed more attractively than the others. That's okay, but how do you know which candy has the most nutritional value or the least calories? I need to know that stuff.

Services have to start telling us, "For one-stop shopping, this file group is good, and for broad-based coverage, this one is good, and for up-to-date currency use these." They should annotate them somehow, or give us new kinds of file selection aids. I'm not talking about the obvious choices, like going to Trademarkscan for a trademark search. I'm talking about the individual personalities of the files, and what they're good for. I know the people in customer service know exactly what databases are good for what. I wish they could somehow codify that for us. Of course, the services will come back and give us a million reasons why they can't do that because of their royalty arrangements. But face it, not every database that's loaded is going to be the best file in the universe, and if we're going to be serious about this, we need some help.

How would you describe your own search style? Do you have one?

I think everyone develops their own approach. Barbara Quint delineated this very well in her series in *ONLINE*, when she talked about the grasshopper and the ant. Both styles—and there are variations on both of them—are legitimate. The ant searcher might be much more valid in technical areas and the grasshopper in business. An ant searcher who's trying to search on a breaking-news kind of business subject is going to have a hard time. She's going to have to get in there and muck about, because there *is* no right, logical way to proceed as there tends to be in medicine or engineering.

For really difficult and cutting-edge-concept searches, I believe in just diving in and swimming around and seeing what you can pull out. I'm definitely a grasshopper searcher. Grasshopper searchers might waste money sometimes, but ant searchers often waste time. It amounts to the same thing for a lot of people.

I love the searches that you just don't think are going to work. You wonder "*How* am I going to do this?" You think about it for a while, and maybe you look up a few things, and then you go online and *bang*—it just jumps off the terminal at you. That's really rare.

It's particularly inspirational to me when a search does work out well. I think of it as the result of a cooperative effort between me, an experienced searcher, and a huge, gigantic, lumbering computer with millions of documents that I somehow or another managed to convince to give me what my client needs. I think of my own little computer as a conduit into these huge things, which I picture as twelve stories high.

The most rewarding kind of search is where you're able to conceptualize, before you begin, exactly how you're going to solve the problem, and it just flows. One thing leads to another, browsing headlines brings up exactly the right phrases that you need to continue the search, and you flow into the next concept, the next database, and the one after that. That's a wonderful feeling. It comes with training, of course, but it also comes with expertise, being confident in your searching skills. You either know where you're going with it, or you don't. But you trust in the fact that it's either going to work or not. If it's not working you realize that quickly, get out and regroup. If it *is* working, you go with it, wherever it takes you. It's a real adventure.

SUPER SEARCH SECRETS

On tracking search projects...
We have an erasable wall chart where we log in each job as it gets sold. It lists the job number, subject, client name and company, budget and due date. We erase each project when it's invoiced. There's also a rolling file, a cart with hanging file folders that we make up in advance with job numbers....So you've got a search form, a file folder and a board.

On estimating search costs...
I have a big clock in front of my desk....We also use kitchen timers, for estimates in particular. I'll set the timer for 15 minutes. When that bell goes off, I don't do another thing except maybe quickly come up with a final price. If you're a good, curious searcher, you can get so involved in your estimate that you don't come out until you've solved the whole search problem....We sometimes have to pull ourselves back to reality and remember that no one is paying for this yet.

On favorite databases...
PROMT is the first place I go, usually, for an industry overview. If the client doesn't have enough money for PROMT, I go to Trade & Industry Index....For one-stop shopping, I go to PROMT.

On planning search strategies...
In certain rare cases, I begin by making notes on paper...usually after I've done a preliminary search....What a preliminary search does is tell me whether I'm in the right

universe. Am I using the database I need to be using? Will I be able to actually produce an answer? I mostly do that by printing titles. Sometimes I start with CROS in Data-Star or DIALINDEX in DIALOG, to help with file selection.

On documentation...

The most important guide is the Predicasts code manual. Next is *Business Periodicals Index*, then the database documentation, the bluesheets and so on....We use *Fulltext Sources Online* a lot, and we've ordered the other BiblioData publication, *Newspapers Online*. We also keep a rolling file of newsletters, tip sheets and things...

On output from a OneSearch...

...when I get the OneSearch results, I always type the first couple of hits FROM EACH database in the title format. Using the FROM EACH command is important, because it shows you a cross-section of what you're getting.

On being a grasshopper searcher...

For really difficult and cutting-edge-concept searches, I believe in just diving in and swimming around and seeing what you can pull out. I'm definitely a grasshopper searcher. Grasshopper searchers might waste money sometimes, but ant searchers often waste time.

CHAPTER 6

CAROL GINSBURG:
SUPPORTING THE GLOBAL DEALMAKERS

Carol Ginsburg is a Vice President in the Global Merchandising Department at Banker's Trust in New York. She is responsible for the overall operations of the Corporate Information Center and the SEC Document Center.

Tell me what your position involves, and how you came to be at Banker's Trust.

I was hired in 1982, when the bank decided they needed to have information to "do deals," as they call them in this business. The large centralized library had been closed in the late 1970s, so I was hired to start an electronic library. "Electronic" at that time meant a 300bps Texas Instruments terminal with the little rubber ears that you clamped the phone receiver into, and the thermal paper that we grew to hate.

We eventually moved up to PCs. As electronic information became available, we acquired more of it. We were one of the first libraries to get CD-ROMs. When electronic mail became available to the bank, we hooked into it as soon as we could, and I learned quickly how to download searches and upload them through the e-mail system.

We serve Banker's Trust worldwide. We started with a staff of three and now have a staff of twenty. We're open Monday through Friday, 8:30 a.m. to 9 p.m., and 10 a.m. to 6 p.m. on Saturdays. Besides the volume of work itself, we require a large staff to cover all those hours. There's another library in London with which we network closely, and one in Sydney, Australia, with which we're in touch primarily through e-mail. We use e-mail heavily to provide information to the Tokyo and Hong Kong offices as well as the European offices. We're kind of a secondary service to the European office; they go to the London library first, but we are the reference point for Los Angeles, Chicago and Houston as well. To serve them, along with e-mail, we have standalone LEXIS/NEXIS printers in each of the domestic offices. We do the searching here, but the passwords are associated with those printers, so the results print out there. In fact, I can do a search here on Park Avenue, and it will print out downtown at the Wall Street location.

So, we are very heavily networked. We've also had a local area network in place since the mid-1980s. The first thing we did on the LAN was our internal automation—our check-in, serials, acquisitions and cataloging. Everyone on my staff has access to the network. We've also integrated a charge-back package. We charge for everything that we do internally. Every search that we do is recorded, along with the time and what databases or hardcopy were used to answer the request. Then, once a month a disk gets passed to our controller's office with the charges. It's soft dollars, funny money, but it covers our costs and that's our goal.

Who are your clients? Are they primarily the principals who are putting the deals together?

The front line are the analysts and associates who were hired to do what they call the grunt work. Certainly we deal with folks on a more senior level, but the people whom we deal with primarily are the junior staff people, who then put the research together and pass it on to the senior folks. But what's nice, if you're here long enough, is that some of those junior people become managing directors. So then we have this rapport with people who know how to use the library and understand what we do, who are now fairly senior in the organization.

How do your search requests come in?

The bulk of the e-mail requests come in from Tokyo and Hong Kong. But most people call, and the people who work here walk in as well. Probably 50 percent of the requests come in over the phone and in person, maybe even 70 percent, and then the other 30 percent by e-mail. There is a plan to put our search request form into Lotus Notes so that they can just fill it out and submit them that way, through the network.

What kinds of requests do you typically get?

There are a lot of generic questions where you just plug in the name of a company or whatever. Even industry searches become routine if you're going into your favorite files, the ones where you feel you're going to get the best hits. But the more interesting, difficult ones really call on the skills of a good librarian. A lot of those questions are not going to be answered 100 percent online, they're going to be answered with other kinds of research, partially online and partially by making phone calls. I see information coming in by fax and Federal Express and so on, as well as online. Sometimes you just do what we all learned in library school—pick up the phone and call a trade association.

There are plenty of challenges, though. We're doing a lot more work now for our Latin American department, and trying to get very concrete information on various industries in Latin American countries, or company financials where there may not be any. Those are the areas that take a lot of concentration, and we may not come up with a really good answer. They just don't have the same traditions and requirements of disclosure that we do in the U.S. Our bank is at the forefront in Eastern Europe and, again, those are new areas for us. We're looking at new resources. There are some pretty good sources on NewsNet and on DIALOG for Eastern Europe and Latin America.

As far as typical searches are concerned, I just did a request for 30 days' worth of articles on a particular company and an acquisition that they made in Australia. That was straightforward. I found two articles that described it and they were perfect. There was a request for articles about the Chicago River flood and the businesses that were affected. The interest was primarily in business continuity. That request was from the part of our bank that deals with risk, our own as well as the client's.

We do a lot of SDI, current awareness searches. We do quite a few daily ones where we download the headlines of the *American Banker* and send them out electronically. I think some of that may be replaced in time by NewsEdge, the Desktop Data service that delivers information through FM radio transmissions. We have it on our local area network right now, which means it's beamed in to everyone subscribing to it who has a node on the network. They can get the headlines at seven in the morning.

You mentioned that you charge everything back. Do you discuss budgets with your requesters?

We make it very clear to them that direct costs get billed. Database charges never fall on my budget line; they are always split out among the requesters. The other thing we do is charge out librarians' time at $160 an hour and clerical staff at $100 an hour. As high as it may sound, it's meant to recoup our expenses. I'm billed for our telephone, for our rental space here on Park Avenue, along with staff salaries, phones and computers. All of that hits my expense code, and our goal is to just reallocate it. In fact, $160 may not quite be enough because we charge for the actual time only, so if it takes me five minutes to do a search, you're paying just one-twelfth of $160 an hour.

I do a major orientation, with a slide presentation, for the new analysts and associates who start every summer. I go over what they can do themselves, and give them estimated costs for searches of all of the different databases. I try to make them aware, not to discourage them from asking us for things, but to let them know what the relative costs are, and that we charge for our time as well as the online costs. Occasionally, departments don't want to incur expenses, but very rarely do I get a call back on a charge. People just accept it as part of the cost of doing business. So I'm assuming that they feel they're getting value for the dollars spent.

We've been doing this a very long time. Since we're part of a department, but we serve the bank worldwide, it's necessary that people who use us pay for our services. That's how we've been able to grow and flourish and provide new products, because people are paying for them, they're willing to pay.

What online systems do you use, and for what kind of searches?

The top services that we're using are DIALOG, Dow Jones, NEXIS, Securities Data and DRI, followed closely by INVESTEXT, TEXTLINE, NewsNet, Spectrum and M.A.I.D. M.A.I.D. is the U.K. system for consumer-oriented market research reports. The protocols and so forth aren't so terrific, but there's some really meaty information in there. We also use DunsPrint; we run all of the D&B credit searches here.

Do you have favorite files for certain kinds of questions?

I go into PTS PROMT and Trade & Industry ASAP almost without thinking about it. We like Trade & Industry ASAP a lot, not just because the indexing is so good, but because we know we're getting full text. We also use NEXIS quite a bit, though it isn't as precise and we're always a little bit concerned about the pricing. We're looking at flat-fee pricing with them. I did go into flat-fee pricing with Dow Jones. But if we could only have one system in the whole world, it would have to be DIALOG, because of the diversity of files and the precision of the search language. As DIALOG becomes more full-text oriented, it becomes just that much better. Of course, NEXIS is trying to be more like DIALOG and DIALOG is trying to be more like NEXIS, so the lines are blurring.

Do you tend to go straight for full text when it's available, as opposed to having people evaluate cites or abstracts first?

Not at all. With NEXIS, and DIALOG too, we print keyword-in-context formats and let the user get back to us. The exception is when it's somebody so high-level that we don't want to inundate him or her with paper at all, in which case we make the evaluation ourselves. With Dow Jones we print paragraphs selectively; it's the same idea.

If a file is up on more than one system, what determines where you search it?

Since we have a flat-fee pricing agreement with Dow Jones, I told my staff not to search DataTimes directly anymore, but to do it through Dow Jones because it's included. But the flat-fee consideration brings up CD-ROM, and that's really interesting. In an ideal world, we would do as much searching ondisc as we could and then go online for the update, but we don't have the time. So the CD-ROMs are primarily for the end-users. We have Business Dateline, the Wall Street Journal, and we've had ProQuest since it became available. I think it's a terrific tool, with the business periodicals and the general periodicals. But I wouldn't say that we're using CD-ROMs in place of online.

Between DIALOG and NEXIS, with budgeted pricing I think we probably tend to go to NEXIS, but not for everything. We wouldn't search Predicasts there. Why would you search PROMT on NEXIS when you can do such precise searches on DIALOG? Plus DIALOG has a fuller backfile. The system we search is partly determined by where the requester is. If they're in a place like our Los Angeles office, where we have a NEXIS printer and they need it that minute, we are apt to go right to NEXIS because they'll be standing by the printer waiting for it. Sending the results by e-mail works fine, of course, but it takes more time and ties up our staff and equipment.

We're also piloting Hoover, a product produced by SandPoint in Cambridge. It runs under Windows and Lotus Notes. I think of Hoover as a more sophisticated Turbo NEXIS as far as simplified searching is concerned. Our choices there are a company profile or business topic research. A company profile is just what it sounds like. You put in the name of a company, whether it's public or private, a ticker symbol if it's public, and Hoover goes out to predetermined databases, currently in DIALOG and Dow Jones //TEXT, and brings back articles.

The business topic research is more of an industry search, or a company search with another concept added. You compose a request and it takes you through it, with online help screens. It works in background, so I can log off and go back an hour later and see if the results are there. It has the functionality of Lotus Notes, which means you can cut and paste material, move it elsewhere on your hard drive, e-mail it to somebody, that kind of thing.

I don't have a really clear-cut opinion of Hoover yet. I like the fact that the people at SandPoint come to the library and work with you on the kinds of databases you want to use. Hoover is meant to take away some of the humdrum requests that the librarian gets. When CD-ROMs came out some people felt that they were going to take away our jobs, that they wouldn't need librarians any more. Probably when printed books came out they felt the same way. I think you have to look at Hoover as something that, if your company wants to bring it in, you should be part of the team and not fight it, because I don't see it as a threat at all.

Let's talk about the more involved kinds of searching you do. When you're planning a strategy for a complex search, how do you go about it? Do you consult a lot of documentation before going online?

Our preparation is a combination of looking at documentation and calling help lines and conferring with each other. There's a lot of years of experience here, and people tend to turn to someone else and ask, "Have you ever done this? How would you do this?" and work as a team.

What about the search itself? How, typically, do you build a search? Do you think in terms of getting the requester exactly what he or she asked for, or do you go broad and then narrow in?

Very often requesters don't *know* what they want. It's "give me three years of General Motors," when what they really need is the latest press release. So, first, it's an exercise in trying to get them to focus on what they want. Sometimes, it's straightforward, like an article in yesterday's *Wall Street Journal.* We really don't want to drown them in paper, so if we can force them to be specific, we will try to do as focused a search as possible. Sometimes they really do want a lot of general information, but we never print full text on large searches. If it's really large, we end up giving them only headlines, which, granted, doesn't give them much to go on in some databases, but it may just be enough to make a selection from. With NEXIS, we always save the search and ask them to come back to us the same day, and then we just go back in and print out what they've asked for. With the new budgeted pricing, taking it in stages like that is a time-saver.

What happens when you've simply gotten too many hits? How do you cut it down? And what happens when you get too few?

For too many hits on NEXIS we do a FOCUS, which lets us narrow down the results and look at just the hits that contain the new term, without losing the original set of documents. Then we start modifying by adding "within so many words of" whatever keyword seems relevant. You have to cut it down somehow; you don't want to hand somebody a search with 300 cites; it's not fair. So, usually, we try to winnow it down ourselves. If they tell us to do a year's search on a company and it turns out to have too many cites, we cut it to six months or something like that. Date limiting is often our first recourse.

If we get little or nothing, on the other hand, what we do next depends on the search. If it's a subject search, we try synonyms and related concepts. But if we're looking for a small, private company, sometimes there is no other way to do it; there *are* no alternatives. We dance from one database to another to see if anything else turns up that we might have missed. That's a pretty big dance when you start going into all of the full-text systems. But that's what we would do, we wouldn't just stop with one. We might start with DIALOG, then go into NEXIS, then Dow Jones. If we think it's foreign, we go into Reuters or one of the European systems.

We do a lot of searching for the private banking group. What they're looking at are people's names. The first place we go is NEXIS because it hits so many full-text newspapers and regional publications. We sometimes have to go back and say, "Look, we've done everything, we've looked at *Who's Who* and various printed sources, too. This is just a wealthy individual who's been very careful not to appear in the press," and they accept that. You can only do a credit report with the person's permission and a Social Security number, so we don't get involved in any of that. We do background searching on people in published sources, see if they've turned up in the business section and that kind of thing.

How do you decide when a search is finished?

It's hard to say. If we get 50 or 75 citations and we're giving it to them in a keyword-in-context or paragraph form, that's usually enough. Sometimes just twenty is enough. If we get what seems like a reasonable number and it appears to answer the question, we don't knock ourselves out unless we've been told to check every possibly relevant source. We're processing so many requests every day that we just can't run like that. What would happen if we started to do that on a slow day—Christmas, for example, is very slow here—and then it got busy again in January? They would start expecting us to do super amounts of work all the time. I think that would be a problem. Besides, the expense is too great. I don't think there's any point to that.

We talked a little bit about search output, and I'd like to come back to it now. You mentioned that you do a lot of electronic print delivery. Do you ever print out search results?

Yes, we do that, too. We all have LaserJets, so the finished product looks nice no matter what. We don't include our search strategy, although we usually keep a record of it in case we have to go back and replicate it. Since we work in shifts, there's sort of a tag team mentality here. If I run something for you and you come back to my colleague who's working that night and want more, she can always look up the strategy I used.

When we send something by e-mail, we clean it up, too. There are hard carriage returns and funny characters that have to be stripped out. For that we use Metro, which is an old Lotus product. We don't bother to strip out codes and ISSNs that appear in each record. We do take out the search strategy and the accounting information, and we usually add a note of explanation like, "These are abstracts. If you need anything full text, please indicate by 'document equals' number." Sometimes we give them a sample of what we need back from them to get the full text. I ask my staff to put a tag at the end of every search that says, "A service of the Banker's Trust Information Center, 212/454-DATA," with our e-mail address. I think it looks professional to include that tag, plus it's a little low-key marketing for us.

Another thing we've done is to have a stamp made with a disclaimer statement. It says, "Information has been obtained from sources believed to be reliable. However, because of the possibility or human or mechanical error by our sources, Information Center does not guarantee the accuracy or completeness of any information. It is not responsible for any errors or omissions or for the results obtained from using such information." We did that because once we got some bad information from one of our vendors and the search results were wrong. They were going to put it into a client presentation and at the last minute someone realized there was something wrong. It's not that anybody's going to sue us, but we want people to know that all we can do is obtain the information. We can't be responsible for its accuracy.

How quickly do you typically turn projects around?

As fast as the user needs. A typical project runs around one to two hours, and if they need it sooner than that, they get it. I'm very hyper, and I tend to hire people like me, so everyone on the staff seems to be like that, too. We're very responsive, within reason, of course. You get to know who's crying wolf, saying, "I need it in the next ten minutes for a meeting," and then it sits in the box, waiting for them to pick it up, for a week. We know the next time that person comes and asks for something, that their "ten minutes" is really not ten minutes. If there are other priorities, that person is not number one.

In general, we're very responsive to time needs. Some of my staff think that we've spoiled people. It could be relatively quiet during the day and at four o'clock the phone starts ringing because they know we have staff here until nine. Well, some of us leave at five, some leave at six, and it isn't fair for everything to bunch up at the end of the day. At one point, we said that things requested on Fridays after three wouldn't be ready until Monday. But you can't be inflexible in an institution like this; you have to do what you have to do.

Tell me about the most frustrating search you've ever done.

I was just dealing with it when you called! This is the one that's freshest in my memory, anyway. It was *logistically* frustrating more than anything else. I got a request at nine this morning that was due at eleven, so I figured, all right, this is what's on my desk now, I'll just do it. This is for somebody downtown, in our Wall Street location. On the face of it, it was very simple; it was that request for articles about the Chicago flood that I mentioned earlier. I chose to do it in Dow Jones because I wanted access to the newspapers on DataTimes as well. There was a lot there, 252 stories after I date-limited it. I e-mailed the hit paragraphs to her, which took a considerable amount of time. In retrospect, I probably should have printed it out and faxed it down, but I sent it by e-mail.

She didn't call back until 1:30 or 2:00 to tell me that she couldn't get it out of her e-mail system. I told her that she'd have to call the support desk. It turned out that she had a bad modem. She finally was able to print it out, and she called to tell me which stories she wanted in full text. She only wanted about ten, so I figured that wouldn't take long. I went back in and was running it in full text, but then she said, "I also want the *New York Times.*" I had figured there were so many stories, and a lot from the *Chicago Tribune*, that they wouldn't need the *New York Times*. But I said, "All right, I'll run a NEXIS search for you on the *New York Times* and print it out." Then she said, "I want it all in full, I don't want you to send me abstracts because now I need it immediately."

If she had only gotten back to me when she *said* she needed it! The thing was waiting for her at 11 o'clock in the morning, but here it was four hours later. Anyway, I e-mailed her the ten full-text articles she wanted, and I was in the process of doing the NEXIS search when she walked into my office. This meant that she had come up from the downtown office. She said, "Now I'm here, I need it here." Well, I had already used the password associated with the downtown printer. I was annoyed at this point. I said, "I'm already sending it downtown." She said, "Well, I'm going to be here and I'm going to be in a meeting and I need it."

So I saved the search, logged off NEXIS, and went back into my own e-mail, which fortunately saves anything I've sent for 90 days, and printed out a copy of the full-text that I'd already done and e-mailed to her. Then I went back into NEXIS and instead of printing to the remote printer associated with the password, I printed it to my local printer here. She said she'd pick it up later, after her meeting.

In the meantime, we got a call from her boss who said he wanted to see a copy of everything we had done. I went back into NEXIS—I had printed out about eight of 20 stories, after going through them individually because some of them weren't relevant for her purposes—on the same password. I saved the search, did a select, printed out in full the stories I'd printed out for his subordinate, only this time I sent it to the remote printer downtown so that he could get his copy. I went back into my e-mail, I found the message I had sent her with the ten other articles, and reforwarded it to his mailbox. I was able to get them both what they wanted even though they were at two different locations.

It's all in a day's work.

I was very tense when you called! They didn't even say thank you. I thought, "Boy, they don't know what miracle work was done." There's a whole generation of people who are used to that kind of speed and immediacy. The more we do, the more they want. There's nothing wrong with that, with stretching and learning and doing, but I don't think they know what reality is anymore. Most of the guys and gals who come in here haven't spent much time in libraries. They spend more time with us than with anyone when they first come. We really have to break them in and do some serious training.

Apart from logistical nightmares like that, the most frustrating kind of search is probably where you have to look for companies with names that create a tremendous number of false drops. Try searching for S.E. Johnson Company when there are so many other companies named Johnson. You've got to do it on DIALOG because you can expand on the company name field. It's really very hard to do on Dow Jones.

Even when we were trying Hoover out we used Lotus Development as a test, and of course it pulled out stories about a restaurant named Lotus and the flower lotus. The person who was doing the demo looked at it and said to me, "Can't you"—meaning us, the library staff—"go through and clean that up?" Hey, that's not what this product is supposed to be about. This is supposed to make end-users information-independent. If they need us to go in and clean up their searches, what's the value?

What's your favorite kind of search? What's the payoff?

It's a thrill to read about something you've researched on the front page of the *Wall Street Journal*. Internally, we get what we call pink sheets. When a deal closes, they report a couple of paragraphs about the deal and which officers closed it. That's when we remember doing all those industry searches, and we know that it was leading up to this. We just closed a deal with the largest producer of school bus bodies, and we were searching school buses up the wazoo. I thought this was wonderful. We know we're contributing to the bottom line, we're helping those deals get done, and it makes us feel very good. Occasionally someone brings us a tombstone ad announcing a deal that they felt we were particularly helpful on. It's a nice thank you.

Another payoff is just being able to explore new information technology. I'm a believer in technology; I think it's what makes our jobs and our profession a very interesting one. No two days are alike. I'm very open to trying new things, but I think we need to remember the basics, too. We had an intern from one of the graduate library schools and all she wanted to do was go online. My librarians, who are wonderful searchers, all started at the beginning using books. I think it's very important for people to remember that many of the files that we searchers think are so wonderful are grounded in hardcopy. It's not a bad idea to look at a print version to understand how it's structured and what's there before we hit the computer keys. But I love searching, and I love computers. They enhance what we do and let us become much more productive.

SUPER SEARCH SECRETS

On delivery of search results...

To serve [our other locations] along with e-mail, we have standalone LEXIS/NEXIS printers in each of the domestic offices. We do the searching here, but the passwords are associated with those printers, so the results print out there. In fact, I can do a search here on Park Avenue, and it will print out downtown at the Wall Street location.

On charging back expenses...

We've also integrated a charge-back package. We charge for everything that we do internally. Every search that we do is recorded, along with the time and what databases or hard copy were used to answer the request. Then once a month a disk gets passed to our controller's office with the charges. It's soft dollars, funny money, but it covers our costs and that's our goal.

On favorite databases and systems...

I go into PTS PROMT and Trade & Industry ASAP almost without thinking about it. We like Trade & Industry ASAP a lot, not just because the indexing is so good, but because we know we're getting full text. We also use NEXIS quite a bit, though it isn't as precise and we're always a little bit concerned about the pricing. But if we could only have one system in the whole world, it would have to be DIALOG, because of the diversity of files and the precision of the search language.

On narrowing results...

For too many hits on NEXIS we do a FOCUS, which lets us narrow down the results and look at just the hits that contain the new term, without losing the original set of documents. Then we start modifying by adding "within so many words of" whatever keyword seems relevant.

On name searching...

The first place we go is NEXIS because it hits so many full-text newspapers and regional publications.

On formatting search output...

I ask my staff to put a tag at the end of every search that says, "A service of the Banker's Trust Information Center, 212/454-DATA," with our e-mail address. I think it looks professional to include that tag, plus it's a little low-key marketing for us.

On disclaimers...

...have a stamp made with a disclaimer statement. It says, "Information has been obtained from sources believed to be reliable. However, because of the possibility or human or mechanical error by our sources, Information Center does not guarantee the accuracy or completeness of any information. It is not responsible for any errors or omissions or for the results obtained from using such information."

On turnaround time...

A typical project runs around one to two hours, and if they need it sooner than that, they get it. In general, we're very responsive to time needs.

CHAPTER 7

TERRY HANSON: MANAGING ONLINE RESOURCES

Terry Hanson is
Sublibrarian for Electronic
Information Services at the
University of Portsmouth in
the United Kingdom.

How many of your colleagues in the library are online searchers?

There are ten or eleven of us who do online searching. We take the classic subject specialist approach; we divide the areas into social science, which is myself; the built environment, which is environmental studies, building and construction and architecture; business and management; and humanities. There are two humanities people, in fact, one covering languages and the other covering literature and related areas. We also have three science specialists, covering chemistry and physics, life sciences, and engineering-related areas. Each of us is responsible for all aspects of library services, including online searching, in those subject areas.

We serve mainly the faculty and students, but we invite people from the general public to use the library, and they do. We do quite a few searches for the outside world as well as for the faculty and the students. We have a standard scale of charges for external users. Internally, we pass on part of the charge to the faculty and students, but it's heavily subsidized. The user ends up paying maybe 40 to 45 percent of the actual cost.

How do your search requests come in? Do people tend to phone you, or do they walk in the door?

One of the advantages of our subject librarian setup is that we develop very good contacts with the departments we support. Usually, patrons will contact the appropriate subject librarian when they need a search. Most know the procedure. We have a standard form on which they indicate their requirements, something about the funding arrangement—who's going to pay, in other words—and perhaps also a maximum amount of money they might want to spend. We ask them to describe the nature of their subject in two ways, one being an ordinary textual description in just two or three sentences, and the other in the form of a list of what they consider the most appropriate keywords.

Next, the procedure is to invite the person along to discuss the search and work out the strategy together.

Hopefully they will be able to sit in while the search is being done and make sure that everything's going okay. We're always reluctant to do the search in their absence. Maybe it wouldn't matter as much with someone who has a particular search run repeatedly; we'd know what's going on. But a lot of people mistakenly think that the search can be done without them being there—that it's somehow a magical system that knows what they're thinking. We try to encourage them to be present, to take part in the search, so we can get immediate feedback before it's too late. They can say, "No, no, no, I don't want that particular aspect of it."

Do you keep a search log to track projects sequentially, or do you use the search request forms you described for that purpose?

We do both. We keep the forms for quite a while, maybe a couple of years. We keep a log as well, recording basic details like what databases we used, who did the search, a brief description of the project, how much was done, and how many references were downloaded or ordered. We've concluded, actually, that the log is *too* detailed. It seems that we do a lot of record-keeping for its own sake sometimes. Now that this is my responsibility, I'm thinking of trying to cut down on it a bit. It's time-consuming and not particularly useful.

CD-ROM has had a tremendous impact here, too. In fact, the demand for searching now is quite a bit less because a lot of people can do their own searches. We encourage them to do that, so we ourselves don't need to go online so often. That means that our record-keeping is correspondingly less, too.

What topics do you typically search?

I'm a social sciences person, so I do anything in that general area: politics, economics, sociology, social welfare, quite a bit in psychology. I stray across the barriers sometimes into areas like nursing and paramedical-type subjects. The research center has some research projects going on in the area of Down's syndrome, so I get a lot of searches on Down's syndrome related to sleep patterns, or children's behavior, or learning difficulties, or whatever. I do a fair bit in comparative social welfare as well—comparisons of the welfare systems and policies among countries, between the U.S. and Europe, between Britain and other particular countries.

What online hosts do you use?

We use DIALOG, Data-Star, STN, ESA-IRS, and ORBIT. I'm used to the DIALOG command language, so whenever there's an option, I guess I'd go for DIALOG. Data-Star is coming up fast, though; they've got a wide range of databases, and the pricing is quite good. I like the "dot dot" language, which is similar to BRS. I spent some time, several years ago, working at the University of Connecticut. I'd had no experience with BRS before going there. But it was the favorite host in use at the time, so I had to learn it. I got to prefer it over DIALOG for the year or so that I was in the U.S. I'd been familiar with Data-Star before going to America, and when I got back home, my exposure to BRS reinforced my liking for Data-Star.

Are there specific databases that you find yourself turning to over and over again?

The obvious ones for social scientists, like Social SciSearch and PsycINFO, are my most frequently used databases. I also use the Applied Social Sciences Index and Abstracts on Data-Star. It covers social policy and healthcare, and it covers them extremely thoroughly. It's my favorite database at the moment because it serves my needs so well. It covers a lot of American journals, but its focus is mainly Europe, and Britain in particular.

How much do you plan your search strategy before you go online?

In the early days I would always sit down and map strategies out first. We had a software package a few years ago that allowed you to plan the search, write it out on the computer and then send it automatically once you got online. That encouraged forethought and planning. But I must say that now, either out of laziness or more experience or both, for most searches I feel reasonably confident in being able to just go straight online and get what I need. I always have the bluesheet on hand for DIALOG, or the equivalent database sheet for Data-Star, if only to verify the formats or the searchable fields or the nature of the index fields.

Do you primarily do controlled vocabulary searching, as opposed to free text?

I always advocate that controlled vocabulary should be used whenever you can. Some people argue that their researchers' needs are unique and individual, and that controlled vocabulary gets in the way of the individual expressing his or her distinctive needs. I think that's bunkum. Occasionally you do want to do a search that can't be handled by controlled vocabulary, so you should be able to drop out of it and use ordinary free text. That's fine. But I would never advocate free text to the exclusion of controlled vocabulary. I acknowledge that many research studies have been done that show that controlled vocabulary searching fails to come up with *all* the relevant references on the topic. But, nonetheless, in my field at least, you can't do without controlled vocabulary.

Do you do anything in particular in terms of post-processing search results?

We don't do anything fancy to make the search look better on the printout, although we can tidy it up. What we usually do is download and format the records for Pro-Cite, which is in heavy use here. We've worked out a routine for converting records from most of the databases we use into Pro-Cite, and we do that almost as a matter of course. We deliver results electronically far more often than we do in print. Very rarely do we just hand over a printout, although we might give one along with a Pro-Cite database. Both faculty and students, but especially faculty, maintain their own local databases.

Do you have any kind of formal feedback arrangement to make sure that the work you did was on target?

Because we all specialize in certain areas, there are ongoing working relationships between librarians and faculty members. A person generally goes to a specific librarian instead of just one who happens to end up doing the search for them. In other words, we know the person and their subject needs, and have regular contact with that person before and after the search. So that kind of feedback, that kind of knowledge, is coming in all the time.

What about the issue of quality? Do you run into substantial problems in database content or file structure or standardization? Do you feel you have to work around these or warn your requestors about them when you deliver a search?

Two points come to mind. One is the lack of controlled vocabulary in certain databases; I think that's a real problem in trying to put together a good, quality search. The other has to do with our need to reformat records and download them for inclusion in Pro-Cite databases. With some files conversion is very hard, and this really comes down to how consistently the data is presented in the source database. For example, data in the source database may be jumbled into one field, making it difficult to separate the individual elements for the destination Pro-Cite database. With some databases it's very easy, because of the way they present the information, and in some it's very hard, practically impossible.

What do you particularly like about the search process itself? What attracts you to online searching?

It's easier, more powerful, more flexible, all of those things together. You have more control over the information. The more you understand the concept of databases and how they're constructed, the better searcher you become. It's a matter of power and scope and control over resources—to a degree that would not have been possible a few short years ago.

SUPER SEARCH SECRETS

On searching with the requestor present...

...the procedure is to invite the person along to discuss the search and work out the strategy together. Hopefully they will be able to sit in while the search is being done...We're always reluctant to do the search in their absence....a lot of people mistakenly think that the search can be done without them being there—that it's somehow a magical system that knows what they're thinking.

On CD-ROM...

CD-ROM has had a tremendous impact here...the demand for searching now is quite a bit less because a lot of people can do their own searches. We encourage them to do that...

On planning search strategy...

...for most searches I feel reasonably confident in being able to just go straight online and get what I need. I always have the bluesheet on hand for DIALOG, or the equivalent database sheet for Data-Star, if only to verify the formats or the searchable fields or the nature of the index fields.

On controlled vocabulary versus free text...

I always advocate that controlled vocabulary should be used whenever you can. Some people argue...that controlled vocabulary gets in the way of the individual expressing his or her distinctive needs. I think that's bunkum. Occasionally you...should be able to drop out of it and use ordinary free text. That's fine. But I would never advocate free text to the exclusion of controlled vocabulary.

On post-processing of search results...

What we usually do is download and format the records for Pro-Cite, which is in heavy use here. We've worked out a routine for converting records from most of the databases we use into Pro-Cite, and we do that almost as a matter of course. We deliver results electronically far more often than we do in print.

CHAPTER 8

ROBERT F. JACK: MEATBALL SEARCHER

Robert F. Jack is Senior Online Systems Specialist at the NASA Center for Aerospace Information, formerly the NASA Scientific and Technical Information Facility. He is also the founder and Director of Technical Services for BBM Knowledge Access Services, Inc. in Baltimore.

What happens when a search comes in? How do you respond?

Occasionally people at the facility come into my cubicle and say, "Bob, can you do something for me quickly?" More often, I get phone requests from people working at NASA headquarters. I've got a lot of these people more or less housebroken in terms of "Tell me *why* you're looking for it." I always say that the first question is "why?" not "what?" Actually, the first question is, "Who's going to pay for this?" But the really important one is "why?" The "why" will *tell* you the "what" if you give it enough thought.

There are so many classic cases like when somebody says, "I want information on solar heaters for swimming pools." You go into a solar energy database and retrieve a great deal of information about the technology of solar heaters and swimming pools. But if this person is trying to sell these damn things in your city, that's not really the information he's looking for. He needs to know who has swimming pools, what the local regulations are governing the installation of this kind of equipment, and what kind of permits you need.

You miss his perspective completely if you don't ask "why?" The "why" colors everything I do: my choice of databases, how much of my effort I'm willing to invest in it, and what this is going to be worth. If this is something that's going to involve a $30 billion project down the pike, fine, we'll pull some plugs on it. If it's just to punch up some conference paper, that's a different kind of application.

I helped develop a search request form for the NASA Applications Center. It was as much for accounting as anything else. We wanted to make sure we listed the databases we used, the number of hits we got, and some estimate of costs. It included the search statement, which was always expressed in the form of a problem rather than "looking for information on." Questions like how far back to go in the literature often become apparent if you've got your "why?" nailed down. I get concerned when people insist ahead of time on limitations on a search, because it might hurt them. They think they want only the last two years, only English, or only this source.

Sometimes people tell you, "I've already searched here. I've already searched DIALOG." I love people like that. *Nobody* "searches DIALOG." There are hundreds of files on DIALOG. If they tell me they've searched something that I think should have the answer, then I ask them, "Okay, you did this yourself, you did this with user-friendly software, or you had someone else do this for you?" They come back and say, "My kid did it." "Now, wait a minute," I say. "Okay, there's a lot of friendly front end software. But do you want a kid driving your car with front end software?" On the other hand, I might say, "Oh, you had *that* person do it. Okay, I trust them, I think they probably did a good search."

If it's an important search, you'd better have somebody do it who knows what they're doing. If I don't think I can do it, I try to recommend somebody I think can. There's got to be an intellectual honesty about what you can and can't do. There's no accreditation in this business. Anybody who's got a password can legally say, "I'll do a search for you." If the medical community was run that way, people would be taking antifreeze for a head cold.

Yet we realize, even if we're not always able to articulate, that there *are* standards. We all operate under a different set of assumptions and expectations about the process. Is this good enough? How do we know, in our heart of hearts? How do we objectively tell if something is *not* good enough? I think that's going to be a really big issue. Sooner or later, somebody is going to get sued. A patient is going to die on the operating table, a bridge is going to collapse, or a plane is going to crash.

As far as I'm concerned, if somebody can do the little searches by themselves, they should go ahead and do them. It's the first-aid approach—you have a boo-boo, you put a Band-Aid on it. You don't go tracking down Dr. Christiaan Barnard for surgery. Take two aspirin and don't call me in the morning. But if it's screwing us up, if it's going to kill somebody, if it's going to cost $30 billion of the taxpayers' hard-earned money, if it's going to throw 10,000 people out of work if you get it wrong, *then* call. For God's sake, *don't* do it yourself, because the costs of being wrong are too high.

That may sound arrogant on my part. I'm just saying that I've got enough faith in myself to do it right. I also know that, under certain circumstances, I would be crazy to do it. I recognize where I'm living. I'm terrible at toxicology and stuff like that. I do not have a real good chemical background and I know it. But remember, I'm the guy who wrote an article called, "Meatball Searching." Frankly, I've got a lot of faith in the meatball approach to doing things. I'm willing to wade through a certain amount of stuff to get the right answer, if they don't mind 49 bad hits to get one perfect one.

Barbara Quint calls herself a "grasshopper" searcher as opposed to an "ant" searcher. How does that map to what you call meatball searching?

In some respects meatball searching is ant-like in its approach, but it's not blindly ant-like as Barbara suggests. Barbara suggested a classical MEDLINE searcher as the ant. "Let's have our pre-search interview now. Let me sit here and get my *MeSH* thesaurus. Now let's look at all these tree structures. I'll sit down and before we go online, I'll show you what the commands look like and what we think the postings are going to be."

I'm not organized in that sense. I'm a lot more flexible. "This didn't work. Quick, what's next?" I always try to keep a couple of things in the back of my mind. I'm not afraid to crap out of a database. Once something happens to convince me that I'm on the wrong track, I'm out of it. But I'm never afraid to try something. Part of that is having access to a lot of databases. "Okay, we didn't find what we wanted on suicides in PsycINFO; there's an interesting little database in Canada that's all about suicides. We'll check that out."

That's the neat thing about having access to a really large body of stuff. Name a subject and there is a database about that subject or a subject that's real close to it.

How I approach a search depends on my gut reaction to what a person is telling me about his information needs. If he's not finding anything, then I've got to proceed with a dual approach. I need to remember that this person may not know how to look for the information. On the other hand, he may have done a pretty thorough background check, so it might be harder than I think, and take a lot more brainpower.

I always operate on the premise that a search is never really done. If I do the search and give the person the results, unless they're under some incredibly tight time limit, they can come back and say, "Okay, do you think you can find more like this one?" I see a search as an ongoing online-offline process.

Searching is just following leads. If I'm getting a huge amount on a subject, I sometimes run it against a whole series of peer review journals in that subject area, to whittle it down. Or if the person says, "I get these magazines, don't look there," then I may turn around and limit that stuff out.

Specifying particular journals is one way of targeting results. You can't do it with every search, but from time to time it's a very useful technique. Sometimes certain publications are available to a person, and they ask, "What does the *Journal of Astrophysics* have to say about this?" You can bet it will be a lot different than what *National Geographic* has to say. On the other hand, if I'm talking to a ninth-grader, then *Aerospace America* or *Aviation Week* may be okay, but *Journal of Spacecraft* might be a little too sophisticated.

You said you have access to a lot of different databases. What online services do you use?

Funny you should ask, because we just canceled access to a dozen or two dozen online services for budgetary reasons. In some cases, we were paying $40 or $50 a month for the privilege of having a password, and I hadn't touched them in a year or two. So we canceled them. I was just making a list of all of the services I've used at one time or another. I counted more than 40, but right now I've probably only got passwords on ten or twelve.

NASA RECON is probably 75 percent of what I use. I use DIALOG, too. If I'm looking for information that RECON doesn't cover, like descriptions of microcomputer software, I go to DIALOG because it has some software directories. For company information, I can pick up the Dun & Bradstreet files on DIALOG.

Since I had to teach myself a lot of the online services I've used, I started making mental connections right away about how the command languages are alike. So I'm not intimidated by that. If it's not on DIALOG, I have no problem going to ESA-IRS because the command language is so similar. If I can't find it in BRS, well, AUSINET is based on STAIRS, too, so I'll try AUSINET. Once you realize there are really only 15 or 20 command protocols out there, you stop thinking that a host in Japan, Australia or Denmark is a stumbling block. They'll give you a password just as easily as DIALOG will, sometimes more easily. So, with access to 40 or 45 different online systems, if I needed a narrow search, chances were good there was a database that would cover that subject.

Knowing where to look, how the information is going to come out, and what it's going to cost, is a big part of the process. ESA charges an extremely low connect rate and a little more per citation. If I know I'm out of my element or may make a lot of typos, ESA is a good place to go because I'm not penalized while the clock is running. If I'm only going for 15 or 20 really good citations, but I know it's going to take three hours of keyboarding to get them—a lot of EXPANDs, browsing, cross-comparisons and whatnot—it's definitely the place to go.

There are times when knowing system capabilities gives you more power in selecting the best place to look. That goes back to the "why" of searching. If I only want a couple of good references, that's what WILSONLINE is for. Cruise into WILSONLINE for some citations. WILSONLINE is good when someone says, "I'm not looking for real technical stuff," or "It's out of my field." Give them the information at a level they can use.

How do you plan your search strategy? Do you make notes before you go online?

I do make notes. I tend to listen for buzzwords and technical jargon. Part of the reason for that is that I'm not very technically-oriented myself. If someone mentions a part of an aircraft that I'm not familiar with, I say, "Is that part of the wing?" I let them guide me to the appropriate terminology.

RECON has a nice capability to help you through that process. It's a feature called "Frequency," which is also the basis of the ESA-IRS ZOOM command. You can create a set, then do a "Frequency" on the indexed terms. It shows what the controlled vocabulary looks like for that set. If I don't know what "photovoltaic" is, I can do a title search and then a "Frequency" on the resulting set. It shows the main index term. Then I can structure my search around that term.

Do you do much full-text searching?

I like to do full text, although I've never really felt as comfortable with it as I do with abstracts. For a while I had passwords to many of the full-text systems. I had NEXIS, VU/TEXT, NewsNet and DataTimes, among others. When I was doing a lot of technology transfer stuff, people would say, "I thought I read something about Joe Schmoe, who's got some kind of patent for doing something with adhesive tape." The best way to start is to find out what it was this person *really* read.

For current events, though, I don't particularly care for the newspaper files because the duplication drives me nuts. Between the wire services and the large number of newspapers online, there's way too much crossover. One story from Associated Press might be picked up by many newspapers.

If I have to do that kind of search, I go just to UPI or AP. Or I might pick one highly reputable newspaper in the right geographic area. I grab the wire service stuff, and next get the newspapers in that area. But I NOT out the Associated Press and UPI as sources, to make sure I'm getting the local slant on things. What did the local newspaper reporter say, not the UPI stringer?

It's important to look at the bibliographic information in the record before you start throwing it out. I love to use DIALOG's KWIC format for that. "Wait a minute; this thing is only 50 words long? Forget it." I use Format 2 with KWIC so I get the headline, word count and the edition, plus a good look at the text to make sure there's enough meat in it. Doing that gives you the chance to say, "Let's look for the one filed late Saturday afternoon; that's the one that will run on Sunday." Or look for the article that's 20,000 lines long because that's going to be this week's definitive article on the subject.

Do you do any multifile searching?

I do on DIALOG, almost all the time, in what I regard as my classic kind of search, the technical abstract kind of searching. I love it, too. I make up my own categories. I almost always use DIALINDEX first just to make sure I can safely eliminate some databases.

Usually I check NASA RECON first, so I already have the stuff from DIALOG's Aerospace Database. There's a lot of overlap between the Aerospace Database and INSPEC and COMPENDEX and other technical files. So, I make sure I search Aerospace Database as one of the first files. Then I pop in NTIS but NOT out the STAR subfile, which is the NASA report literature, because I've already got that from RECON. Next I try to structure the other databases. If I think they're going to be comparable, I put the cheapest one first. That's not the deciding factor, though. I have some other approaches to decide the general order of information. I'm always careful not to do too much mixing and matching of database types, like mixing abstract files with full text or directory ones.

I try not to waste time deduping stuff that does not have a lot of duplicates in it to begin with. You need to mentally anticipate where those are going to be. You're going to have a lot more duplication between ABI/INFORM and Trade & Industry Index than you are between ABI/INFORM and MEDLINE, so why waste the effort? You've got to weigh the extra expense of five duplicate citations at 50 cents apiece against the time it takes to process the dedupe.

Oddly enough, I like including magazine indexes in technical searches. Most people, when they say, "I need a search on something," first read about that subject in *TIME*, *National Geographic*, *TV Guide* or *Playboy*. A couple of years ago, somebody asked for a search in a business management technique. I found things in *Journal of Accountancy, Journal of Management* and so on. I thought, "Oh, this looks marvelous." He came back to me and said, "You didn't find the article that was in *Newsweek*."

They may already have seen it, but they want to see it in your search results, because it guarantees that you did a good job. That may be the best article for them, too. I certainly can't digest 30 pages of a chemical article. Something from *Newsweek* that explains why dioxin is dangerous is much more appropriate to my level of understanding. If I do a search and don't find anything, my gut reaction is that I did something wrong. I don't assume that there are holes in the database.

What's your first recourse if you do come up with nothing?

Usually I grab one of the other searchers and say, "Okay, this must be blatantly obvious. What did I miss?" Half the time another perspective is exactly what you need.

If I really come up with nothing, I print out the session and say, "Look at this. This word doesn't show up in any of these sources. Is there another spelling for this? How many z's are in this word?"

Not that it happens that often, but when I go fishing, I take anything I can get. "You wanted Agent Purple in Cambodia. Well, I found Agent Orange in Vietnam, that's as close as I can get for now. That's what you're going to get. Now tell me what clues here will help us get to what you really need." I don't have any problem with that approach. I don't regard the search as a failure. Some just take longer than I'd like them to.

That's an awfully positive attitude, Bob.

You have to remember that I've got a couple of things going for me that a lot of searchers don't. Part of it, as odd as it may sound, is that my library background is not very good. I don't begin with too many biases one way or another about the databases. If the subject sounds like it has to do with history, I search the databases with "history" in their names, no matter what. I have eventually learned there are other good places, too. But early on I tended to take a lot of files at face value.

I also learned quickly that no single source is comprehensive. That's not bad, it's just a reality. That taught me the advantage of what Barbara Quint calls format file searching. I use Magazine Index the same way that I use Dissertation Abstracts for almost every search. Sometimes people want popular literature, and sometimes they want dissertations. A dissertation is an enormously valuable document because it was written by somebody who's been grilled by a bunch of Ph.D.s on the subject. The 20-page journal article, on the other hand, might have been accepted because the editorial peer board had some sort of hidden agenda.

There's almost too much stuff online. What you get may not always be real good, but leads lead to leads. I always look at what I'm doing as just part of a process. If I do it really well, it could be the most time-saving and cost-effective part of the process. If some of the results aren't great, then maybe there's one abstract that has somebody's name in it. Then your user can pick up the phone and make a call. Technology transfer teaches us that. What I find online doesn't have to be intrinsically valuable, it just has to lead to something.

You've said that your own background isn't technical. How do you know whether you're on the right track when you are over your head technically?

It depends on how much I'm finding. After I've done a basic subject search and have 20 citations, I'm comfortable. I feel like, okay, something here has to be more or less vaguely similar to what this person is looking for. Sometimes I look at it and say, "None of this looks right." At that point I just dump what I've got to disk, sign off, get back on the phone with the client and see if we can get a better sense of what he needs. It disappoints me when I have to do that, because I think that I must have really done a bad interview job. Now I have to go back and ask the questions I probably should have asked the first time.

But often the individual will look at the cites, and say. "Yes, this is the one good one that I'm looking for." Then sometimes he'll come back weeks later and say, "I got that article, remember? Okay, since then I've come across this. Now, would you look for more articles by this author or other things from this publication. By the way, there's another way to look at this buzzword; sometimes it's not called 'x,' sometimes it's called 'y'." They discover the new jargon that emerges, and you have another hook to fish with.

One thing that I don't rely on in refining a search is the NOT operator. I'm very careful about using NOT. The only time I like to use it is after I've delimited the stuff I've already looked at. I seldom do a search and produce one final answer set unless it's really narrow. I much prefer to deal with several sets.

This is where using multiple files comes in real handy, because no subject truly falls into one single discipline. No search request is really in just one subject area. A search on something in architecture by definition includes human factors, psychology, local government, city planning, materials science and engineering. Your first cut is going to be the stuff from the key sources and the most obvious terminology. The second cut might be the "aspect element" kind of chunks, various aspects of the basic subject. For instance, your search is on something to do with some kind of arch in architecture. So you search on the arch itself. The next cut might be on the materials, what kind of concrete works best. So I search the concrete database because the question really is how to put the bricks together. The one after that might be something about bricks, depending on what you've gotten so far.

Another example is aquaculture, freshwater fish, catfish and so on. Somebody would say, "Well, I'm interested in this particular kind of catfish." Fine, I'll make sure we go into BIOSIS and get a genus and species name we can work with. We get that stuff, and we also find stuff on other genera of catfish. Okay, a catfish is a catfish, for our purposes, so that's number two. And now here's some stuff on filtration of water in aquaculture tanks. Well, the principle is going to be the same whether it's catfish or turtles in the tank, so we'll throw that in there. You end up with several different slants on the information.

Often when end-users are evaluating their information needs, they're overlooking something. For example, someone is going to start an aquaculture pond and needs to know about catfish. Well, he needs to know about catfish, but what does he know about maintaining an aquarium? If I can find some hobby information about people who keep real big aquariums, like goldfish breeders, a lot of the information about filter systems, thermostatic heaters, plant life, and diseases may be relevant. There probably isn't a publication about keeping *this* kind of catfish in *this* size tank in Lexington, Kentucky. You've got to be a little more flexible. If the only thing I can find is about keeping a different species in Uganda, then you use Uganda because it's better than nothing. And unless the laws of the physical universe shift between here and Uganda, it will be useful, too.

Let's talk about output formats.

When I have a lot of hits for clients to evaluate, I give them title-author-source, because the title alone often doesn't tell you much. If I've gotten 100 cites, I give them what I think will be the ten or 20 best with the abstracts. Then I leave the abstract off the others, just to save time and paper, and make it easier to read.

I almost always sort by journal name, too, because that's the way stuff is loaded on library shelves. If I can't sort online by journal name, then I take care of it in word processing afterwards. With full text, I get it in KWIC if what the person seems to be looking for is a factoid. Why make them read six pages if they really only want to know what kind of catfish they have in Uganda?

Do you do much post-processing?

I don't sit down with 600 citations, meld them into a pretty list, and annotate them. I also try not to delete anything that will help me get my hands on a document later on. I need the ISSN, for instance, when I have to order outside our own immediate network. I take out descriptors unless I really think I screwed up the search and I want the client to take a look at them. I remove the indexing terms because if they are there, people second-guess your strategy.

For the same reason, I hate having people sit next to me when I do a search. There are lots of searchers who say you have to have the person sit next to you. No, thank you, I don't need that aggravation. The meter's running and I don't need somebody to ask, "Why did you put a question mark there?" I'm sorry, it just cost $35 to explain what the question mark means. If you want that, I need some kind of device that sits on top of my PC that shows the dollars racking up. You want to sit and chat about this? You want to get a cup of coffee? Fine, at $300 an hour.

I try to move the good hits to the front, remove false drops, move the peripheral stuff to the B-list, that kind of thing. If I highlight anything, I only do it on the paper output. I like cleaning it up and putting in a certain amount of consistency, if I have to, across journal titles and that sort of thing.

If I haven't managed to dedupe everything because of the nature of the search, I pull duplicates, too. If I've run something in DIALOG and maybe ESA, RECON and several other systems, there's no way I'm not going to have duplicates. So I pull those out in word processing, keeping an eye on the quality of the abstract. I like INSPEC's abstracts. I'll always go for those first.

Do you document for your client the search strategy and the databases you used?

Not usually. If what I'm delivering looks like a real blatant dump from a single source, like 300 citations from the same database, I include an idiot sheet, like the DIALOG bluesheet for that database. That helps explain where all that stuff came from, so that it makes sense in terms of slant and focus. For a while I did that for all of my searches; I included a photocopy of the idiot sheet for every database that actually gave me results. I'd give them a list of databases I tried, just to keep them from coming back to me and saying, "Why didn't you look in this one?"

When I deliver results, I almost always put some kind of cover sheet on it. The person who requested the search may not necessarily continue working on it himself or herself. They give it to a colleague, an underling or an intern to work on. So I like giving whoever might end up with it a way of knowing where it came from. If nothing else, they can contact the facility and say, "I never heard of NASA Center for Aerospace Information. Where are you guys and do you have any more of this stuff up there?"

I've gotten away from some of the more formal types of presentation simply because people now know me. When I get somebody new, I feel that I'm sort of marketing NASA's information services to other people within NASA, so then I want to make something that looks nice. At other times, I know that people are looking for a relatively fast response, and it's not worth doing a lot of exotic stuff. If people really want to know which databases I searched, I tell them. It's not a secret. But if I can save time by not having to compile lists, I will. You might search 300 databases in one session; I certainly don't want to list all of those.

If I have a hunch that what I've done is going to be part of some really big project, I archive a copy of the search results on a floppy. I almost always keep an immediate-purpose paper copy. I don't bother keeping the strategy because I know that I would never do exactly the same search twice, anyway. The paper copy I use when people call and say, "I just got this, Bob, do you have your copy there? I need to have Section 3 on that one."

Do you have a formal feedback mechanism with your users?

I work on the assumption that no news is good news. Very seldom do I hear from anyone in the company that I've done something better than expected. In NASA, I've had some very high-ranking people come back and say, "What you did for me was marvelous. It was better than sex. It was the best search that could possibly have been done on the whole planet." Those mean a lot, and they're real rare.

The most meaningful thing you accomplish is that you did a good search. There are other times when the ramifications go a lot deeper. I'm sure other searchers have had similar experiences. "I did this right. I got good, accurate information from the right mixture of sources, and I kept a coal mine from having to shut down." If that coal mine had shut down, 5,000 people might have lost their jobs. I can look at that and say, "I'm not going to get any medals for that. I'm not going to get my name in the paper for it, but damn, I feel good about it. That made it worth getting up this morning."

SUPER SEARCH SECRETS

On the reference interview...
Actually, the first question is, "Who's going to pay for this?" But the really important one is "why?" The "why" will tell you the "what" if you give it enough thought....The "why" colors everything I do: my choice of databases, how much of my effort I'm willing to invest in it, and what this is going to be worth.

On the search process...
I always operate on the premise that a search is never really done. If I do the search and give the person the results...they can come back and say, "Okay, do you think you can find more like this one?" I see a search as an ongoing online-offline process.

On searching current events...
For current events, though, I don't particularly care for the newspaper files because the duplication drives me nuts. Between the wire services and the large number of newspapers online, there's way too much crossover....If I have to do that kind of search, I go just to UPI or AP. Or I might pick one highly reputable newspaper in the right geographic area. I grab the wire service stuff, and next get the newspapers in that area. But I NOT out the Associated Press and UPI as sources, to make sure I'm getting the local slant on things. What did the local newspaper reporter say, not the UPI stringer?

On getting zero hits...
Usually I grab one of the other searchers and say, "Okay, this must be blatantly obvious. What did I miss?" Half the time another perspective is exactly what you need....If I really come up with nothing, I print out the session and say, "Look at this. This word doesn't show up in any of these sources. Is there another spelling for this? How many z's are in this word?"

On using the NOT operator...
One thing that I don't rely on in refining a search is the NOT operator. I'm very careful about using NOT. The only time I like to use it is after I've delimited the stuff I've already looked at.

On searching with the requester present...
...I hate having people sit next to me when I do a search....No, thank you, I don't need that aggravation. The meter's running and I don't need somebody to ask, "Why did you put a question mark there?" I'm sorry, it just cost $35 to explain what the question mark means.

CHAPTER 9

ROGER KARRAKER: THE POLITICS OF ONLINE

Roger Karraker is a journalism instructor at Santa Rosa (California) Junior College and an advisor to the student newspaper. He is also a freelance writer, writing primarily for computer publications.

How did you get into online searching?

I've always liked to be self-reliant. Anything that I'm going to use regularly, I try to learn how to do myself so I don't have to deal with intermediaries. I got really interested in online searching two or three years ago, and I do it in fits and spurts. I do it when I need to, when I'm researching an article or something like that. I search a fair amount of the time just to satisfy my own curiosity on different subjects.

I'm pretty much self-taught. We have a four-week class at the junior college that teaches the basics on how to construct a search strategy and that kind of thing. I took that four or five years ago.

I have academic accounts on DIALOG and NewsNet. Their classroom instruction packages cost something like $15 an hour, including telecom charges, which is just the most extraordinary thing. But, even at that rate, I'm aware of the ticking meter syndrome. It makes no difference, really, what the rate is. Any time there's a connect charge, I'm conscious of it. I think that people will always be conscious of the charge, no matter how low it is.

Do you caution your students that when they get out in the real world it's going to cost a lot more than $15 an hour?

Oh, yeah, I tell them just how incredibly fortunate we are to be able to show them everything at those rates and that this is atypical. I usually teach a two-session strategy; I tell them to get on quickly, get some information, get off, evaluate that, and come back on with a more refined search. So they're thinking "cost-effective" from the beginning.

I emphasize that you have to ask, "What is the end purpose of the search?" In many cases, people are after totally comprehensive information; they want to know everything that's been published on the subject. My searching, because it's usually for newspaper or magazine writing, is a little different. I want to have a sense of what's been published, but if there's one little tiny fact that is in some obscure journal and I miss it, it's probably okay. So I use a different type of strategy, a different approach.

For my needs, the databases don't have to be encyclopedic. I don't have to know everything that was ever written about a subject. I know what I have to do to get a good sense of what's been written, and find the specific information I need. The reality of journalism is that you're going to miss something. You can't find it all. It wouldn't make any difference if I had accounts on lots of other systems, I would get 99 percent duplicates of what I already found. You hit the point of diminishing returns pretty quickly in the kinds of stuff you do for traditional journalism.

Do you usually go to full-text databases first?

I used to because you'll usually want the full text eventually. But I found that those searches tend to take a lot more time, and I get fewer productive hits. Now I usually start with DIALOG File 484, Newspaper & Periodical Abstracts, because that even indexes the *New York Times*. Even if I can't get the full text online, I can at least find out what's been written. I use National Newspaper Index as well, and Magazine Index. When I started doing computer articles, I discovered Trade & Industry ASAP, Computer ASAP, and so on.

I use the DIALOG PAPERS file a lot, too. When there's something you want to write about, you don't know for sure that some reporter somewhere hasn't done something already. But it could have appeared anywhere, not just in the *New York Times*, *Washington Post*, *Wall Street Journal*, *Christian Science Monitor* or *Los Angeles Times*. If you've got one unique term, like the search I did on National Security Division Directive 145, NSDD 145, you can go in with a fairly tight strategy and see what happens. You don't have to look under "computers" or something like that and get 14 million hits.

If you get 50 or 75 hits, how do you narrow it down?

Usually I'll look at a Format 3, which in most DIALOG databases is a full cite minus the abstract, then I go back and look for abstracts, or lead paragraphs if they're newspaper articles. In many cases, I can tell from that if it's going to be right on. Unless it's a 10,000-word piece, I'll go to full text from there. If it *is* a 10,000-word piece, I'll probably look at a KWIC format first to check relevance. If you're fairly knowledgeable about a subject, it's amazing how much information you can get from an abstract to help judge whether that article will work for you.

And, of course, I use the standard ways of narrowing a search with Boolean operators and so on. I may be an end-user, but I'm not a fan of menu-driven systems. Usually they're not as flexible as I want to be, and if I know where I'm going, it's much faster to do it by commands than with menus.

I don't think the online services have really grasped what end-users want. I wish they would realize that they are dealing with a real business here. There's no excuse for small business approaches. I wish they would get out of the way and let some pros handle it. The thing I keep preaching, my mantra in all this, is that computers give you choices and you should have the choice of all of the front ends in the world—to do it whatever way you want to do it—let the computer figure out, invisibly, how to get it done.

I've come to the conclusion that all this stuff should be taught much earlier in schools. Almost everything we do with computers involves some big conceptual changes that cannot be grasped quickly. We should start teaching Boolean searching the way we teach algebra. At the Technology Center in San Jose, they teach fifth grade students how to create their own HyperCard stacks, and then these kids have to create stacks usable by the *first* graders. I'm a big believer in fostering logical thinking way, way down in the school system, rather than trying to do it all in one shot. Today, students get to college and we say, "Okay, we're going to teach you all about databases and Boolean searching in an hour and half a week for four weeks." Forget it.

Going back to your own searching, how do you handle your search output?

I dump everything to disk. I start downloading when I go online so everything is captured to disk automatically. I print out almost nothing. Everything for my magazine writing is done through e-mail, so it all stays pretty much in electronic form. I've actually come to hate having things in paper form because I can't index them or sort them or do anything that I can do much easier in the electronic world.

I have a program for the Mac called On Location, put out by Mitch Kapor's company, ON Technology. It indexes every word in every text file, and it's lightning fast in its retrieval. You can do Boolean searches, too. All I have to do is remember a word or two that might be in any particular file and zip, there it is. I find that to be a much more effective way of filing things than anything I ever had on paper.

I keep things for as long as I think they might be useful, which usually means forever. Realistically, when I write an article, I may only use two sentences worth of material from a very extensive search. It's not so much that I quote the material, although I certainly do that when it's appropriate, but more that it rounds out my understanding of the subject. I get a different perspective by looking at articles in widely different kinds of publications; it helps me triangulate on my own approach. Very often, of course, it suggests sources of people to interview.

From your perspective as an informed end-user, what issues concern you in the field of electronic information retrieval?

One of the things that the information business has to do, if it's serious about reaching end-users, is to tap into the impulse buying kind of thing. I'm really fascinated with this Home Shopping Network. It's just so foreign to me; it's unbelievable. But the concept is that they put something up there and make it appealing. They make it very easy for you to buy, and you run out or call up or whatever, and you buy it. Of course, later you find out that you've got a house full of junk...

Maybe something like the "Home Searching Network?"

The point is, I don't think you should have to have an account on these systems. I think you should be able to call up with a credit card number, or alternatively, maybe a relatively low-cost 900 number, something that is charged back automatically to your phone so you don't worry about it.

What concerns me most, though, is what I call the "politics of searching." Information providers decide which publications to index, and that's a business decision because it costs money to put publications online. What I find is that there is an enormous political imbalance. I would like to see alternative points of view, and the reality is that most alternative or leftist publications are not indexed electronically. My concern as we go forward into a digital world is that to not be indexed electronically is to not exist. I think it would be wonderful for some wealthy foundation that might be concerned about this political imbalance to fund a project to make alternative publications available on a major online service.

I'm concerned about the political angle because most of my own research is concerned with politics. If I choose to use online sources, which I prefer to do, I'm restricted to viewpoints that are available online. That means that what I get comes from one band of the political spectrum. During the Gulf War, I was teaching a special journalism class, and some powerful stuff was coming out of the *Village Voice* and other contrary publications that, to the best of my knowledge, are not available online, certainly not in full text. Luckily, some activists made a lot of that stuff available through various Internet newsgroups. Otherwise we wouldn't have seen it at all.

My perception of most librarians and professional searchers is that they're using databases that are already organized, structured in some way. Yet there's a whole universe of information that exists in the digital world that is outside that. This is where these wide area information servers come in handy. I've been using those through the Internet where a lot of this ephemeral stuff exists. You can do a search through old Usenet newsgroups, for example. Most of the stuff is drivel, but there are things that are valuable and that you wouldn't get any other way. I'm excited about these newsgroups. I consider them a form of alternative publishing, and I think they're going to be an increasingly valuable source of information for people in the information business, reporters as well as researchers. Searchers are going to need to look at them as well as at the traditional services.

I'm also concerned with the limited amount of in-depth material about regional issues. For example, I'd love to see databases that concentrate much more on California information, or even Northern California information. I think we're going to start to see a flood of that kind of stuff, but I'm not sure it's going to come up on DIALOG or BRS. At our college, we put our catalog online six or eight months ago, and now we've got public access and dial-in and Internet access. One of the projects that's underway is to put up a local database of Sonoma County information. As this kind of information starts to become available digitally, as government agencies put their information in digital form, it becomes easier to build a local database. I think we'll start to see a real growth in that kind of thing.

One of the things I'm thinking about is what the electronic newspaper of the future would be like. In January of 1993, we started a dial-up computer conferencing system for the student newspaper. Over the summer we're going to extend it to almost all the Macintoshes on campus. Given the network and a sufficient number of color Macintoshes on campus, we'll disseminate an electronic newspaper that includes not only newspaper but video. There are going to be lots and lots of new sources of digital information online. We don't have the tools yet to turn it all into a searchable knowledge base, but it will be possible.

These are some of the issues I see. I do see these two parallel structures developing: the conventional structured databases being integrated with the ad hoc information sources that have grown up on the Internet and in many local, decentralized places. On campus we're continuing to work with the library and the student newspaper. We don't know exactly what we're doing but we do know that what we want is some kind of a unified information system. Actually, it may not be unified, but my hope is that the user won't know that, that it will be transparent. We're all interested in going in that direction.

Super Search Secrets

On search strategy...

I usually teach a two-session strategy; I tell them to get on quickly, get some information, get off, evaluate that, and come back on with a more refined search.

On favorite databases...

...I usually start with DIALOG File 484, Newspaper & Periodical Abstracts, because that even indexes the *New York Times*....I use National Newspaper Index as well, and Magazine Index. When I started doing computer articles, I discovered Trade & Industry ASAP, Computer ASAP....I use the DIALOG PAPERS file a lot, too.

On saving search results...

...everything is captured to disk automatically. I print out almost nothing....I have a program for the Mac called On Location....It indexes every word in every text file, and it's lightning fast in its retrieval. You can do Boolean searches, too. All I have to do is remember a word or two that might be in any particular file and zip, there it is. I find that to be a much more effective way of filing things than anything I ever had on paper.

On the "politics" of online...

Information providers decide which publications to index...there is an enormous political imbalance. I would like to see alternative points of view, and the reality is that most alternative or leftist publications are not indexed electronically. My concern as we go forward into a digital world is that to not be indexed electronically is to not exist.

On regional information online...

I'm also concerned with the limited amount of in-depth material about regional issues....I think we're going to start to see a flood of that kind of stuff, but I'm not sure it's going to come up on DIALOG or BRS....One of the projects that's underway is to put up a local database of Sonoma County information. As this kind of information starts to become available digitally, as government agencies put their information in digital form, it becomes easier to build a local database. I think we'll start to see a real growth in that kind of thing.

CHAPTER 10

TOM KOCH: SEARCHING AS EMPOWERMENT

Tom Koch is a Toronto-based journalist and author of books on subjects as diverse as electronic journalism (*Journalism for the 21st Century: Online Information, Electronic Databases and the News*, Praeger, 1991), bicycling through Hawaii, and caring for the elderly.

You're an end-user, Tom, not a professional searcher. I'm curious about your involvement with online searching. How did you get interested in it, and how do you use it?

Two of my books deal specifically with the issue of online resources. The first talked about problems with the way news has been done in the past. The second dealt specifically with the way in which online resources can change, and are changing, the narrative form of the news. I also write about caregivers for the elderly, and I work with people who are either seniors or fragile themselves, or who are taking care of elderly relatives. And I write about transportation, both as an academic and as a popular writer.

So I've got three very distinct areas of interest, and for each of these, I do my own research. I also do directed research for student clients, or for my journalist contacts who call and say, "We hear this, where's the story? Can you help us?" The third thing I do is teach. I talk about what an online search is, what it means, how it will affect the work one does, and how to do it.

I'm self-taught as a searcher. I come from an academic background. I learned the old-style academic hand-searching as a student in the late '70s and early '80s. I did a lot of work by going to the library and trying to muddle through something like *Index Medicus*. Then, as a working journalist, I did a medical story that had national significance and I received a request from a lawyer in Mississippi for copies of the work I did in British Columbia. I sent him a copy and asked him how he ever heard about me, and he sent me online printouts from DIALOG, saying, "You're in the database." When I realized lawyers were using these databases to win multimillion dollar suits, I figured that I'd better get online.

This was about 1982. My eyes went bad, which took me out of the full-time news business in the mid-'80s. Searching was a way for me to keep my edge as a journalist. So about '85-'86, I began to seriously transform what I'd learned about traditional research into a knowledge of online research.

For your outside clients, do you work within a pre-arranged budget?

Whenever I start a project for anybody, I give a top level. I ask "How much do you want to spend on this?" If somebody only has $20, $40, $50—some people working in areas like medical research who come to me don't have much money, and other writers don't either—I will tailor it so that my time and their costs are synonymous. Often I approach it as a teaching function. That is, I want people to come to me and say, "I want to learn how to do this for myself, can you show me?" In the end, I'm a success if they go to the library and use the CD-ROM databases for the first time.

But I also sometimes use an independent broker, or one of the in-house search services like Mead and DIALOG have, for a search on a system I can't access myself. Instead of paying a fee to use it twice a year, I get a quote from somebody who knows the system inside-out, and I build that into *my* quote. I go through the same process on these subcontracts that my clients do with me: "I need this much. This is my budget." They say they can or can't do it for that, or they say for X dollars we can give you just the cites; I say fine, I can go to a law library and do the rest myself. I do a lot of library research, probably more than many online searchers.

What kind of hardware and software do you use to go online?

Until very recently the only computer I could use comfortably was a Macintosh. In the mid-'80s it was the only screen I could use for longer than 20 minutes without getting a migraine, and on which I could write in larger characters. I started off with SMARTCOM as software because it was the only one, in those days, that could bring text down larger than 9-point. I would immediately go to 12-point type, which I *could* make out, then later massage it into even more comfortable text for my eyes. Now, with Windows, that's also possible on an IBM-compatible platform, but I've stayed with the Macintosh.

We've talked a little bit about the kinds of searches that you typically do for each of your three careers. Could you go into a little more detail about that?

For my own research, especially medical research, which I did as a journalist and for a book and still do for clients, I tend to use two different databases. I use PaperChase, which is a shell created by Beth Israel Hospital for MEDLINE. It's available both independently and on CompuServe, as a front end filter for probably the largest of all medical databases. Often when I have cases of people who are showing very bizarre reactions, where their relatives will say, "Well, that person's just senile," I can find other reasons.

I worked on a story on the effect of electromagnetic emissions from power lines on an area that had an enormously high rate of childhood leukemia. This was a neighborhood where the mothers noticed that the kids within a six-block radius had an tremendously high incidence of a fairly rare childhood leukemia. The local cancer agency said it was probably just a typical cluster, which means it was random.

So I checked the medical databases, and then I went into a general news database and searched on "electricity or electric and cancer." I found a wealth of stories, including articles that mentioned six cases with over one million dollars in legal settlements in areas where power transformers appeared to have been a specific contributor to childhood leukemia. So I used both a news database and a medical database to pull stuff that would affect those people if they were my clients, but that also provided background for my newspaper story.

Sometimes my areas of concentration overlap. I may write about gerontology for a newspaper. In one case, a news organization wanted a story on driving requirements and vision. I did a medical search and then a news search. Next, I went on CompuServe and found two or three people in the forums who had this specific type of sight impairment and were still driving. With that approach, we got personal interviews. It made a great story.

It's amazing to me that even the most astute writers are sometimes ignorant as researchers. Some of them are extraordinarily research-oriented, but any of us who were trained more than ten years ago learned library-style research. Our first reflex is the book or the journal. Most of the stuff that's available now was just coming out when we got out of school. I recently talked to a newsgroup about the difference between dead stacks and live information, between the morgue and the library. What this stuff allows you to do is access the library instead of the morgue of dead facts. If you're a journalist writing about an area that is moving as fast as biotechnology, for example, anything more than five years old is probably out-of-date. What you really want is articles that aren't in the medical journals but are probably in the ethical journals or the legal journals. Case law is growing incredibly.

If you find the same database, or essentially the same collection of information on more than one service, what determines where you go for it?

Like everybody else, I tend to go with what I'm most familiar with. I also tend to go with what I know is cheaper. That's clearly the subject of some debate among researchers. I've told a lot of people, and they haven't believed me, that it's very often cheaper to go to IQuest on CompuServe than it is to go to Dow Jones or to DIALOG. I want elderly people to be able to go online and say to their doctor, you just gave me these two drugs and together they kill people. It's an enormously empowering thing. But we can't do that if it's going to cost $120 an hour, or because they can't afford to invest 100 hours to learn this or that system.

What databases do you find yourself turning to again and again?

I use National Newspaper Index a lot. I'll go there first if I'm searching for something that happens in multiple locations, for instance, anesthetic deaths. I used to do a lot of work on how people were killed in hospitals. I would look in the Los Angeles and New York papers. I would look in the national papers to see if suits had been filed or court cases reported with large enough judgments to warrant a New York or Los Angeles or even a Seattle summation. It might have happened in Everett, Washington, but it will be in the Seattle paper. It might have happened in Orange County, but it will be in the *Los Angeles Times*. I use them for a first run when I'm looking for national patterns.

Going into the full-text papers is another challenge. I was doing a search on certain issues dealing with coverage of the elderly. There are a lot of elderly people living in Florida, so I went to the Florida papers, and also looked in the Boston and New York newspapers and the *Washington Post* and just did a quick run through with the words "aging or elderly," "Florida," and then the specifics of the issues. I love keywords, because they limit what you get to a rational return. I normally use a broad subject first and then an incredibly specific modifier. You can get 40,000 hits on "aged" or "aging" or "elderly" alone. But if you're searching outside of the South and bring in "Florida" as a search term, you get reports of major nursing home scandals and that sort of thing.

I use proximity operators, especially in an expensive system like Dow Jones. Not being able to afford to stay online long is a real impetus to good searching. Normally, if I plan the search correctly, I don't need too many proximity phrases. I did one, though, on a type of device used in nursing homes and pediatrics, called restraining vests, which they use to tie people either to cribs, for children, or to chairs, for adults. I thought, "No problem, nobody else would be using restraining vests." Of course, with "restraint" and "vest" in the story, I pulled up a whole lot of things about fashion. If I had thought about it, I would have realized that I would get a lot of fashion stories with "restraining." The number of dresses that are apparently restraining is awesome. I never thought of it in terms of vests. My mind was on this one product that I could see in my brain. It was a humbling experience. So I went back and used an adjacency operator to make sure all I got was "restraint" or "restraining" near "vest," which limited it to the specific product I was looking for.

You're unusual in that you're a heavy consumer of both full-text news and the bibliographic medical files, and you integrate the two a lot. How does that work?

What I'm conscious of in these different modes is a sense of geographic scale. If I'm searching the medical literature, I'm searching a database whose scale is basically international. It usually doesn't matter if an article came from a Swedish researcher or a Canadian researcher or an American researcher. Once the knowledge is in the literature, it's there, diffused. But if I'm searching a news-related story, the "regionality" might be important, for legal reasons or whatever. If there's been a court case in Florida and a court case in Texas, the one in Florida, if that's where you're writing, is much more important. If I'm using a newspaper database, or I'm working for a client who says look, my region wants to know about X, then I have to limit it by geographic scale.

A lot of what these databases do is give us, for the first time, control of geographic scale. Sometimes what you want to do, if you're in Florida, is find that this happened and was reported on 15 times in Washington State and California. So you can say, "Nobody here knows about this, but we know that this has happened time and again in these other parts of the United States." Sometimes what you have to do is limit it to a specific county, a specific region, a specific doctor.

So, when I'm searching anything that is news-related, I look to the geographic scale of the story I'm seeking. If I'm looking for a topical issue, like in medicine, it's much less relevant. Then I want to be able to know if this has gotten into the popular or semi-popular literature. If it's been in the *New England Journal of Medicine*, then I know that someone has written about it in the major papers. At that point I go into a newspaper database and search for the topic and the phrase, "New England Journal of Medicine," to find the secondary coverage.

You can do that in business, too. It might have been in a very technical report, but you want to find out if it's been mentioned in the *New York Times* or the *Wall Street Journal*, which means it's a major story. This is true of a lot of the pollution issues. Some incidents involving very serious pollutants will only show up in the technical databases. However, if it's been in the *Wall Street Journal* or the *New York Times* or the *Los Angeles Times*, you can be sure it is something that's been widely commented about in the popular literature—then you know to go to a whole different series of sources to answer your question.

Sometimes I go back to the technical literature at that point because I have to know more in order to advise my client. Also, now that we've finally got the technical literature in our hands, why not make use of it? I mean, ten years ago, to have been able to pull up a primary piece of technical literature, a single Environmental Protection Agency document, that turned out to be the key to the query, would have been impossible. It would have taken months, if ever, to find it. Now I can get five absolutely perfect technical articles, with abstracts, that tell me, and ultimately the client, everything we need to know about what was going on, why it was going on, and where to track it.

When you're looking at search results, how do you evaluate what you've retrieved? Do you get titles first? Do you just go in and get abstracts right away if that's what's available to you?

It depends on whom I'm working for and what the client wants. I prefer, typically, to get an abstract whenever I can. Generally, the abstract provides an evaluative tool which the title does not. I know what headline writers do for a living; I used to do it. I like bibliographic cites in areas that I know and which I can evaluate from the title alone. Some journals in medicine, one or two in business, and one or two in environment I know so well that I know I'm going to want to pull an abstract out.

The evaluative process again depends on who I'm doing it for. If I'm teaching, I'll pull everything with abstracts, sometimes with full text if I can get it, but I narrow the search to the last six months only. Then I use that retrieval as the first test; I sit down with the person and say, "Here's what you can get for the last six months. Is this what you want? How can we hone this better?" On the other hand, sometimes I'm working for a client who says, "Look, we hear this rumor, we know this story. Is this something for us? How can we find the information?" Then I do the evaluation and the stripping myself, write up a two- or three-page summary with the references at the back if they want them, and make a nice little information packet. Of course, they pay for that. So it really depends on who the client is, the parameters of my assignment, and my familiarity with a subject area.

How do your deadlines vary? Do you turn things around pretty quickly?

The deadlines that are stretched out are part of my own ongoing work. Working on a book takes at least a year to a year and a half. When I'm finishing a book in any one of my three areas, I do a search or two just to see if anything critical has come out since I first did my research.

On the other hand, I've had people call and say, "Gee whiz, this is happening!" A newspaper reporter calls and says, "There's been a chemical spill. What is this stuff, is it dangerous, what's going to happen, why are we evacuating, what is a polyphenol bi-chloride?" In a case like that, your first search is going to be really direct. Is it going to kill the reporter who goes out there? Are we going to have 500 people dead tomorrow? Next, there are second and third, even fourth-order searches: Who makes this stuff? Has it ever been spilled before? Has there ever been a ruling on the safety measures required for this? If somebody says kids are dying from X, first you want to find out if that's possible. If firemen are going out there in their space suits and trying to hose something down with water which, when it mixes with water, explodes, you want to know that. You want to pull your photographer back, but not too far.

If you only use this stuff in a crisis mode, though, you miss the real joy of it. That is when you find out that whatever this spill was, there have probably been five other places where it happened, and that the company has made 30 percent extra profit in the last year, that the shipper is not following basic procedures...There are second, third, fourth, sixth-order searches you can do around that one event, as time and circumstances allow.

You're obviously very price-conscious. What tips do you have about saving money online?

At the moment, there seems to be a real snobbishness about the databases you use. People who are really good with Dow Jones or who love DIALOG will go into those systems, even though they may be more expensive than some of the progressively cheaper resources out there. If you're doing this for a living, it makes sense to check the alternatives and then make a very cold decision. As online access points proliferate and different databases are bundled and unbundled, the information will be available in so many different ways that you can almost certainly find it cheaper. It's like, do you want to use a generic drug, or do you want to pay more money so you can say, "Well, I'm taking this drug called X. It's the best and most well-known one." I'm not snobbish; I look for the cheapest place, the easiest place.

You can also look at how you approach the search. I don't necessarily search for the most technical or the most complex article to start with. Most nontechnical clients don't want to know the chemical components of a substance. What they want to know is whether this stuff is going to hurt, who makes it, that kind of thing. If that's what they want to know, that's what I will find for them. If they ask me to find X, but also to see what else there is, I will then search in the most general way possible for those leads. I won't do more work than I'm hired for. A lot of people do. They want to pull out all the stops. That's not necessary, not if you're trying to run a business.

Tell me what you like most about searching.

What is really satisfying, both in my own work and for others, is the degree to which online empowers the individual. It gives them the information that otherwise they would not be able to access. It enables them to know, perhaps, that the doctor, the planner, the lawyer, who speaks so definitively, might be speaking through his or her hat. Years ago, Walter Lippmann, the doyen of American journalists, said "We have to trust them" ("them" meaning the politicians, the officials, the experts), "the books and papers are on their desks." The books and the papers are not on their desks anymore, they're on *our disks*. What I see emerging from this is the means by which individuals can again be empowered by what libraries once were, providers of information for everybody. At the moment, we are the facilitators in that.

What I love about the process is when it informs me and it informs someone else. It's great when somebody says, "I'm not going to need you anymore, I'm doing this myself." We should be happy when people learn to do it themselves, because they will come back to us with the next order, the more difficult stuff, and that's more interesting, anyway.

However, this can be a social movement as well as a business. If it isn't, then we're just part of the same old thing we bitched about twenty years ago, those of us who were bitching twenty years ago. When people don't get that message, I feel discouraged. This has empowered me as a sight-impaired writer. It's allowed me to write more books, and to do hundreds of stories that I would not have been able to write otherwise. That's important. If it can empower me, it can empower anyone.

SUPER SEARCH SECRETS

On the costs of a search...
Whenever I start a project...I give a top level. I ask "How much do you want to spend on this?" If somebody only has $20, $40, $50...I will tailor it so that my time and their costs are synonymous.

On subcontracting to brokers...
But I also sometimes use an independent broker, or one of the in-house search services...for a search on a system I can't access myself....I get a quote from somebody who knows the system inside-out, and I build that into *my* quote.

On choosing a system for a search...
Like everybody else, I tend to go with what I'm most familiar with. I also tend to go with what I know is cheaper....it's very often cheaper to go to IQuest on CompuServe than it is to go to Dow Jones or to DIALOG.

On formats for search output...
I prefer, typically, to get an abstract whenever I can. Generally, the abstract provides an evaluative tool which the title does not. I know what headline writers do for a living; I used to do it. I like bibliographic cites in areas that I know and which I can evaluate from the title alone.

On saving money online...
People who are really good with Dow Jones or who love DIALOG will go into those systems, even though they may be more expensive...If you're doing this for a living, it makes sense to check the alternatives and then make a very cold decision. As online access points proliferate and different databases are bundled and unbundled, the information will be available in so many different ways that you can almost certainly find it cheaper. It's like, do you want to use a generic drug, or do you want to pay more money so you can say, "Well, I'm taking this drug called X. It's the best and most well-known one." I'm not snobbish; I look for the cheapest place, the easiest place.

CHAPTER 11

NANCY LAMBERT: PATENT PUZZLER

Nancy Lambert is an information analyst in the Technical Library at Chevron Research and Technology Company in Richmond, California. CRTC is the patenting entity for Chevron Corporation.

Where does patent searching fit into Chevron's overall corporate structure? Do you serve the entire company?

All Chevron patents are assigned to Chevron Research and Technology, with a few exceptions, and those are primarily goofs. Any patenting activity within the rest of Chevron Corporation gets funneled back to the patent lawyers for processing, and to me for patent information. Patent searching is my main job.

The patent lawyers at Chevron Corporation are among my principal search customers, though I work with the researchers as well. The lawyers come to me for patentability questions and for validity and infringement questions. They also ask a lot of itsy-bitsy legal stuff, like the legal status of this patent, or the patent family of that one, whether this company holds those patents, has so-and-so got a patent infringement suit going with such-and-such other company, that sort of thing.

The researchers more often ask about state-of-the-art patents and literature to support the research that they're doing. Sometimes they're working on Chevron-assigned patents that they already invented.

Backing up a bit to your own professional background, how long have you been with Chevron, and when and where did you learn to search?

I've been with Chevron for six years, and I was with 3M in St. Paul, Minnesota for about 12 years before that. The patent activity at 3M is very heavy, of course; it's an order of magnitude bigger than at Chevron, as a matter of fact.

Most of my training was on the job. I got a B.S. in chemistry at Carnegie-Mellon in 1968, and did some graduate work in chemistry at Princeton between '68 and '70. I graduated from Columbia University with a Master's in library science in '71. After I graduated, I worked for Columbia for three years, in a little Population and Family Planning Research Institute that was attached to the College of Physicians and Surgeons. You could say I started learning searching my last year there, because we had an in-house database that looked and felt a lot like DIALOG. But my searching experience was pretty limited until I got to 3M.

Back to the present, how do your search requests come in? Do requesters walk in, e-mail you, send you memos, call you on the phone?

All of the above. Some tend to be a little more formal and send written requests, but not that often. Even when they do, we inevitably have a long telephone conversation during which I give them a thorough grilling about what it is they're really trying to find out.

Can you take us on a walk through a generic reference interview?

That's a toughie because, if you'll pardon me blowing my own horn, I really am a very good reference interviewer, but I'm not quite sure that I can put my finger on *why*. I can tell you that, if they come in with lists of keywords, I always back them gently down to point zero—*beyond* the keywords, and out again in a different direction. What I need from them is a thorough description of the technology. This always tends to be a learning process for me. I've learned most of my petroleum chemistry on the job here, and a lot of it from interviewing the people who ask for searches. I have to understand the technology that they're interested in; I have to know what they're talking about.

Next, I find out what they're trying to get out of the search. This is not always what they *say* they want when they come in and ask for a search. Sometimes they're trying to second-guess the system; sometimes they're assuming that we can't do this and we can't do that, and they're often not correct. So it's very important to find out what they want to accomplish. I try to get a general background: Is there a specific patent that they're trying to invalidate? Are they worried about infringing someone else's technology in this area? Is it a patentability question, meaning, is it novel, can we patent it?

After that, a certain amount of negotiating often goes on: "Well, this database can do *that*, which is not exactly what you wanted, but this is about the closest we can get. This is why we can't do exactly what you wanted." Or, "Take a look at this list of lubricants and pick the ones you're interested in having me search in the context of your question."

I generally don't try to teach my requesters how to use databases, but I try to educate my frequent requesters, particularly, so that they have an awareness of what can and can't be done. Patent liaisons, for instance, use me a lot. A patent liaison is someone with a laboratory background, usually a Ph.D. in chemistry or whatever, who has moved out of the lab and into a position where he or she has also learned patent law. All of our patent liaisons are also registered patent agents. The job is pretty much what it sounds like. They are the liaisons between the patent lawyers and the researchers. They know much more about the technology than the lawyers and know much more about patent law than the researchers.

Depending on the type of patent search, there are always some basic bibliographic-type questions: What countries are involved? How far back do you need to go? If it's a company search, do you know of any other names this company has had in its history, and do you want me to search for them as well? I have to have a pretty good mental pattern of all the possible ranges, the different branches I have to explore, the ones that are appropriate for the type of question I'm being asked.

Do you use a checklist or search request form?

We do, indeed, have a search request form. It's one that I designed shortly after I came to work here. We also use it to input search request information in our computer log. The stuff that has to be keyed in is lightly shaded on the form, and it appears on the form in the order in which it has to be keyed in. There's a lot of space for search details, and basic questions like country coverage, language and date coverage. We also ask for known references; that's a very important one: "Do you know of any good art in this field?" If they do, the first thing I do is plug the known patent into the system and see how it's been indexed. The form also has a checklist of the major databases we use, plus space to fill in the names of others we might use.

From the computer log, we can search on, and generate some statistics based on the title and keywords we've assigned to each search. There's also a series of standard descriptors, broad technology areas like polymers, biochemistry, computers, petrochemistry, petroprocessing, fuels, lubricants, gases, health, pollution, and so on. We'll assign as many of those as are appropriate to a particular question, and those are handy for retrieval, too. Then we divide by type of search: literature, patents, competitive intelligence, current awareness, and manual searches. Of course, we also include basic information like the requester's name and division number, the charge number, when the search was assigned, when it was needed, when it was finished, how long it took to do it, the databases that we searched, and so on.

What online services and what databases do you use most heavily?

As far as online services go, our use is about 85 percent ORBIT, 10 percent STN and the rest mostly DIALOG. I use QUESTEL a little bit, not very much. In terms of databases, almost every patent question gets into Derwent's World Patents Index at some point.

Certainly the file I use the most, and the reason I use ORBIT the most, is the American Petroleum Institute (API) patent file, which has been merged into the Derwent World Patents Index. This is a wonderful, wonderful situation, because it is a true merger of the records. It took an enormous amount of agony and years of work for the people at ORBIT and API, who would probably never have tackled it if they had known how much work it was going to be. But it is worth every penny as far as I'm concerned, because it allows us to do true multifile searching. We can come up with a search strategy that combines both Derwent and API parameters. Derwent is very strong in some areas, such as chemical substance indexing. API has excellent controlled vocabulary indexing for all the petroleum concepts. There are a lot of other enhancements on both of them, and the two, together, make a very powerful database for any downstream petroleum-related question.

"Downstream," lest you ask, is everything that happens to the oil after it gets to the refinery—all the petroleum processing, the products, that kind of thing. "Upstream" is everything involved with the petroleum-finding and digging-out industry—exploring for the petroleum, getting it out of the ground, enhanced oil recovery, well logging and so on. I do quite a bit of patent searching on the upstream side as well, some wonderful/ghastly mechanical searches.

For downstream questions, I usually use the IFI Comprehensive Index as well—that index's strongest point is how it handles polymers. I use Chemical Abstracts, of course, for both patents and literature. Chemical Abstracts is particularly good when I have a question that would get me a ton of garbage in a more generic file—the registry numbers let me do much more precise searching. One has to keep in mind that Chemical Abstracts isn't particularly comprehensive, though for some kinds of searches that's okay.

I use the U.S. patent files for any kind of patent citation searching, INPADOC for patent family and legal status searching, and Derwent for that kind of thing also. I use the

Claims Reassignment & Re-Examination file, the INPADOC legal status file and sometimes the LitAlert file for various kinds of legal status questions. A lot of those are exclusive on ORBIT or heavily on ORBIT anyway.

On the upstream side, TULSA is the major petroleum file. That's also, for all practical purposes, exclusively on ORBIT. There is a version on DIALOG but it doesn't go back far enough, and it doesn't have abstracts. Any given question is usually going to involve several different databases, at least if I'm going to do any kind of civilized search rather than just a "quick and dirty" one. I do a lot of cross-file searching.

Do you go for full text immediately, if it's available, or isn't that a factor in the kind of searching you do?

No, I don't go straight for full text. In fact, I prefer the shorter format files because they have better indexing and they're easier to search. I've been on LEXIS maybe twice in my life. I'm not a big advocate of full-text patent searching. The patent writer is his own lexicographer by law. He doesn't have to use any kind of accepted terminology. He can use anything he darn well pleases as long as he defines what he means and he's consistent within that. A patent lawyer will take advantage of this to obfuscate deliberately, so as to make the patent less retrievable. They have to disclose, but they don't to make it any easier for their competition than they have to. So we're far better off depending on controlled vocabulary and concept coding than we are with free text in patents.

Obviously you're going to ORBIT for content as much as anything else. What else determines what online service you go to for a particular search?

They say that people tend to stick with the system they learned first. I'm an exception to that rule, I guess, because I did learn DIALOG first, but I like ORBIT better. It has a very elegant, very concise command language that lets you get stuff with a minimum of keying. It's quite flexible. You don't need a lot of parentheses. You can pre- and post-qualify; you can change prequalifications after the fact. ORBIT does have some major pain-in-the-neck features also, mainly because of its file construction. You can grow old and gray waiting for it to NEIGHBOR on an obscure field, and if you're searching on heavily-posted terms, you can sit there for quite a while, too. But it's an indispensable system for me, largely because of the GET command. That's basically a statistical searching capability that's been available on ORBIT for years.

I use ORBIT's statistical capability quite a lot, as a search aid as well as for actually generating statistics. For example, if I have some horrible mechanical upstream search where I'm looking for a particular type of well logging device, I will do what searching I can in TULSA, which has indexing terms that get right at that technology. Then I do a PRINT SELECT on the patent numbers—PRINT SELECT is similar to MAPping in DIALOG, but I think it's more straightforward—bring them in through the Derwent file, and do a GET command on the International Patent Class (IPC). What that does is rank the International Patent Classes that have been assigned to all the patents in that technology, according to their frequency of occurrence. It's very handy, a really quick way of looking for IPCs to supplement the search in a broader file.

I do something similar in the CLAIMS files; I do GETs on the U.S. patent classes. If someone comes in and says, "I want a search on Mobil and Exxon and Texaco and this particular technology," I will usually ask, "Why just those companies?" The person will say, "Because they're the major players in this technology," and I will ask, "How would you like me to do a general search on the technology without putting in company names, and get you a ranked list of the companies that actually have the most patents?" Sometimes that produces some surprises for them.

Those are examples of a very basic type of statistical searching. When you get into the fancy stuff, you have to be very careful that you know enough about the databases, and about different countries' patenting practices, and about different *companies'* patenting practices, to be aware of problem areas that might give you statistics that seem to imply something they shouldn't. You should know enough about these things to be able to recognize when something's fishy.

DIALOG, of course, has duplicate detection, but not in the patent files. It has OneSearch, which is relatively useless in the patent files. I'm not that big a fan of OneSearch in general, because it ignores the individual strengths and weaknesses of the separate databases. Also, it can disguise the fact that, in one database, the search strategy has given you five clean hits, and in another, 150 pieces of garbage. You can't tell what's going on without going into the individual databases, anyway. There are some times when OneSearch is useful, though. I've used it on all of DIALOG practically, when I'm looking for a really obscure person or company, or when I'm desperate to find anything and have no idea where to look. Particularly, I look in DIALINDEX, which I think is great; I wish ORBIT had something equivalent to that with all of its capabilities.

How do you plan your search strategy?

Quite extensively. What I do is pile my desk ten feet high with all the search aids. I have my office very nicely organized, as a matter of fact. All the things that I use all the time—my Derwent manuals, my IFI thesauri, my API thesaurus, my TULSA thesaurus, my *U.S. Manual of Patent Classifications*, my international classifications, my DIALOG, ORBIT and STN user guides and database sheets, my Chemical Abstracts search tools—are where I can reach them when I'm sitting at my desk. I pull down one thesaurus or code book after another, and I formulate my searches pretty thoroughly before I go online. For that, I use the white space on the search intake form. You should see the wild and wonderful cryptic notes I make on these things—no one else could possibly make any sense out of them. I have my own symbols for AND and OR and LINK and so on.

How do you actually build a search? Do you think about it in terms of its component parts?

Normally what I do—and I think all this out beforehand—is divide the question into its essential subconcepts. Often that involves a great deal of discussion with the customer: "Do you want to limit to this concept, or to that concept? Would you like me to do a cut for this concept but not limit to it?" By "cut" I mean isolate that particular aspect and the references that focus on it, so we can go back to them individually if we want, but not throw away everything else in the process. Then I work up a search strategy that captures all the subconcepts, individually and separately. Finally, I go online and create the sets, and combine and recombine them, depending on the results I'm getting.

I can give you an example; this is one that I've written about for *DATABASE*. It was a search in TULSA on the toxic effects of oil well fires. First, I came up with the terms "oil reservoir," "oil field," "crude oil," "oil well," "oil spill," "oil seep," and "oil waste."

That covered the "oil" concept. Then I used "toxic effects" and "health," which are both hierarchical term headings with many narrower terms under them, or posted to them. That took care of the "health" concept. Then I put in "well fire," which is a more specific term, and "combustion," "combustion products" and "accidental fire," all of which are more generic terms. Each of those was a separate set.

Next, I keyed in all the "oil" terms, just kept on keying line after line until it was all entered, and that was set number one. Then I keyed in "toxic effects or health," and that was set number two. Then I keyed in "combustion or combustion products or accidental fire," that was set three. Then the very specific "well fire," which made set four.

After that, I combined sets one and two and four to get the "oil well fire health and toxicity" angle, and looked at how much I got. Then I combined one and two and three NOT four, to get what additional material there might be on oil fires other than well fires.

That's fairly typical of the way I approach a search. I key in a set for all the synonyms for every subconcept, and then add the subconcepts together. What I do next depends on how much I've gotten to this point. If I get five hits when I AND all the subconcepts together, that will be the narrowest cut. Typically, I decide which subconcept is *least* necessary to the search or *most* likely to be artificially limiting, to be restrictive in ways that could risk missing good stuff. I get rid of that subconcept, AND the others together, NOT out what I've already seen, and see how much else I get.

When you present the results to the client, do you walk them through the process the way you've explained it to me?

Yes, and usually I annotate each set, or each cut, with a descriptive title. I outline the concepts for each, in an English sentence rather than using the actual search language and all the key terms. On the example I gave you, I would have said "toxic effects of oil *well* fires," and then "toxic effects of oil fires, other." I try to make sure that all the Boolean concepts are included, but in a statement that the customer will understand.

Just to summarize, I create subsets with as many synonyms as appropriate, key them in, and AND them together to get the most appropriate stuff. Then I back out the most restrictive set, and see what else I've got. If the most restrictive set got a hundred hits, though, I look at them to see if they're relevant. If they are, I print them and tell the customer, "Here's what I got with the most restrictive approach. Here's what I didn't get. How much more do you want to look at, or is there another approach we can take?" Searches are always open-ended.

I almost never pull hundreds or thousands of references in a single shot. I only do that after talking it over with the requester and making sure that this is an acceptable approach, that he or she has some way of screening those references. We don't have the staff here to provide the kind of analysis that, for example, Exxon, Amoco, Dow Chemical, and DuPont do. They have much larger staffs; I think DuPont has a group of something like ten or eleven Ph.D. chemists who do nothing but patent analyses and reports. We have *me*.

If I do retrieve a ton of references, I usually make a strong effort to do it in layers the way I just described. This way the stuff that is more specific and has a higher probability of being relevant is separated from the "Oh, by the way, you'd better look at this, too" stuff. Then this second-level information is separated from the "Well, this *might* be worth glancing at, but I'm not sure" stuff, which would probably be another level below that.

What does your end product look like? How much do you clean it up before the requester sees it?

If it's a question in which I am getting a lot of false hits and I can't screen them out while I'm doing the search, I will go through and get rid of them by hand afterwards. This happens more often with literature searches than with patents. I sometimes order offline prints when there's a lot of material, and when the requester is willing to wait a week. But for the most part, I download search results, move them into WordPerfect and clean them up. If I find something that looks particularly good, I either move it to the front or mark it somehow.

I have a lot of little macros that will do things like put on a pretty title, highlight the titles of individual documents to make it easier to scan, put the requester's name and charge number on every page, and write "Search Results From The CRTC Technical Library" in large, bold print on top of every page. We make sure that we get our due credit.

How do you determine when a project is completed? Given the nature of your work, I would imagine that some searches might stay "live" for years.

My customer and I will have negotiated, right at the beginning, which databases I'll search. I've explained the advantages of each one, or I've said, "This is a good one for TULSA," or "This is a good one for API." I've asked, "Do you need to get the pre-1964 U.S. patents? Do you need very current stuff? Do you need foreign, or just U.S., or both?" Usually it's both. We've negotiated all those parameters and decided what databases to start with, and we've decided just what approach I'm going to take.

When I've finished all the searches that we decided on and gotten everything into some sort of package, I call the customer and let them know. If they are here at Chevron Research they usually come over. I give them the stuff, explain what I did, and give them a little cheat sheet, which is a sample Derwent printout with all the fields labeled and explained. I ask if they have any questions, invite them to let me know, when they've had a chance to look at it, if there's anything else they want me to do for them. About 80 percent of the time, that's the end of it.

The patent lawyers are in San Francisco, not here in Richmond, but I can send their results quickly, too. When I'm finished with the word processing, instead of printing the results, I upload the files and send them by VM, which is our company electronic mail system. They have the option of receiving them directly, in e-mail. But most of them don't want that, so I send the VM files to a laser printer in the city, one floor up from the patent lawyers' area. That way, they have pretty laser prints made right there, the same day. That's much better than worrying about mail getting lost or sitting around in the mail room for three days.

It sounds like you're in regular, close contact with a group of people whose information needs you know pretty well. Do you find it necessary, under the circumstances, to follow up on searches after you send them out?

I seldom follow up in a formal way. Now and then, if I have doubts about the search, I call, or I send a note saying, "I know this isn't complete; take a look and let's talk about it." In a situation like that, I follow up. But if I feel it's the best we can do, I explain it to them and leave it up to them. If they have any more questions or suggestions, we do another iteration.

We used to send out a little questionnaire with the final search results. The problem was that the patent lawyers never once sent theirs back. The ones that did come back always said, "Yeah, everything was fine, I got what I wanted." It didn't really accomplish anything except to give us some warm fuzzies, so we've kind of stopped doing it. At this point, we don't really have any objective measure of how happy our customers are with our searches. I depend on my own interaction with my customers, many of whom are repeats, to be able to sense when something isn't right. It's pretty subjective but it seems to work.

What's do you see as the downside of being an online searcher?

I get frustrated with the databases and the online services because they're not changing fast enough; improvements take so long. I've been one of the more vocal patent information people at various users' group meetings. I have a pretty good grasp of what needs to be changed, and I can make some pretty directed suggestions.

Unfortunately, a lot of what I'd like to see are things that just can't be done that easily. Certainly the indexing, the database changes that I want would involve a great deal more intellectual effort than the producers currently put in. I suspect that some of the system changes I want would involve an awful lot of computer power that isn't there at this point. Some of the hosts still don't have both-way proximity; you can't say "these words within three words of each other *and* in either direction." You can get a "sentence" operator that works on words in the same sentence, but if you want to get a bit narrower than that and still have both-way proximity, you can't.

Now let's turn it around; what do you *like* most about your job? Why are you an online searcher?

I like it because it's a wonderful intellectual jigsaw puzzle. It's a great deal of fun to take chemical structures and processing concepts and break them down into pieces, and put the pieces back together in such a way that they produce good stuff out of the database.

I like being a patent specialist. In fact, I have resisted becoming a generic reference librarian here at Chevron. I have no hesitation about giving business-related searches to one person and technical searches to someone else, and keeping the patent stuff for myself. I like feeling, "This is where *I* can search." It's nice to know that you're doing the best job that can be done in these particular databases. There are a limited number of patent databases and they are fairly sophisticated, which means it's a universe that you can get a very good hold on with time and practice.

It's not exactly an esoteric niche, either, where you can just play around and indulge yourself. It's something that's crucial to the organization.

It is esoteric, in the sense that the work of the organization itself is specialized, and patent searchers are specialists within a specialty. The point is that when you have to cope with the entire world of literature databases, and the entire world of printed reference sources, it's impossible to develop that level of expertise. You just can't do it, you can't know them all. I much prefer operating in a smaller and more in-depth universe.

You would think that a person would get bored with a field as relatively narrow as this, but I don't. Despite all my grumbling, the technologies, the tools that I use in my job, are changing incredibly fast. When I think of what patent searching was like in '74 when there were virtually no online databases for patent information, versus what we've been talking about here, it's amazing. I just look forward to more changes all the time. It keeps things exciting.

SUPER SEARCH SECRETS

On the reference interview...

...if they come in with lists of keywords, I always back them gently down to point zero—*beyond* the keywords, and out again in a different direction. What I need from them is a thorough description of the technology....Next, I find out what they're trying to get out of the search. This is not always what they *say* they want when they come in and ask for a search.

On favorite databases...

Certainly the file I use the most, and the reason I use ORBIT the most, is the American Petroleum Institute patent file, which has been merged into the Derwent World Patents Index. This is a wonderful, wonderful situation, because it is a true merger of the records.

On full-text files...

No, I don't go straight for full text. In fact, I prefer the shorter format files because they have better indexing and they're easier to search.

On searching ORBIT...

...I like ORBIT better. It has a very elegant, very concise command language that lets you get stuff with a minimum of keying. It's quite flexible. You don't need a lot of parentheses. You can pre- and post-qualify; you can change prequalifications after the fact....it's an indispensable system for me, largely because of the GET command.

On planning search strategy...

What I do is pile my desk ten feet high with all the search aids....All the things that I use all the time—my Derwent manuals, my IFI thesauri, my API thesaurus, my TULSA thesaurus, my *U.S. Manual of Patent Classifications*, my international classifications, my DIALOG, ORBIT and STN user guides and database sheets, my Chemical Abstracts search tools—are where I can reach them when I'm sitting at my desk....I formulate my searches pretty thoroughly before I go online....You should see the wild and wonderful cryptic notes I make...

On formatting search results...

I have a lot of little macros that will do things like put on a pretty title, highlight the titles of individual documents to make it easier to scan, put the requester's name and charge number on every page, and write "Search Results From The CRTC Technical Library" in large, bold print on top of every page. We make sure that we get our due credit.

CHAPTER 12

ANNE MINTZ: MULTIFACETED SPECIALIST

Anne Mintz is Director of Information Services at Forbes Inc., publisher of *Forbes* Magazine. Her responsibilities include the licensing of electronic database products as well as supervising the information center. Anne is a highly regarded speaker and an award-winning writer on data quality and other online issues.

How did you get started in the wonderful world of online searching?

I don't know how I became a librarian, but in 1971 Rutgers gave me a master's of library science degree. There weren't many online search systems then, just the New York Times Information Bank. They did teach us systems analysis and about mainframes, but not a whole lot else. My first introduction to online was in 1974 or thereabouts. I saw an ad announcing that Predicasts, whose print products we used a lot, were online with something called DIALOG. They were training people for $25. All you needed was a dumb terminal running at 300 or 1200bps. Our leasing department was down the hall, and they had a dumb terminal they used occasionally. They said I could use it with their modem as long as it was on a different password and bill. My office manager said, "Sure, you can go to this training session for $25. Just don't tell anyone you know how to use it." So I went and learned how to search Predicasts, which was then essentially just the F&S Index, File 18 on DIALOG. The rest is history. My user number on DIALOG was 1343. It hurt to give it up when I left Lazard-Freres in 1986.

I got to Forbes by a fluke. To make a long story short, I started there in July, 1986. They hired me to "do something about that library." It took me three or four years to actually get "it" done.

Before that, on my fourth day on the job, the executive vice president called at 9:05 and asked to meet me. I made my way across the huge expanse of his office, and he was very gracious, welcoming and chatty. At one point he sat back, and obviously he had something he wanted to show me and ask me about. I was dying. He asked, "What do you know about this?" He took this piece of paper and he handed it across his four-foot desk. I was convinced, like new employees everywhere, that he was going to discover now that I was a total fraud. Halfway across the desk I recognized the Information Access Company letterhead, and I thought, "Oh, thank God, I know the company."

It was a letter about their license agreement concerning *Forbes* on their full-text files. He told me he thought that more could be done and he wanted me to discuss it with them. I said, "Well, I don't know the details, but of course Forbes is a publisher. This is about your relationship with them as a publisher and not as a customer. I know the company and I understand the relationship, but I don't know anything else about it." Apparently I passed the test with flying colors because I acquired a new aspect to my job, licensing negotiations. Four days on the job, and I was no longer just running the library and the in-house automated index to the magazine. I was also negotiator for secondary rights online, and later for film and disk. It works because I understand the products from a customer's point of view. I'm also the contact person for the Copyright Clearance Center as a publisher, not a customer.

From 1989 until just recently, when the library school closed, I taught the online classes at Columbia, too. So, in addition to searching on the job, I also had to keep up in order to teach. That was very, very good for me. If you were to sit down and learn NEXIS now, you would not have the same problems you used to. Now you see a set of 27 items and you can select 1, 3, 5, 7 and 9; you never used to be able to do that. In DIALOG, you can go into DIALINDEX and SELECT FILES ALL. Then if you put in the name of a person, product or whatever your search query is, it will search every database and tell you the results in each file. Next you can rank your files to put the most productive ones at the top, save your search and execute a OneSearch just in the ones where you know you're going to find something. You can do it economically, not just financially, but in terms of time as well. You can search *all* of DIALOG. That never used to be feasible. That used to be one big difference between Mead and DIALOG, but not anymore.

What I'm saying is that people learning online now learn *differently*, and teaching people to learn differently has been good for me. I search differently than some people on my staff who have been searching for ten years.

What communications software do you use?

I have SMARTCOM III and a 9600bps modem, because I work with our full-text files at Forbes. Everybody else uses SMARTCOM II. We don't use DIALOGLINK because we search too many different systems. We search Mead, DIALOG, Baseline, CDA Spectrum for stock ownership profiles, RLIN, Data-Star, DataTimes, VU/TEXT, Dow Jones, Info Globe, and Reuter TEXTLINE, which will be folding into both Data-Star and DIALOG. Mead and Baseline each have their own software, too.

Front end programs like Mead's and DIALOG's aren't useful to us. Being able to type ahead of the first search query doesn't save us anything, because the first query isn't the time-waster. It's when you get back a response that you have to think about what to do next. The meter is ticking all the time, even if you do have that little buffer to type in. The buffer is useless at that point. The time that we take is not in typing; the time we take is in *thinking*. DIALOGLINK may have features that are worthwhile, but they haven't shown me anything compelling yet.

How do you and your staff keep up-to-date on enhancements and new databases on all those systems?

Six of us are searching on a regular basis. We decided a long time ago, almost from the outset, that it was not productive for each of us to keep up with everything. So we divvied up the systems. One person gets DIALOG, one person gets NEXIS and all the others are doubled up. One person gets Reuters and VU/TEXT and another one gets Data-Star and DataTimes, and so on. Their primary responsibility is to file the documentation for their systems, to annotate the changes, and to keep that documentation up-to-date. They are also the primary contact for the customer sales person for that system. At our weekly reference staff meeting, if something unusual or important has happened or is going to happen on a system, it is that person's responsibility to bring it to our attention.

Whom do you serve within Forbes? Who are your search clients?

When I first got there, my mandate was editorial. Five years later it's a very different story. We do work for advertising, promotions, circulation—believe it or not—legal, tax and real estate. These are all departments within the magazine. Then there are the other magazines, *American Heritage*, *Forbes FYI*, *Forbes ASAP* and several other publications.

What's the first thing you do when a requester walks into your office? How does the reference interview go?

We say, "Hi, how are you? What are you working on these days?" I'm not kidding. We make sure that we talk to them as equals, as team members. We see ourselves as part of the team that puts out their story, and we make sure they do, too. So we ask them how they are. We say, "I haven't seen you lately." And it works. It humanizes the relationship, and we get a lot more out of it. We treat them like people and not like clients because they *are* colleagues.

When you slow down and actually interact before you get down to business, it puts your client at ease. *They* slow down and think, "You know, I really *do* have 30 seconds more." When someone asks "How's your father?" or "How's your kid?" or "How was your trip to Japan?"—you know, that has been a marvelous technique. It puts us on equal footing with the writers, and they treat us very nicely. Then we say, "What are you working on?" We don't just take their request. We ask, "What kind of story is that?"

It sounds like that's the transitional question.

It is. "What are you doing? I know you want me to help you on this story but what is this for?" When you say you want a list of the richest people in Philadelphia, I ask, "What is the project? I need to know more about that." I can't just answer that question. I can spend a day on that, I can spend a week on that, I can spend five minutes on it. You tell me the question; you tell me the purpose. Then I will figure out how much time to spend on it and what level of questioning to ask you.

We begin the reference interview in a very strange way, saying, "Tell me more! Oh, that's interesting, tell me more about that." So we ease into it in a pretty subtle way. They know the transition has taken place when the staff member picks up a pen and starts filling in the reference sheet. "Who's this for? What's their phone number? What's today's date? When do they need it? What's the question?" At the bottom of that sheet it says, "Action taken: Question answered, citations sent or articles copied. Any or all of the above."

Are you in a charge-back situation?

No. Zero. Nothing is charged back to departments. It's all the magazine. If something is more than $100, I make a note about what it was for. Once in the five years I've been here, and it was recently, someone asked for a very specific search. It cost us a lot of money on DIALOG but we got the answers. It was a brilliant report—*that* we charged back to *American Heritage*.

Are requesters aware of how much a search is going to cost even if they don't have to sign off on it? Do you ever talk money?

Money is discussed only if we know that it's going to cost a *lot* of money. First, you can't put a price tag on a story you didn't get. If a search helps bring in that story, it's well worth every penny. I can justify the hell out of VU/TEXT, DataTimes, Mead and all the full-text papers on DIALOG because it means that our writers don't have to get on an airplane and go to some city and go to the newspaper morgue. Even if they were flying in to interview a chief executive the next day, they wouldn't have to spend an extra day in that city at either the public library or the newspaper library. We can take that request, get the information from the local newspaper, and give them either key-word-in-context or full-text articles about what they were looking for, without their spending an extra night in town. That's $100 right there, plus $35 for food, plus a day of their productivity.

It's obvious that what we're doing is useful, and there's no need to justify every penny spent. To budget, I can just say prices have gone up x percent in the past year—Mead raised their prices four percent—add an overall five percent to online for the same amount of information. This year I hope to save a little money because we went to the Data-Star fixed price plan. If we don't, we won't continue with the plan. Mead is now doing fixed pricing. Now I'm going to have a much easier time with the budget.

You've mentioned some of the topics you search. How about giving me some particulars?

You name it; we do it. We do an enormous amount of work for Steve Forbes, the owner, for his Fact and Comment column. We have to know all about history, economics, and what's going on in the government. We have to be able to find the volume of the Great Lakes and the length of the Volga River. We have to be able to find Barbra Streisand's home address. We have to be able to locate all kinds of amazing nonbusiness things because Forbes entertains. They have Fabergé eggs and art work. They have real estate. They own an island in Fiji. We publish *Forbes* in four editions in four languages now.

We need an encyclopedia for a lot of those things. This is Reference 101. It is not a business library; it is a social science library with a business bent. As you can imagine, we've had to build up a pretty good print collection, too. We don't allow end-user searching except on compact discs, so we need to have a library that is usable at three o'clock in the morning. That is, unless I want to get a phone call at home. The library is open to end-users 24 hours a day, 365 days a year. We don't close the door. So, let the reporters have a book catalog to look up books, periodicals and pamphlets in one place. Let them have a line of shelving where the books are in cataloged order. Let them have an alphabetical list of company files and subject files. Let them have microfilm, microfiche, paper copy or whatever they need. And let online be primarily for searching and not document delivery.

Journalists are different from bankers, lawyers and accountants. Journalists are in the research business, and we want to let them do their research. That's why it's important for us to be their colleagues. We are all in the research business, but we do it differently. We're complementary to each other.

Do you have favorite databases for particular kinds of questions, ones that you find yourself turning to again and again?

The vanilla question in the Forbes library is, "Has this story been written yet?" Particularly by the *New York Times*, the *Wall Street Journal*, *Forbes*, *Fortune* or *Business Week*. Has this story been covered in the business press? If it has, we don't publish it, unlike our competitors!

However, if a story on the same company, person or industry *was* written and we disagree with it, we will go at it with a vengeance. Then we need to know what's been published in the past two to three years on this particular topic by the business press. We clip the business press for our vertical files, so that at three o'clock in the morning someone can go to the company file and get the annual report, proxy statement and the latest major articles from the *New York Times*, *Wall Street Journal*, *Forbes*, *Fortune* or *Business Week*. If there's not a file, we also have every annual report, 10-K, 10-Q, proxy and 8-K on CD-ROM from Disclosure. We have annual reports back to 1986 on microfiche, if you need an annual report on any traded company. We have *Reader's Guide* back into the '60s, *Business Periodicals Index* from the beginning, the *Wall Street Journal Index* back to the 1960s, the *New York Times Index* back to 1957, *Facts on File Yearbook* and *Index* back to 1946, and *Congress and The Nation* back to World War II. We have all of *Moody's Industrials* in microfiche, and in hardcopy for ten years. All this is end-user accessible. I believe in microform. We have it on film, and the writer can get to it. If the paper runs out, it's plain paper, so they can reload it like a photocopier. Online is a supplement to what they can do themselves.

As far as the online sources are concerned, I use Nexis CURRNT a lot, for those "what's been written" questions. I also have what I call the big three—UMI, IAC and Predicasts. From UMI, we use Business Dateline or Newspaper & Periodical Abstracts more than we do ABI/INFORM. From Predicasts, it's PROMT and the Newsletter Database. With IAC, we have some of their products on disc, so usage depends on the month. We mostly use Trade & Industry Index, and then NEWSEARCH for the up-to-date stuff.

You've negotiated fixed-price contracts on a couple of online services, and you've divided primary responsibility for each service you use among your staff. How do those factors affect which system is used for any given search?

I guess I'm sending my staff a mixed message: You are to use the most cost-effective system you can, but you are not on a budget. Yes, you are to answer the question in the most *effective* manner you can, but there are other factors involved besides money, like quality of output and quality of the search itself. Time is a factor, too. If you're already on DIALOG, don't logoff and go to Data-Star to do an IAC search, because it's going to cost you as much to logoff, logon and track your time as it would be to keep on going or to do a OneSearch.

I tell them never to scrimp on quality. If you believe that this is a NEXIS search, then spend the money. If you need to search all of NEXIS at once, use OMNI, and never let me tell you not to. It's your judgment and your question. I'll know by the bill and the feedback—by your reputation upstairs—if you're doing a good job. If that's what it costs, that's what it costs. You're super searchers, and I trust you. That's what I hope I'm telling my staff.

I treat them like grown-ups. They make good decisions, and I learn a lot from them. If I tell them they have to go on a NEXIS diet, they go on a NEXIS diet. Other than that, I don't tell them how to search, unless I tell them a more *effective* way. I don't tell them when to go where, unless I see on their research sheets that they're not doing something they should be. It might be, "Why didn't you just pick up the phone and call the Commerce Department, instead of flailing around online?" I ask them to use their judgment. They are very good at that. I've got a staff of super searchers. There are six of us on the Forbes online staff. We cross-train. We talk to each other all the time about things we discover we can do or problems we run into.

What kinds of reference tools do you use, database documentation and that sort of thing?

We use everything, especially the print tools. My copy of *Fulltext Sources Online* was dog-eared by March, and it just came out in January. I personally use the Cuadra database directory, though my staff doesn't as much. We all use the DIALOG bluesheets and the database sheets for Data-Star. I tell people never to go online without a bluesheet unless they already know what they're doing. We do not use the DIALOG database chapters. We're familiar with the structure of the files we use most, and once you know the structure on DIALOG, you know the file. If you know an IAC file, it doesn't matter what service a database is on. If you know the service and the structure of the file, you know there's a company field. You know that there's a date field and a byline field. If you know Dow Jones, you know that the author is in the headline field. If you work for the press, you know that Dow Jones calls them headlines, not titles.

Let's talk about search building and actual online strategies. How do you build a search? How do you know when to start really broad and comprehensive? When do you zero in?

Unless you have a very specific set of parameters, my personal philosophy is to look for the broadest way of getting at it, and then narrow it down. In many cases, when you cast a wide net, you wind up with only six hits. You want to look at the six hits. If there are only six and you've cast a wide net, you've done it. There are always ways of going narrower if you have to. It's easier to go narrower than it is to broaden. If you find one hit that's reasonably close and look at the title and the index terms in a free format, then you know how to reevaluate. You can't do that unless you've started broad to start with. You have to have that pool of possibilities to begin with.

Browsing doesn't hurt; don't be afraid to browse. Data-Star lets you type FREE and you get whatever the free format is in that file. On DIALOG it's almost always Format 6 or 8. On Mead, looking at cites only costs the fairly low hourly connect time.

Most people assume you always start searching with a SELECT statement. My approach, knowing what I know about errors in databases, is to teach people EXPAND. I believe before you do anything on any file, particularly IAC or Predicats files, you EXPAND. You're dealing with typos of all sorts, hyphenation, punctuation, spacing problems, input errors on the part of the database publisher, and a lot of mistakes in critical places like the company name field. EXPAND the hell out of it. For that, you're not paying by the search statement; you're paying by the minute. EXPAND, it doesn't cost much. Look at the variations, look at the possibilities, look at the related terms, and look at the "used fors" and the "broader thans" and all that other stuff. Home in on what you really want before you go get it. Relying on SELECT makes sense in the sciences; the world is more organized there. But I'm in the humanities and social sciences. When you're in the less precise, more natural language-oriented disciplines, you have to look at all the possibilities.

We do a lot of free-text searching though, even in files with good indexing. Natural language used by the abstractor or the journalist gives you more access points. Headlines are useless unless you're looking for a specific cite. They're not written to be descriptive, but to get you to read the article. You've got to be able to combine controlled vocabulary, like company field or descriptor field, with free-text terms.

Natural language is one of the most wonderful creations on earth. It gives everybody the ability to express themselves. It was not meant to be codified like scientific, botanical or zoological information. If I want to say "pension plan" and not "retirement plan," I want to be able to say it. If you want to categorize it your way, you can bloody well index it. I think you're going to see people like Mead Data Central asking if they should be indexing their full text. I think all the systems are going in the same direction. DIALOG went in the direction of loading newspapers, and Mead is going in the direction of indexing because everybody knows you can't search full text without controlled vocabulary because of the vagaries of natural language. That's what makes a writer an individual. I wouldn't want any editor to take my article and put it into politically correct writing.

I intentionally put the word "zen" in the title of my article, "Quality Control and the Zen of Database Production." (*ONLINE,* November 1990, pp. 15-23.) I used the word appropriately, but I chose that title because I wanted a whole lot of people to get a false drop when they search the word "zen" without a modifier. If they don't modify it with "Buddhism," they're going to get my article, thank you very much. I wrote an editorial in *DATABASE* back in 1989 where I used the word "yen" intentionally: "...if you have a yen for crackers." I wanted it as a false drop. "No, this story is not about Japanese yen." If somebody just puts in "yen" and thinks they can get away with it, they're going to come up with my hit and pay a royalty to Jeff Pemberton, the publisher. It's an "in" joke. Natural language is an expression of a particular human being, a unique expression. If you want to have some control over it, that's what indexing is all about.

I think when end-users confront that problem they will start having more respect for librarians. My boss is the executive vice president of Forbes. He's not a database searcher, and he will never be. He's brilliant. He was asking about all of this full-text delivery and why we couldn't let the writers use it. He was playing devil's advocate. I said, "What if you were looking for an article about factory automation, and our automotive guy had run a story on General Motors and how it automated its plants using robotics? The story is about factory automation, but if the writer didn't say "factory" next to the word "automation," it would not come up. And he said, "Oh, if I say 'retirement plans' and you say, 'pension benefits'..." I said, "Exactly." He "got it." He asked me how I knew this stuff, and I told him, "That's what we *do.*"

Do you go for full text whenever it's available?

If they just want an *answer,* no, not if they want to know how long the Volga River is. But one of the points about using online in this environment is that we cannot go to press without checking our facts. If it comes from another periodical, that's not considered "checkable." *Moody's* is checkable. *Facts on File* is checkable. *Congressional Quarterly* is checkable. The *Wall Street Journal* and the *New York Times* aren't checkable sources. They may not have checked *their* facts. We don't rely on publications like that. We don't rely on a McGraw-Hill newsletter even though it's considered authoritative. We get an independent verification before we go to press with a fact. We don't use it as fact unless it's from an independent source. An online search to close a story isn't going to help unless it's in a directory file or something like that. That's an entirely different sort of searching. That's why we have a lot of those sources in print and other formats, so that the writers can have access to the information without needing an online search.

We do over 500 online searches a week. Fact-checking is one thing, but editorial uses online for background, leads and subtleties. They use it to make sure that another publication doesn't say what they were going to say. Or they use it so they can say, "Ha, *Business Week* really screwed up this time." Or they say, "I guess I'd better tweak my story in a different direction." Newspapers are where we get color for stories, local color. We might be able to pick up a quote by the guy's next-door neighbor. Local papers are a source that a lot of people really like, along with Business Dateline. We go for local stories, not the major business press.

Full text is also searching for the needle in the haystack. I gave my students a wonderful question for full text. The example I used was: "Rumor has it that in 1988, Marilyn Quayle was considering running for her husband's Senate seat in Indiana. Was this reported in the press?" I told them to search the PAPERS file in DIALINDEX and rank the output. The point of the exercise was that the whole article doesn't have to be about that topic. It can be a mere sentence. That is why you use 3,K (Format 3, KWIC) on DIALOG or KWIC on NEXIS. Don't worry whether it's a major part of the article. If it's mentioned, it's in the press. This was a great example of how very different searching full text is from searching bibliographic files. The Quayle thing was written about a lot—in two sentences in the *Washington Post* here and three sentences in the *Washington Post* there, but you got a very good picture of it. And yes, she *was* thinking about running. But it was never a feature article in itself. So it's very important to know that about full-text searching. It doesn't have to be an full article about the matter. It can be the last paragraph, but if it's there, it's there. You'd never see it unless you searched full text and looked at the results in KWIC.

How do you know what system to search?

It's just experience and intuition, I think. We hired a young woman several years ago, an entry-level librarian. She was pretty good. After six or eight months she said, "I really have a sense of this, I think I'm doing great, and I don't understand why people always ask for two to three years' experience." Three years later, when she left to go into another master's degree program, she said, "You know, Anne, now I understand what they mean when they say they want two to three years' experience, because now that I have it, I know what I didn't know." The truth of the matter is that until you understand when to search what database, you *don't* know. How do you learn? Experience. Just plain old experience. You have so much knowledge that you haven't really articulated to yourself. You know this about that system. You know that Mead is great for needle-in-the-haystack searching, and you know that DIALOG is better for a mix of controlled vocabulary with free text. You know that Data-Star is going to be better for expense control if you don't need the most up-to-date thing possible. You know that DataTimes is best for Gannett newspapers. We need it all, and we need to know how to mix and match.

I personally can't learn DataTimes. I make no bones about it. Everyone else on my staff loves it, but they use it a lot more. I know the "dot-dot" commands because I trained in BRS in 1983. So my solution is to search DataTimes with the "dot-dot" commands through the Dow Jones gateway. My staff all laugh at me. On the other hand, they all had a hard time learning Data-Star because they hadn't learned the "dot-dot" commands. Data-Star was intuitive to me because I already knew them.

Anyway, that's how I know when to search on what system. Intuition. However, there are thousands upon thousands of little factoids that went into making that intuition possible, and that's known as experience. That's very hard to convey. It's like trying to quantify the knowledge of a New York cabbie that says when to make a left turn *here* to avoid traffic, as opposed to a right turn that's more direct. It's knowing when to take the Drive rather than Central Park or 8th Avenue. Experience. There's a learning curve, and after you've reached your peak it levels out and you don't think about it. So when somebody interviews you and asks how you make that decision, you say, "How the hell should I know?" I just do it. That's what I *do*.

That's why teaching has been so good for me. My students ask much more basic questions than my staff does. So when they ask, "Why would you search it that way?" I answer, "If you search it the way you suggest, it's obvious that you're going to get 367 hits. That's always too many unless you're searching for a Ph.D. candidate. Twenty-five is the limit of anything you want to look at." Knowing that rule of thumb is a function of real-life experience. The students also force me to confront some of my own assumptions and to take them apart.

Getting back to the search process, how do you know when you're done? Is that something you decide, or does the requester?
When we get the answer, we're done. The answer is always in the last place you look, by definition. But if you don't find the answer, or if you only find part of the answer, or approaches *to* the answer, you type a "logoff hold." Then you pick up the phone, and ask them to come and see you. You say, "Okay, this is what I got. Here's the problem." And they say, "Oh, you know what? I forgot to tell you blah blah blah," or "Ooooh, that's interesting. See if you can find so-and-so's name."

Sometimes not getting the answer is the answer. Meaning, they haven't told you what they needed to tell you. Or maybe it doesn't exist. The inverse is what I'm most concerned about. When you've gotten zero hits, how do you know it's really zero hits? That gets into the quality thing. How do you know whether it's your fault, the database's fault, or the online service's fault?

What kinds of quality problems do you see in the course of searching?
I can take both a short-term and a long-term view. The short-term view is that the errors and the quality problems I mind the most are the ones where you get duplicate citations, misspellings and the "selective coverage" garbage, where they don't index a publication cover-to-cover. An article might be in the *San Jose Business Journal* but you won't get it in Business Dateline because they didn't choose to include it. That, and the sloppiness, are short-term issues.

The long-term quality problem I see is one of access. You have to know where to go to get everything. A journalist at Forbes cannot possibly navigate all the multiple systems to find what he or she is looking for. The information is there, but they don't know how to go about getting it. What's worse is even if you know that the full text of the *Wall Street Journal* is only on Dow Jones, you still can't get it if all you know how to search is NEXIS. Long-term, there's got to be some way of enabling you to search each system, whether it's through a common command language, a gateway or whatever. There has to be a way to find what you want and get it without having to learn more than one way to search.

The way the system is structured now, everybody has treated the text and the indexing separately. Mead is thinking about whether or not to index this stuff. That's a quality issue for me. Are they going to do it well? Are they going to index everything? Who's going to do it? What level of indexing will they apply, and what are the terms they're going to use? Are they going to be consistent with anybody else's? These kinds of questions are going to be resolved internally in the major search services. We're going to be stuck with their decisions. They may ask us what we want, but they're still going to make decisions that aren't consistent with their competitors, because they think they have a better way. They want you to use *their* service. That's being very short-sighted. It's understandable from a business perspective, but they're not helping you get access to what you need.

Inconsistency in indexing is probably our most debilitating problem. Soon after we began using Data-Star instead of DIALOG for certain things, somebody complained to me that Data-Star had a problem. She had searched for articles on United Way, had limited it to the company field and gotten very little. She was less familiar with Data-Star, so she assumed it was their fault, and wanted to go back to old familiar DIALOG. But it wasn't a system problem, it was a database producer problem. IAC sometimes put United Way in the company field, and many times they just put it in the descriptor field. That's inconsistency. We run into that a lot. It's important to know when it's the host service and when it's the database producer screwing up.

Are there habits you can cultivate to approach searching critically and to anticipate routine lapses like the ones we've been talking about?

Do what you can do offline. Have the printed search aids by your desk while you're searching. For example, if you're doing a full-text search, have Ruth Orenstein's book, *Fulltext Sources Online*, right next to your search machine so that you can tell which search service to go to to find the full-text source. Don't go onto DIALOG without a bluesheet in front of you. Use the field limitations. That's what they're there for. You have to understand the concept of basic index and additional index. Those are on the bluesheets, too.

You can't possibly do a good online search if you don't know what you're searching. If the author isn't part of the basic index and you don't use the author field prefix, AU=, you're not going to come up with the author, even if there are 27 entries for that author in that database. It doesn't matter how perfect your keywords are, if you're not searching the appropriate field you're going to get a completely wrong answer, or no answer at all.

When I go to trade shows, I like to go up to a database producer's booth and give them a real search that I've had, and say, "I'd like to find this." That's another tip. Go to that exhibit floor armed with a search that you want done, maybe two or three different types of searches. Go up to everybody with the same questions, so you can see exactly how they do the search and exactly what features they use. Just walk in there and say, "Can you help me with a question?" You can learn a lot.

The other thing you can do when you go to a trade show is walk up and ask, "What's new on your system?" That way they'll start telling you not only what's new now, but what's coming down the pike. That's very useful. It also sensitizes you to be aware of those changes when they're finally announced. "Oh yeah, that's the thing I saw demoed."

Getting back to procedural matters, what about turnaround time? Are there stories that you work on as long-term projects, or is everything pretty fast-paced around there?

Other than the special issues of the magazine, most projects are very short-term, by which I mean 24 to 48 hours. They either want to *get* the story or *kill* the story. If it is going to be killed, they don't want to have worked on it for a week first. We do vanilla requests immediately. A vanilla request is something like "I'm doing a story on Black and Decker. What has the press said about them?" For that we do the vanilla response, which is to go to Trade & Industry, InfoTrac, our files, and maybe NEXIS, if necessary. We search to see if the story's been done, or if *any* story has been done. If so, we retrieve the references, have a clerk find and photocopy the articles, and send them to the writer. Sometimes they get Federal Expressed to a bureau. Sometimes they are faxed. I hate getting international requests by fax. We get it in the morning when we come in; they've faxed it 18 hours earlier in their life, not in our life. For us it's Tuesday, but for them it's already Wednesday when we get it and it's Friday by the time they get our package. So for them it's a three-day turnaround, and it's not good enough. But we can't fax 30 articles every time, so we bump heads occasionally. Is that what you mean by "fast-paced?"

I think you've made your point, yes. Do you have any kind of formal feedback mechanism, or do you work with people so regularly that you know when something is wrong?

Yes to both. We know when something's wrong because our clients are very direct people. They're journalists. They don't beat around the bush. They want to get their story. The feedback is direct, and we try to get them to tell it to me, not to their boss. I don't want to hear vague complaints filtering down about "that library." Again, it's a *human* process. Writers are human, and librarians are human. When someone new comes in and they see that there are five people under "research" on the "who does what in the library" list, they ask "How do I know who to go to?" My response is "Go to each of them once or twice and see whose chemistry works best for you." They're all very good, and if they don't know how to do something, they ask each other. We all learn from each other.

What do you think makes a good searcher?

It's not really accurate to say it's seat-of-the-pants know-how, because it's not. Even though we do search in seat-of-the-pants fashion, we forget how much we know. We have level upon level upon level of knowledge—about file structure, about the producer of the information, about the quality of that producer, and about the structure of their database. We forget how much we know. But we are a fount of information before we even sit down at that terminal.

A really good online searcher has to be slightly neurotic. You have to be neurotic to think of life in terms of controlled vocabulary. I don't want to control the world of knowledge, because I also want free text, natural language and freedom of expression. I'm a total egalitarian. When my researchers go online, I want them to think creatively because that's the way people have written. I also want them to be detail-oriented, because that's the way librarians organize knowledge. To be a really great online searcher, you've got to be both.

That's why I'm the perfect person for this job. I'm off-the-charts creative, but I'm also off-the-charts detail-oriented, and that's a rare combination. That's why I'm a good searcher. I can understand that you need to limit *this* kind of term to the descriptor field, but you need to have *those* kinds of terms in free text. You have to be able to think of all those things at once, and understand it. Some people learn it and some people can't. Those who can't are just okay searchers, they're adequate, probably even above-average. A really great searcher is both detail-oriented enough to be a cataloguer part-time, but also spunky enough to be a great reference librarian. That's why the best online searchers come from special libraries, especially smaller special libraries, where they have to do more than one thing in their jobs.

I'll tell you about one of my biggest challenges. One night at 7:30 a fact-checker called me and said, "I need the title to this book verified because we're transmitting in half an hour." The book was printed in 1913. It was written by so-and-so. It had to do with the production of cotton. It wasn't in *Books in Print* so I had to go into RLIN. I could have called someone at UCLA who hadn't gone home yet and asked them to do me a favor. But I didn't do that. I said, "I am going to fumph my way through an RLIN search." And I fumphed my way onto RLIN and, without wasting very much money at all, found that it was in fact a book. It was published in 1913 by that author, but the title they had was a couple of words off. I said, "This is the way Yale cataloged it." The checker was impressed enough to say, "If Yale has a book from 1913 by that author, with *that* title, it's good enough for Forbes."

The point is that I needed to use a highly sophisticated catalog database that I had never searched before. I had to figure out what I needed to know, minimally, to search it. I had to know how to find what I needed to know in the documentation. Can you truncate? Is Boolean searching allowed? What is the field structure?

When I teach online searching, I say that there are seven things you need to know about a databank. If you know them, and you know how to search one databank, you can search any new databank. You need to know how to logon and off, begin a file, and truncate. You need to know what the Boolean operators are, and in what order they're processed, or you need to know how to nest, how to use parentheses. You need to know how to get output. You need to know how to look at the basic index if there is one. Oh, and you need to know whether you can do iterative searching, set-building.

Those are the things you need to know about an online service. If you know how to look up those answers in the documentation, you will be able to make your way through a basic search. That's what I try to *educate* my students about, instead of *train* them with. I figured out how to do an RLIN search based on knowing how to do those things, and I succeeded. You have to understand what an online databank is, and what a computer can and can't do. You have to know what artificial intelligence is and isn't, and how much smarter you are than the machine. That's what makes a good online searcher.

SUPER SEARCH SECRETS

On search software...

I have SMARTCOM III and a 9600bps modem....Everybody else uses SMARTCOM II. We don't use DIALOGLINK because we search too many different systems....Mead and Baseline both have their own software, too.

On using a type-ahead buffer...

Being able to type ahead of the first search query doesn't save us anything, because the first query isn't the time-waster. It's when you get back a response that you have to think about what to do next. The meter is ticking all the time, even if you do have that little buffer to type in. The buffer is useless at that point. The time that we take is not in typing; the time we take is in *thinking*.

On the reference interview...

We make sure that we talk to them as equals, as team members. We see ourselves as part of the team that puts out their story, and we make sure they do, too....We begin the reference interview in a very strange way, saying, "Tell me more! Oh, that's interesting, tell me more about that." So we ease into it in a pretty subtle way.

On search costs...

Money is discussed only if we know that it's going to cost a *lot* of money. First, you can't put a price tag on a story you didn't get. If a search helps bring in that story, it's well worth every penny. I can justify the hell out of VU/TEXT, DataTimes, Mead and all the full-text papers on DIALOG because it means that our writers don't have to get on an airplane and go to some city and go to the newspaper morgue.

On favorite sources...

I use Nexis CURRNT a lot, for those "what's been written" questions...we use Business Dateline or Newspaper & Periodical Abstracts more than we do ABI/INFORM. From Predicasts, it's PROMT and the Newsletter Database. With IAC....We mostly use Trade & Industry Index, and then NEWSEARCH for the up-to-date stuff.

On browsing...

Browsing doesn't hurt; don't be afraid to browse. Data-Star lets you type FREE and you get whatever the free format is in that file. On DIALOG it's almost always Format 6 or 8. On Mead, looking at cites only costs the fairly low hourly connect time.

On using EXPAND...

...before you do anything...you EXPAND. You're dealing with typos of all sorts, hyphenation, punctuation, spacing problems, input errors on the part of the database publisher, and a lot of mistakes in critical places like the company name field. EXPAND the hell out of it. For that, you're not paying by the search statement; you're paying by the minute. EXPAND, it doesn't cost much.

On searching full text...

Full text is also searching for the needle in the haystack....the whole article doesn't have to be about that topic. It can be a mere sentence.

On going to conferences...

...Go to that exhibit floor armed with a search that you want done, maybe two or three different types of searches. Just walk in there and say, "Can you help me with a question?" You can learn a lot. The other thing you can do...is walk up and ask, "What's new on your system?" That way they'll start telling you not only what's new now, but what's coming down the pike. That's very useful.

On being a good searcher...

...think creatively because that's the way people have written....be detail-oriented, because that's the way librarians organize knowledge. To be a really great online searcher, you've got to be both.

CHAPTER 13

MARYDEE OJALA: HOOKED ON ONLINE

Marydee Ojala is head of Ojala and Associates. She is a columnist for *ONLINE* and *DATABASE* magazines, and a frequent speaker at online conferences. This interview was conducted shortly before she moved her base of operations from Overland Park, Kansas to Park City, Utah.

How did you get into this crazy business?

I was a corporate librarian for many years. I worked for Bank of America and it was there that I learned about online searching. I've now been self-employed for five years. I find that much of what I learned at the bank still is valid, though things are changing rapidly, as we know. But the real basic training—how to do a search and how to think about approaching a search—I got at Bank of America.

Were you self-taught or did you have a mentor there?

We had a large staff for a corporate library. There were three professional librarians. When I arrived at the bank both of the other librarians had gone through formal DIALOG training. Bank of America signed a contract with DIALOG in 1974, which was very early, particularly for a business library. So it was always a forward-thinking group. When they signed the contract, their peers all said, "You're crazy. That's only for scientific/technical libraries. Business libraries don't use this stuff." Which, of course, is ridiculous now, but at the time it made sense.

When I joined the bank, we had DIALOG and the New York Times Information Bank. Shortly after I got there, we signed up with SDC, which was a pain because our equipment couldn't make the handshake correctly. We had to dial long distance to Los Angeles to get connected.

In 1974, we didn't have PCs, of course. We were using dumb terminals. The other radical thing the bank did was to start searching at 1200bps, which, again, people told us we were crazy for doing. "What's the matter with 300bps?" they asked. So, we were pretty much on the leading edge there, too. No reason to go slowly if you can go fast.

I learned at 1200bps, and I learned by looking over other people's shoulders to watch what they did, then sitting down and just winging it. Later, I went to formal DIALOG training. The Information Bank did not give formal training at that time in San Francisco.

What does your business consist of? Are you still doing a lot of searching, or is it mainly consulting these days?

It's really a three-pronged business. Part one is research, which is primarily online searching. Part two is consulting, which means going into an organization and advising them on their information needs and information flow. The third part is writing. The research I learned basically by working at the bank. The consulting, to some extent, I also learned at the bank, because one of the things that I did there was outreach to other departments. I helped them get their information organized.

I remember helping organize—not really a library although they called it that—for the corporate real estate department. It contained wallpaper and paint samples. The bank also sent me to England to do consulting for the London office, to help them organize their information and determine which online sources they should be using.

The consulting I do is about how you make people think about using information and how you organize it in a usable fashion. I think it's surprising that people who are very intelligent and knowledgeable in their own field lack that organizational ability. Perhaps it's because they've never thought of it, or may not have been brought up thinking that way, or maybe they're just not interested. You go into an organization and they say, "I just don't understand where things are kept. We get three copies of these magazines, and I can never find the one I want." There are very simple solutions to this. I'm used to thinking that way, and they're used to getting a magazine and tossing it in a corner.

Let's look at the online component of your business. How do your research projects come in?

I would say 80 percent comes in by phone, and that phone call may be followed up by a fax or a letter. The other 20 percent comes by e-mail. That's a sizeable percentage, and it's growing, partly as I become more visible online in places like CompuServe. It's a name recognition thing that, surprisingly, is turning out to be a business generator.

Tell me how you handle the reference interview. How do you find out what the client really needs to know?

There are differences in reference interviews depending on whether it's a new client or an established one. I have some clients who call me all the time, and almost before they open their mouths I know what they want, because I've done things for them before. It's like, "I know what you want and I know where to go. Just give me the topic." They understand how I work, so there's no explanation required. It's just, "I need this."

What do you say to a new client?

Sometimes new clients, if they've been referred by word of mouth, are already into the process, because their friend or colleague has described what I do. Then there's less explanation required. One guy continually calls me, and every time he tells me how highly our mutual friend regards me. He almost never gives me much work, but he calls and strokes.

With a brand-new client, the first question really is, "Why are you, Marydee Ojala, qualified to do the research that I want done?" They want to know why I think I can do it. Not so much *how*, but *why* do I think I can solve their information problem? Most of them have never met me and never will. Ninety-five percent of my client base is not local. I will never, ever meet them. They need reassurance that they're not making a horrible mistake.

Very often, they have never done anything like this before. Occasionally, though, they have left a corporation where they had access to a library, and now they are on their own. Those instances are nice because I can say, "I do what your corporate librarians did." The Bank of America connection has been very valuable. When you say, "I spent all these years with Bank of America," that validates your competence as a researcher. Few of the people who call truly know what online is, so there is an educational process that goes on.

Do you find yourself going into the particulars of how you're going to do a search? What do you say when a client asks, "Can you pull this out of your computer?"

I tend to describe format, and I do it more as a series of questions than as a set explanation. "Do you want recent news releases? Do you want financials? Do you want full text or a summary?" I don't use the word "abstract," I use the word "summary" because "abstract" doesn't mean anything to most people. I say, "I can get you wire stories, and I can get you newspaper stories. I can get you summaries of magazine articles." A lot of it is finding out in what format they want the information. You can't just flat-out ask them that because they don't know what's available, so you have to give them some choices and let them tell you what they want. I must say that there are times when they tell me exactly what they want, and I absolutely ignore it. People will say, "I need a D&B on such and such a company." It turns out that they don't really want a D&B, they want news stories about the company, but "D&B" has become generic for "business information."

How do you negotiate budgets?

I'm very flexible. People sometimes ask, "How much do you charge?" I don't answer that question, I walk around it. Sometimes people ask, "How much will this cost me?" which is a much better question and is usually the way I walk around the other one. "Well, for this project you can either pay me by the hour or you can pay me by the project." Somehow, I work in the question, "Do you have a budget for this project?" When pressed, I quote my hourly rate, and I adjust for out-of-pocket expenses. In other circumstances, I simply say, "If you have a budget cap or an amount of money you want to spend on a first look, let's do that. Then we'll review what we have and see what the next step should be."

I often do projects in stages like that. People like the idea of a cap because it's a budgeted amount. They can go back to their boss and say, "Okay, for $200 we get this." I rarely get an open-ended go-ahead, although I did get one not too long ago. I was in a meeting, and the client said, "We absolutely have to have this." That was the first time I ever heard a person actually say, "Money is no object." I was flabbergasted.

Assuming you have a fixed budget, how do you divide that up in terms of time versus online cost?

My rule of thumb is that I'm going to spend half my time online and half my time offline. That's the way it works out. I couldn't have done this when I started, but now I can tell you that's almost always the way it's going to be.

How do you keep track of projects? Do you keep any kind of formal log book?

I don't keep a log book. I do have a request form. I use the same form in two different colors, pink for reference and green for writing projects. So I can sort of eyeball my stack of papers to see how much writing I have and how much research I have. It's a quick color check. I use the form itself essentially to write down the request and to remind me to get an address, a phone number and fax number.

I have one client for whom I have six phone numbers—an office phone, a home phone, an office fax number, a home fax number and a car phone. I forget what the sixth one is—maybe his pager. One guy called me from a car phone to make a search request. While driving around in a strange town in a rental car, he proceeded to get stuck in the middle of a parade. He tried to tell me what he wanted to know about this particular technology, then he stopped and said, "I'm lost. What's going on? There's a float in front of me!" I had never before done a reference interview with someone who was in the middle of a parade. I have done reference interviews with other people on cellular phones where their voices fade out as they go under bridges. I once did a reference interview with a consultant who was relaying information to *his* client, so he was sitting there with a phone at each ear—and his client was calling from an air phone.

What's a typical project for you?
No project is typical. I do primarily business searching, although business sometimes does slop over into technical. Someone has a technology and wants to know if anybody else is doing this kind of thing. That's partly a technical search and partly a business search. I do a lot of news searching for public relations firms. PR firms want to track who picked up the press releases they wrote. Or if they know an issue is coming up and their client is involved, they might want to track what public reaction has been to this issue in the past. Are we going to have a problem before we spring this on people? In that regard, I've been doing environmental searching and a lot on the insurance industry. The other thing PR firms want is background on potential clients.

For the PR people, I often use real-time sources like First Release on DIALOG and NewsNet's NewsFlash. I like the way NewsFlash is set up. It's very fast. I check it every morning; it might just take three minutes.

I use Federal News Service when clients want to find out what's happening in Congress and when hearings are scheduled. For insurance and other heavily regulated industries, the BNA files have been great. Cable television is another one. For that, we just tracked what happened to a particular bill in the Senate and then in the House. I was at a trade show the week that the House was supposed to be working on cable TV, so I would stroll down the aisles and ask the exhibitors, "Would you search cable TV for me?"

The other thing that I get asked—this is one of those things where you never really know what the person needs—is "I need a 'think piece' on such-and-such." "Think piece" can mean anything you want it to mean. I had one guy who said, "I want an in-depth study of this topic, but I only want one article." Sometimes what they're looking for is a philosophical view as opposed to a lot of nitty-gritty details.

What that kind of request involves is picking the database you think is most likely to have the type of source material the person wants. It's not so much the subject or the format of the database, but the sources, the kinds of journals that tend to carry those "think pieces." I've taken to asking people, "If you were to find this ideal article you're looking for, where do you think it would be published?" I had a guy the other day tell me that *Computer Reseller* was where the think pieces show up. I would never have thought of that, and he was right. That's a case of trusting your client's expertise. If they subscribe to a journal, they have a sense of what's in there.

This particular person happened to be very knowledgeable in his own field, which is a high-tech area. But I've had other people who were just exploring something that was brand-new to them. You can't trust their instincts because they don't know what they don't know.

You must have favorite files for certain kinds of questions.
I like the way ABI/INFORM has added full text along with the abstract. I have clients who do not want full text for all the references they get. I do not automatically go to full text. I've sort of created an abstract format for full text. It doesn't work everywhere, but sometimes you get really messy searches where the subject is ill-defined and you just can't pin it down beyond a certain point. So you end up with a lot of garbage that you can't really NOT out because if you did you might be NOTting out valuable things as well.

So I started to define my own output format. In DIALOG, it's Format 3, lead paragraph, KWIC, and I set the KWIC value in my user profile to 50. So the type command is T/3,LP,K followed by the records you want. You have to go back, clean up some of the KWIC portion, and take out the trailing parts that don't pertain. It's not a perfect technique, but it works reasonably well. You get a lot of information to help judge whether the document is relevant without having to spend all the time and money it takes to get everything in full text. Format 3 gives you the cite. The lead paragraph tells you where the article started and what they had in mind in the beginning. Then KWIC shows you your search terms in context.

What other databases do you use a lot?
I have gradually grown to know and love Newspaper & Periodical Abstracts from UMI. It gives wide geographic coverage of the United States. The abstracts are short, and it tells quickly how much coverage there's been on an issue. I get cites from there and then go selectively to full text.

If the same file is up on more than one system, what determines where you search it?
Software has something to do with it. I learned the Dow Jones system a long, long time ago. For the files I can get on both Dow Jones and DIALOG, I usually go to DIALOG, though, and I go to Dow Jones for their financial exclusives. So it's a combination of system familiarity and features—and how I feel that day.

Cost is a factor, too. But part of that is my ability to do the search well, not just the system's ability to deliver it cheaply. If I can be more efficient on one system than another, higher connect charges don't matter as much.

What kind of references do you have close to your terminal? What do you look at before you go online?
What I have most handy are the catalogs from the online hosts that tell me what the file name acronyms are. I think, in general, the database producer literature is more important than the host systems' literature. It's more specific. I use DIALINDEX a lot, too, to remind me what files I should be looking at that I've forgotten about.

How do you plan your search? Do you make notes before you go online?
I make notes for some topics. For others, I don't bother. Not that I haven't thought it out ahead; I have. It's just that sometimes I've actually written it down and other times I

haven't. It depends on how complex it is. I had one the other day where someone wanted a lot of information on about fifteen different companies that his firm wanted to check out as partners or potential buyers. Of course, I had the list of companies in front of me so I could be sure I had them spelled correctly.

I actually write down command sequences as reminders sometimes. Dow Jones and DataTimes have each modified the same basic software in a slightly different fashion. Every once in a while I do something on Data-Star (which uses the same software, too) that works on Dow Jones, and it comes back and tells me "You can't do that." The same thing happens with BRS.

Do you ever build your search strategy offline and then upload it?

I know a lot of people upload at least their starting search statement, but I don't. For me, there is something about typing my search ideas online that is part of the rhythm of the process. It gets me focused and thinking about what's going on. It's really psychological; you logon and get into that mental state of doing it, and doing it as effectively and efficiently as possible.

When you approach a search, how do you decide when to start broad and when to go in with all the terms you think you'll need? Do you use a building-block sort of tactic, or try to go for perfection on the first round?

Sometimes you think you're going right for perfection and then you hit something really bizarre that you hadn't thought of. I once was asked to look at a St. Louis-based company, and the client was primarily interested in the local and the national press. The company name sounded extremely unusual, and I figured I didn't have to do anything special. It turns out that there's a health center named Mallinckrodt, a street named Mallinckrodt, and so on. Not being from St. Louis, I did not realize that the company, and probably the family, had donated a lot of money and had a lot of civic things named after them. So my first cut gave me a very large number of hits that I was not anticipating, and when I looked at them I realized why. I had to go back and be much more specific to confine my results to the company name. Yet in a different kind of database, like the Wall Street Journal, I wouldn't have run into that problem. I would have gotten just the company.

Normally, though, I have found that when I start broad, I have a tendency to go *too* broad. Then I waste time because I'm constantly eliminating things rather than building. So I usually start narrow and then broaden out, with synonyms and alternative concepts, or by removing qualifiers that turn out to be too restrictive.

How does searching full text differ from searching bibliographic files? Do you make use of whatever descriptors there might be, or do you go for free text right away?

It depends totally on the database. Business Dateline has wonderful descriptors and category codes. They have put intellectual effort into that database, and it shows.

In that Mallinckrodt example, how did you cut out the extraneous references? Did you just skim titles?

Well, one thing I did was add in a few other company names—the question was Mallinckrodt in relation to these other firms—and use a much more restrictive proximity operator to put them closer together. That pretty much knocked out all the irrelevancy.

The trouble with company searching in full text is that I really don't like putting "Company" after a company name. It takes a long time to search, and a lot of newspapers don't bother to put it in anyway. It might be Inc., it might be Co., it might be Company. Mead is handy for that sort of thing because they have those equivalencies built in. DIALOG and DataTimes do not.

Do you do a lot of multifile searching?

I use Dialog's OneSearch. I don't like most of their preformed categories, though. I like FIRST, the continuously-updated wires, but others I don't like because they mix databases that have different formats and they include databases that I don't think should be included.

Do you exclude certain files from the OneSearch category, or do you make up your own?

I almost always make up my own with the exception of FIRST and PAPERS. But even with PAPERS, I've taken to adding File 635 (Business Dateline) and File 636 (Predicasts Newsletter Database), so I get the business journals and the newsletters.

In the course of a search, how do you evaluate your results?

If I'm not really sure that I'm on target, then I tend to look at the descriptors and see why I've got either too many or too few. Or I scan titles.

How do you refine when you've gotten a huge amount?

When I've gotten a huge amount, I generally look at the descriptors if there are any. I look at the titles if there aren't any descriptors, and find out what in the world is going on. You sometimes forget that an acronym could mean something else, or that a search term can have other meanings. If you scan five or six titles, it's usually really clear what you did and you just sort it out.

That's the "whoops" factor.

Yes. I'll never forget the time—this was at the bank and unfortunately I had the person hovering over my shoulder—the client was looking for individual retirement accounts, and she insisted that I put in IRA. So I got stories on the Irish Republican Army and a whole slew of people whose first name was Ira.

How about when you've gotten too little? Is it usually a matter of a faulty search strategy, a wrong spelling, or what?

I have not encountered the problem of wrong spelling very often. On occasion, people have given me a company name as an acronym, and the database does not use the acronym. More often the information just hasn't been collected in the form the client wants, or with the spin that he wants to put on it. It's just not going to turn up; it doesn't exist.

Do you often find yourself checking back with your client during a search or do you just sort of shoot things through?

I check back if I'm not finding anything, or if I'm finding a whole lot more than they thought there would be. Those are the calls I like to make because people generally are very happy to get that kind of call. It's the ones where you have to say, "I didn't find anything," that are difficult.

How do you decide when you're really done with the search, other than the fact that you're out of the client's money?

I think that's the primary thing. I'm either out of money or I'm out of time because their deadline is too short. Sometimes "short" is within the next two hours. Or "Can you get this today?" Then there's the diminishing-returns factor. I always explain to people that what they get is going to depend heavily on how much they can spend and how much time they have. If they want more, they're either going to have to open their pocketbooks or expand the time frame.

But there are times when people have a very distinct request. They know, for example, that something is going to come across the wires. They've talked to a wire service reporter, and they want to have that story as soon as they can, so for that you're constantly checking the wires to see when it comes over. When it comes, you're done.

How do you typically get your search output?

I generally download right on the spot. When I order offline prints, I order them delivered electronically. I haven't gotten paper from an online host in probably three years. I either fax the results if they're short, although there are people who want 50 pages of fax. I have no idea why; I wouldn't. I also use Federal Express; I do a lot of Fedexing. Very occasionally, for a very good local client, I hand-deliver the results.

What formats do you typically use? You mentioned that not everybody wants full text, even if it's available. How much post-processing do you do?

I almost never print descriptor terms. I strip extraneous codes. On full text, I run a spell check for typos and words that were scanned incorrectly. I correct mistakes because otherwise the client will think *I* made a mistake. I also bold key points, particularly company names, or if the concept is buried way down in a long article.

If I find I've got one good paragraph in an otherwise irrelevant article, I create my own KWICs, with ellipses to show that I've edited out some material. That way, my client doesn't have to go through the whole thing.

I was doing a search once on legislation about restricting telemarketing and what telemarketers could do, and I found a perfect one-paragraph explanation. It was in the middle of one of these summaries of recent legislative actions. The headline was about spaying your pets. Before you hit the telemarketing paragraph, there was a paragraph about spaying, a paragraph about the speed limit, a paragraph about every little legislative thing that had happened. The article went on for six pages. So I picked out the paragraph I needed. But I couldn't change the headline.

How do you present your search results to the client?

I almost never prepare a presentation-quality report because so many of my clients want the results so fast that they really don't care. I always do a cover letter, though. Sometimes it's nothing more than, "Here's the article you wanted." Generally speaking, though, a cover letter recaps their search request. "Here is the information you requested on such-and-such, and here are the databases I searched." I do that even if I know that they don't care what databases I used. I do it partly for my own documentation, and partly to let the client know that I searched a lot of different files. Sometimes you don't really get that much information, but you do a lot of searching and have to charge for your time. So if they see this long list of database names, it lets them know, at least, that you did in fact *work*.

I don't recap my search strategy, because clients wouldn't understand it. In five years, I've had one person who said, "Please append your search strategy at the end of what you send me." One person—and he was a chemist who used to work for a large corporation and was a DIALOG searcher himself. I occasionally paraphrase the strategy and say, "I used the keywords you suggested plus these others that occurred to me," but I only do that if some of the results look funny and I want to explain why.

Do you send an invoice with the search?

It depends very much on the client. I have some clients who call multiple times in a month and I bill them at the end of the month. I have some clients I joke with about running a tab. If they use me enough during the month, I actually can do more for them for less money because I don't have to worry about a minimum. I can do something that takes ten minutes and just add it to their overall bill, whereas if they call just once for a ten-minute thing, then I have to charge a $50 minimum.

I prefer to bill at the end of the month. Some people want me to send the invoice along with the search. The problem with that is that if they come back to you and have questions or want it modified, you end up spending half an hour on the phone with them that you can't bill.

How do you track online costs for billing purposes?

I just jot them down as I go, or capture the session summary, and then write it down on the search form. I keep all of that kind of documentation on the search request form and add it up as I go along to make sure I'm not going over budget.

The search results themselves I keep on disk for a week or so, until I'm sure the client has gotten them and looked them over. Sometimes I just send citations or abstracts. If they come back and want full text, I just have them give me the accession number. I use that to pull the cite up on my screen and make sure it's what they want.

What about tips for cost-effective searching?

The first thing is to know what the database has in it before you go online. Check the documentation. Offline preparation saves you money online. Be sure of your strategy before you go online. I often do what DIALOG calls a "save temp." If the system gives you the option of holding your search temporarily when you logoff, get in the habit of doing that, just in case you do have to go back to it.

FOCUS, on LEXIS/NEXIS, is a wonderful money-saving feature. You use FOCUS when you're doing a rather broad search. As long as you have under 1,000 records, you can use the command FOCUS to specify a word or phrase that wasn't in your original search, and it will show you just the documents that contain that word. In a way, it creates a subset of your search results, like what Mead calls a modification, but without losing the original search. So if you want to look at different aspects of an issue, you can use FOCUS instead of paying for multiple searches.

You can take a broad subject, say the last three months in telecommunications, then look at what's going on that's legislative and what's going on technologically. You can focus on those various aspects and pull out of your main set only the records that have to do with one or the other. In a way, it overcomes the objection that DIALOG-oriented searchers have that you can't build sets in NEXIS.

Another money-saving tip is to watch the discount programs for certain databases, the free files of the month, and so on. Watch the ones that the online services offer, too. On Data-Star, for me in the Central Time Zone, any connect time after twelve noon is discounted $20 an hour.

The telephone training that both Data-Star and Mead are doing is a good way to learn how to be a cost-effective searcher. So is simply phoning the online service and saying, "This is what I have to do and this is how I think it ought to be done, but is there a cheaper way to do it?" I've had online hosts save me bundles of money by pointing out easier ways to do it. You're paying for those support costs one way or another, so you might as well take advantage of them.

What do you love about searching? What do you hate? Why are you doing what you're doing?

I suppose you could say I have a love/hate relationship with online databases. They can be so useful, but sometimes they are just plain cantankerous. There are days when I am convinced that I possess some sort of jinx; every single database I go into presents me with a glitch. I was once asked to find all companies in one state that had subsidiaries in another state. The week before I got this project, the database I needed was reloaded. You guessed it, the reload eliminated the fields that were essential to doing the search. They *knew* I was going to be asked to do that search and they *deliberately* made it impossible. I'm kidding, of course, but it does seem that the databases change so rapidly that keeping up is a real challenge.

Another frustration I have is with the customer service departments of online hosts and database producers. They often seem to put people on the phones who have never done an online search, or who are brand-new hires. UMI/Data Courier used to have their indexers fielding customer service calls, but they don't do that any more. On the other hand, Predicasts has always done pretty well for me with their customer service personnel. The U.S. Data-Star office has excellent customer service.

The quality of the information I retrieve is of great importance to me. It is annoying when producers and hosts don't seem to take responsibility for building quality into their products. The quality of customer service is one aspect of overall quality. The rest of it includes accurate financial data in directory databases, no misspellings in scanned-in full text, correct citation information, abstracts that truly reflect the sense of the original article, and things like that.

What do I love about online searching? The thrill of unearthing something the client thought didn't exist. Putting together a really interesting picture of a company, industry or topic. Speed; being able to pull down a story from a newswire database seconds after the reporter wrote it, turning around and zapping it to my client. Creating linkages between data elements the way I want, rather than the way a print publisher decided I wanted it. Anonymity; no one knows what questions I asked of the database, so I can preserve the confidentiality of what my client has asked me to find out.

Finally, there's the intellectual element. I honestly believe that anybody can learn to do an online search. But I don't believe that everybody can be an expert searcher. You have to be creative and knowledgeable, not just intelligent. You have to out-think the databases, and you have to completely know the complexities of the online services. You have to enjoy problem-solving to be a good searcher.

People who are good searchers have to be patient and be willing to laugh at some of the glitches that other people would take much too seriously. That's not to say it isn't serious; it can be very serious. But it helps to be able to put things in perspective and even see the humor in some of the foul-ups that occur.

Online searching, having access to so many databases containing so many disparate pieces of information, gives me the ability to know what's going on in the world. I can check on companies, look up obscure points of interest, figure out who the experts are in a field, even research my kids' illnesses, and find the background on the latest educational theories their teachers are discussing.

Information empowers. Having online databases at my fingertips empowers me on a personal level, and my clients on a professional level. The feeling of knowing that you can find almost anything you want—that's a pretty heady experience. I guess that's why I'm hooked on online searching.

SUPER SEARCH SECRETS

On search requests...
I would say 80 percent come in by phone, and that phone call may be followed up by a fax or a letter. The other 20 percent come by e-mail. That's a sizeable percentage, and it's growing...

On estimating search costs...
People sometimes ask, "How much do you charge?" I don't answer that question, I walk around it....I work in the question, "Do you have a budget for this project?"...I often do projects in stages...People like the idea of a cap because it's a budgeted amount.

On the reference interview...
I've taken to asking people, "If you were to find this ideal article you're looking for, where do you think it would be published?"

On output formats...
...I started to define my own output format. In DIALOG, it's Format 3, lead paragraph, KWIC, and I set the KWIC value in my user profile to 50....You get a lot of information to help judge whether the document is relevant without having to spend all the time and money it takes to get everything in full text....If I find I've got one good paragraph in an otherwise irrelevant article, I create my own KWICs, with ellipses to show that I've edited out some material.

On thinking online...
...there is something about typing my search ideas online that is part of the rhythm of the process. It gets me focused and thinking about what's going on. It's really psychological; you logon and get into that mental state of doing it and doing it as effectively and efficiently as possible.

On OneSearch categories...
I almost always make up my own with the exception of FIRST and PAPERS. But even with PAPERS, I've taken to adding File 635 (Business Dateline) and File 636 (Predicasts Newsletter Database), so I get the business journals and the newsletters.

On printing search results...

I almost never print descriptor terms. I strip extraneous codes. On full text, I run a spell check for typos and words that were scanned incorrectly. I correct mistakes because otherwise the client will think I made a mistake. I also bold key points, particularly company names, or if the concept is buried way down in a long article.

On saving money...

Check the documentation. Offline preparation saves you money online. Be sure of your strategy before you go online.

On being a super searcher...

...I don't believe that everybody can be an expert searcher. You have to be creative and knowledgeable, not just intelligent. You have to out-think the databases, and you have to completely know the complexities of the online services. You have to enjoy problem-solving to be a good searcher.

CHAPTER 14

RUTH PAGELL: ONLINE MENTOR

Ruth Pagell is Associate Director of the Lippincott Library of the Wharton School of the University of Pennsylvania. She is also Adjunct Associate Professor at the Drexel University College of Information Studies.

What kinds of users do you serve?

Our clientele now is mostly M.B.A. students. We also work with a couple of hundred faculty members. Our primary goal at this point is end-user training. We do an incredible amount of training, and that means that we've got to know about the systems we're training people on. I was speaking to a colleague about this. His comment was that maybe the "super searcher" of the future will be more of a consultant than a researcher.

We're doing less hands-on searching here, and more training and consulting. There's definitely a move toward end-user searching. You can see that vendors are going that way as well, in terms of flat-rate pricing and special deals for new users and for after-hours use. We information professionals will have to evaluate what our roles are. I'm not sure it's any easier being a consultant than a full-time searcher. Then you've got to know everything that's out there, at the same time that you're doing it less frequently yourself. That means we've got to read about it all. We have to stay up-to-date on sources, techniques and new features.

It's a lot more challenging now, because when somebody comes in and asks us a question, we don't just jump onto DIALOG. We have to look at all the choices, and then tell them, "This is really the best one for you to use." We have to be able to back up our advice and then show them how to do it. Then we have to have some alternatives in the background in case that doesn't work.

That's an interesting perspective. Tell me a little bit about yourself in terms of background. What did you do before you got to Penn, and where did you learn to search?

I actually started out in a public library. Then I became reference librarian in the business library at Drexel University. I learned to search there on one of those old Texas Instruments terminals.

What's your search setup like now?

For our students, we have four computer stations in the library itself where end-users can come in and search. We have everything from a new Gateway PC to a couple of horrible old clunkers, including an original PC XT. For software, we use CROSSTALK, with all the passwords loaded in. We use Datastream and ReutersLink software for accessing financial data, but we don't use any of the other system packages like DIALOGLINK, because we search too many systems. Currently, we search at 2400bps. We're going to start doing as much as we can on the Internet. We've given faculty passwords and they're getting to NEXIS via the Internet. From my office, I can search via the Internet. But it doesn't help to dial in through the Internet if you're still dialing in on a 2400bps modem, so we'll definitely upgrade our modems soon.

Tell me how you approach the reference interview.

With the students, we conduct a generic kind of training that applies to all online systems. We talk about how you construct a search, how you put the different pieces together, and how to use Boolean logic and connectors. We talk about doing field searching and truncation. We try to explain the importance of being able to put a title on something. What I mean by that is, if you can actually specify what it is that you're looking for, then you have some sense of what you need to do online. If your concept is still too fuzzy to put a title to, maybe you're not ready to sit down and search.

If we think a subject is too broad, we say to the student, "You know, you're going to get too many hits. What other concepts do you want to tie this to?" You really don't want to search on "finance," especially in a financial database. Maybe they say they want "finance" and "stock," and we say, "You're still probably going to get too much. What *aspect* of stocks are you looking for?" We keep asking them questions until we think they've gotten to the point where they're going to get a quantity of information they can deal with.

If it's too narrow—if they come and say, "We're interested in the effect of Tuesdays on the stock market in Japan in November of 1948"—we say, "No, no; let's go up a few steps. You're never going to find anything that specific."

Do you find that they develop a sense of what's appropriate and that they become more efficient as they go along?

Well, one of the first things that you have to learn when you're running an end-user search service is to close your eyes and bite your tongue. But, yes, we find that some of them are really good. They sit down the first or second time and really seem to get the hang of it. They say, "I don't think I need your help anymore. I feel comfortable doing it myself." That's fine, but some of them never learn. Some of them never get beyond AND and OR.

Are you in a charge-back environment there?

The students pay $5 per half hour, so the searching is heavily subsidized. Faculty, depending on what sources they're using, pay different rates. So, in fact, there is a charge-back to faculty.

Do you actually talk money to them? Do you negotiate a budget, or is it a matter of saying, "You're asking for the moon, you're junior faculty and we can't do that for you?"

If a faculty member is doing a survey, and they want to identify all the restaurants in Pennsylvania so they can send out a questionnaire, we point out that it's going to be incredibly expensive. In fact, for one faculty member who's doing some kind of questionnaire with banks, we helped develop a sampling methodology, using the Dun's files, to bring the project into line with their budget.

Occasionally, somebody will say that money doesn't matter, but that doesn't happen too often. Actually, the faculty doesn't search as much as I think they should, because they are concerned with the fact that it costs *something*. Whether they worry about how much it costs depends on how large a grant they have.

But yes, we do talk money. To the students, we try to explain what they're getting in real dollars. It's very hard to convince somebody who asks, "Why should I pay $5 for this when I'm already paying $20,000 a year in tuition and fees?" that the $5 is giving them at least $200 worth of information.

Aside from finance and stocks, what subjects do your end-users search?

They have a lot of marketing-related questions. Many of the kids are doing marketing projects, and some are *real* projects. Either they're intending to carry them out, or they're working with small businesses or with import/export people. Someone was looking at exporting a notebook computer to Japan. Someone else was interested in exporting push-pins to South Africa. Another student wanted to set up a jazz music club in France. A whole class on consumer behavior used M.A.I.D., which specializes in market research reports, because it included demographics. We do a lot of company-type searches, mostly for students' future employment. They look for profiles of specific firms or firms in a particular industry. We get a lot of requests for time series data, not only financial but also economic time series. We do lots of management things, "soft" subjects, and strategic-type topics. We've gotten into FDA regulatory filings for some project or other.

You've mentioned some of the systems that you search. How about a quick run-through of all of them?

DIALOG, Dow Jones News/Retrieval, Data-Star, NEXIS, BRS, NewsNet, Reuters FinanceLink, Datastream, and M.A.I.D. Obviously, we use some more than others. We can gateway to DataTimes through Dow Jones.

What databases do you use most? I imagine, with all the marketing projects, that Predicasts would be a big one.

Right. We actually ended up getting Predicasts on CD-ROM, but we still use it very heavily online. We use Business Dateline a lot, especially for information on small companies. We use Dun's Market Identifiers all the time, because so many kids are doing projects that involve screening for companies that meet particular criteria.

If the same file is up on more than one system, as Dun's is, what determines where you go to search it?

It depends on several things, including what the student knows and feels comfortable with, and if they have a preference. It depends somewhat on who's helping them. Some of the people on my staff are more or less comfortable with certain systems. It depends on the question, too. If you're screening, you're better off screening on DIALOG than anywhere else, I think. I find it easier to screen on sales and to rank things in DIALOG, and to do a tabular report, which you can't do on Data-Star. We discovered that with the D&B files, for instance, it's sometimes easier, if you're looking for several discrete items, to put them into a report format. You'll get a lot more in a lot less time than if you ask for the full record, and it's a much more compact, usable format. So, for anything that requires a report format, it's DIALOG. For anything where you're going to have to expand on a company name to verify it or to account for all the variations, we usually steer them to DIALOG, too.

If we're looking at INVESTEXT, then I always recommend Data-Star. It's easier for somebody who's not a good searcher to deal with a full report, which is how Data-Star has it formatted. On DIALOG, they have to remember that they're getting pages out of a report. Also, if the kids have searched ABI/INFORM, which we have mounted locally, the Data-Star software is familiar to them. The CD-ROM uses BRS Search software, which is much closer to Data-Star than to DIALOG.

So it's a combination of factors. Does cost ever enter into it?

We have flat rates because we're academics, so there is some cost differential among the systems, but none, really, from the students' point of view. Another thing that is important, though, is when we think they're going to need more than one database, which system is going to have the better related files? Once they're in there already, what else will they want to check? So you really have to look at the entire search.

You mentioned CD-ROM. How do you feel about CD-ROM as a search medium compared to online?

I have a problem looking at online as online or CD-ROM as CD-ROM. We should be looking at all the possible ways we can get the information, and not just focusing on online *per se*. We direct people to what we think is best under the circumstances. CD-ROM certainly has made some difference in our use of online. Getting ABI/INFORM locally-mounted obviously had a huge effect on what we were doing online. Getting Predicasts on CD-ROM made a big difference, because a lot of students were going online just to get the PROMT files, and they no longer have to do that.

I see a lot of libraries tying so much money up in CD-ROM, when for the price of one CD, they could be accessing a lot of different online databases and getting more current information in the process. We take a mix-and-match approach. We tell somebody to try ABI/INFORM or PROMT locally to see what's available. Then if they don't get enough, they can take some of the terms they've found and use them to construct an online search. Sometimes they just use online for full-text delivery. It's not an either/or situation between CD-ROM and online. We just try to find the best way to deliver the information.

How do you approach building the search strategy itself?

I do it completely differently when I'm searching for myself than when I'm instructing kids. When I'm searching for myself, I try to combine as much as I can in a search statement. When I'm training, I use a building-block approach. I say, "Try it this way. Then you can AND it together. If you get too much, you can bring it closer together with a proximity operator instead of the AND. You can play with what you've got."

I think they're much better off, when they don't know what they're doing, trying it one step at a time. They make a lot of typos and they get frustrated. Also, beginners tend to want to enter the ultimate search right at the outset and to get everything at once. They ask, "Can't I just put all the terms in at the same time?" I say, "You can, but if you don't get the results you want, then you don't know where the problem is." Also, if they're not that familiar with the databases, it makes more sense to break it down, search one file at a time, and see where something turns up.

Do you do a lot of full-text searching, or do you use full-text files more selectively for document delivery?

I go directly to the full-text files, especially for "quick and dirty" searching—of which I do a lot. I'm not doing an "ultimate" search in most cases. Often, I go to the full-text files, especially the news files on NEXIS, because I'm looking for something really new and current. By the time something gets into an abstract or index file, it's already old.

That's one of the trade-offs, indexing versus currency. Tell me how you approach full-text searching. As we both know, if you don't know what you're doing, you can really get in trouble.

I try to think of the terms that might be used for a single concept, and I OR them together. Then I try to think of some logical number of words apart that my different concepts might appear. Sometimes I guess wrong. Usually I'm too broad; I get too many hits. Then I go back and ask that the terms appear closer together within the same search. I usually look at a few cites right off the bat if I'm in NEXIS, or I look at titles or Format 8 in DIALOG. Sometimes I go back and ask for the country name, say, to appear in the headline. With newspapers, I might qualify my terms to the lead paragraph.

If I'm really trying to do a definitive search, I look at the articles I've gotten to this point to see what other search terms I might have missed. When we're searching a descriptor database, we tell people that, when they've gotten a couple of good articles, they should look at the descriptors, and then go back and try those descriptors to see what else they might pull up. It's the same principle.

Searching is definitely an iterative process. You go in, you don't quite get it, and you keep tweaking your strategy and going back. It's interesting to watch the students. Somebody might sit down with what looks like a really difficult search, and they just hit it right the first time. Of course, then they walk away thinking "Boy, this is easy." And then you get something that seems like it should be really easy, and it's not. I might go away for a while and think, "Well, how else can I approach it? What other angle could I use? What have I missed here?" I keep coming back and coming back at it. Unfortunately, I notice with our end-users that, if they don't get it, they often just walk away, period. They don't realize there are a lot of other approaches. That's a real problem. If I can intervene, I do. I ask, "Did you try this way? Did you try a different term? Did you try a different database?" *I* try them all, but I know that *they* don't, and sometimes that's discouraging. If they get negative results once or twice, they're not going to come back.

The librarians all serve as search consultants on a rotating basis. Their function is to help the people who are doing searches. The consultant will sit with students while they're running the search, if that's what they want. The problem is the ones who think they know what they're doing and then don't ask questions, or are too proud to ask. That's definitely a factor. Wharton School students consider themselves the cream of the crop, certainly, and it's hard for a lot of them to ask for help.

Do you download search results directly, or do you order e-mail prints?

If it's an expensive database, like Dun & Bradstreet, then we do e-mail prints. We usually turn things around in a day or two, when the library staff is doing the searching, so it depends on how soon they need it. But we try to do e-mail prints if possible.

I'm curious about how much post-processing you do. I've found among my own clients that the business and management types don't want to see things like CODENs and ISSNs, and certainly not descriptors. How much time do you spend cleaning up search results before you deliver them?

For faculty, we do a lot of post-processing. We might easily spend three times as much time doing post-processing as we do running the search in the first place. I take out all of the garbage. You know all those control characters you get when you download a Dow Jones search? It's a disaster. I clean all that out. For NEXIS, we use the Lexform software to clean it up, then we put it in WordPerfect. We take out extra spaces, we put in real page numbers, and take out the "Page 2 of 12" kind of thing that you get on each document. We add some headings and weed out any hits that look really irrelevant. Then we print it out on a laser printer.

Occasionally, we might do something like bold or highlight key points, but not routinely. How much we do depends on whether it's for somebody who is really familiar with this stuff. If they're comfortable with it, I don't bother. If it's somebody I'm trying to impress, or it's his first search, then I do a little more.

We also find that a lot of the faculty don't like anything that comes from online in ASCII text. They still want to see the original article, or at least a photocopy. So if we can get it from Business Periodicals On Disc, which is an image file, that's what we do. They consider that the same as a photocopy, so that's okay. The other thing I've found is that they don't want electronic delivery of search results. They want it in hard copy. It would save so much time if I could just send them the file in e-mail or at least send them a disk. I guess they're just not comfortable with the medium.

When you deliver a search, do you document what databases you covered and what strategy you used?

I try to do that routinely. I paraphrase the search strategy; I explain it in English.

Do you follow up to make sure that the search was on target? Or do you assume that no news is good news?

It's informal. If I see a problem when I'm working on a search, I immediately call the faculty member and say, "This is what I'm turning up," or "Let me give you a sample and you tell me if you think this is okay." I've been trying to do this long distance with somebody who's on a year's sabbatical in London. She asked for *everything* on business ethics. She wanted me to download some 300 NEXIS articles, and that's just not do-able. So I've been trying to get her to narrow it; I've been sending her examples and waiting for her to look at them and tell me what she really wants. There are some faculty I work with all the time, though, and I've gotten a pretty good sense of what they're looking for.

What problems do you run into with regard to database quality, completeness and reliability?

You name it. I was teaching my marketing class at the library school, and I wanted to see what the Trinet company directory files look like since American Business Information took them over. I didn't want to redo my share-of-market overhead, because I did it just a few months ago. I've been using the beer industry as an example for three years now, and I think I know the beer industry pretty well. But a company showed up in the database that I'd never seen before. I thought, "I don't believe this. This is the first time I've tried this file and I'm getting this weird record." The company was showing up as the third-largest beer company. I spent the better part of a day trying to figure this out. I checked them out in the SEC filings, and I checked them out in D&B. I looked in all of the updated files on mergers and acquisitions to see if something had happened that I didn't know about. They do have some kind of a wine distributorship. It's like their fifth-ranked secondary SIC code, but I didn't turn up beer anywhere else. So it must have just been miscoded at the most basic level.

It worries me when I stumble across something like that when I'm not specifically looking for quality problems. If I find a mistake very easily, it makes me really nervous, because it's so random. You know, how good is the *rest* of the database? You have to wonder what the percentages are. That's why I always warn my students about accepting this stuff at face value.

Then there was the problem I've written about, where I was looking for the largest food companies in Europe. I was searching D&B International, and all the largest companies were showing up as being Yugoslavian. It turned out, after a whole lot of looking and searching, that the reason was that the dinar, the Yugoslavian currency unit, had been deflated and revalued. There was a time lag between the exchange rate that Dun & Bradstreet uses and the date for the total sales, so we were looking at 1988 sales and 1990 exchange rates, which of course threw everything out of whack. This happens quite a bit in files that are not really geared for financial analysis. They can't do what you really have to do, accounting-wise, which is to use some kind of average or year-end exchange rate for the period of the sales. You just can't use these databases for ranking, at least not reliably.

Where do you go when the financial data has to be absolutely accurate?

I look in more than one place. I look in DISCLOSURE, which we have on disc. I look in Extel, because I think they have a good handle on financial information. If it's stock data, we probably use Dow Jones if it's U.S., or Datastream or Reuters if it's international. The students aren't as attuned to that kind of thing as they should be. They tend to accept what comes out of the computer without much question. They're usually in a rush, and they're not looking at it when they walk away. Then maybe at three in the morning when they're writing their paper, they discover the data doesn't make sense. But in terms of actually evaluating the quality of the data, they don't seem to be doing that much.

Now, *I* notice right away if something looks like a load of garbage, and I try to do something about it. As soon as I see something that looks weird, I check it out in a second place. If the second one is different, then I go to a third source because you can't be sure which one is right and which is wrong. A British company might report "profit" as profit before taxes, while a U.S. company would list profit after taxes. You often have to go to several sources to make sure that you have the right line. I wish more people did it.

It's really important, when we run into quality problems, that we get back to the host systems and the database producers, because if we don't tell them, they're not going to know. We have to work *with* these people. Sometimes we tend to treat them as adversaries, and they're really not. They're our friends. There are certain people I know I can talk to on the database producer side, although sometimes they're defensive at first. There are certain databases where I've come to expect better quality, and others where I just know that I'm going to find some funny results no matter what I do. If I'm going to use D&B International to rank companies, for instance, there are almost always exchange rate problems. So I just expect certain things, and keep an eye out for things that I know might cause problems. What I find with students, unfortunately, is they don't want to hear about a lot of this. This is an information professional's problem. They just have to get their assignments done, and they don't want to hear about different accounting standards for different countries.

What makes a good searcher, Ruth? What do you enjoy about it?

I think a logical mind makes a good searcher. Searching is a really logical process, from my perspective. Some people are good at it and some people aren't. For some people, it's probably an art, and they do it okay. For some people, it's a science, and they do it okay, too. Other people just don't seem to be able to think in terms of pulling a whole lot of ideas together. I've seen people who've been searching for years and years and years, who never seem to get it right. Some people don't understand how a database is constructed, and they can't see how it searches. Maybe that has to do with knowing something about computing, but I'm not sure how important that really is, because some good searchers know nothing about computing. For me, it's like a detective puzzle. I like detective stories and I like puzzles. You're holding a lot of clues in your head simultaneously, fitting them all together.

I find some searches very interesting and others boring. The ones I find interesting are of two kinds. One is interesting because I'm interested in the subject itself, and I find myself getting caught up in it. The other is interesting because I know that the search itself is going to be a challenge—I won't be able to come at it directly. Either there is no single database that specifically covers this topic, or there's no clear descriptor term, so you have to come up with your own creative strategy. I enjoy things like that.

Searching *per se* is just a small part of what I do now. In terms of students and training, I get a lot of satisfaction when I see somebody I helped come back and do more searching and do it well. I love it when it's obvious that they've gotten interested in it and they want to know more. I feel as if I've passed along my own enthusiasm and they've gotten it, somehow.

SUPER SEARCH SECRETS

On search software...

...we use CROSSTALK, with all the passwords loaded in. We use Datastream and ReutersLink software for accessing financial data, but we don't use any of the other system packages like DIALOGLINK, because we search too many systems.

On the reference interview...

We try to explain the importance of being able to put a title on something....If you can actually specify what it is that you're looking for, then you have some sense of what you need to do online. If your concept is still too fuzzy to put a title to, maybe you're not ready to sit down and search.

On using the REPORT feature on DIALOG...

If you're screening, you're better off screening on DIALOG than anywhere else, I think. I find it easier to screen on sales and to rank things in DIALOG, and to do a tabular report, which you can't do on Data-Star....You'll get a lot more in a lot less time than if you ask for the full record, and it's a much more compact, usable format. So, for anything that requires a report format, it's DIALOG.

On CD-ROM...

We should be looking at all the possible ways we can get the information, and not just focusing on online *per se*....CD-ROM certainly has made some difference in our use of online....I see a lot of libraries tying so much money up in CD-ROM, when for the price of one CD, they could be accessing a lot of different online databases and getting more current information in the process. We take a mix-and-match approach.

On search strategies...

When I'm searching for myself, I try to combine as much as I can in a search statement. When I'm training, I use a building-block approach.

On searching full text...

I try to think of the terms that might be used for a single concept, and I OR them together.

On searching...

Searching is definitely an iterative process. You go in, you don't quite get it, and you keep tweaking your strategy and going back.

On quality...

If I find a mistake very easily, it makes me really nervous, because it's so random. You know, how good is the rest of the database?

On being a good searcher...

I think a logical mind makes a good searcher. Searching is a really logical process, from my perspective. Some people are good at it and some people aren't....It's like a detective puzzle....You're holding a lot of clues in your head simultaneously, fitting them all together.

CHAPTER 15

NORA PAUL: NEWS RESEARCH SYBARITE

Nora Paul is Library
Director at the Poynter
Institute for Media Studies
in St. Petersburg, Florida.
She was formerly librarian
at the *Miami Herald*.

**The Poynter Institute sounds like an interesting place.
Tell me a little more about it.**

The Poynter Institute is a non-profit educational
organization that conducts seminars for working journalists.
Most of the seminars are a week long, but there are a couple
of six-week sessions that focus on journalism studies—
helping working journalists develop their techniques in
writing and editing, journalism ethics, newspaper graphics
and design. There's a broadcast area and a media
management area, each of which conducts its own series of
seminars each year. We've just added a news research area.
In the past we did just one seminar a year on news research;
next year we'll be able to do three. Part of my mission in
coming here was to spread the word about what I see as the
role of research in the development of the news product.

**What's your professional background? Are you a
librarian by training?**

Yes, I got my masters in library science from Texas
Women's University. I spent about a year and a half in the
science and technology and business areas of the Houston
Public Library. Another woman, Jennifer Reavis, and I saw
that the demand for information from the business
community was really high, so we quit and started an
information brokerage company called Freelance Research
Service. This was around 1975. We searched BRS and
DIALOG, and we ended up doing a lot of document
delivery—going to the university to pull the full text
because the databases just didn't provide it back then. We
found it hard to do enough business in information
retrieval, so we branched out into corporate library design
and records management. But both of us really loved doing
the information searching. There just wasn't the demand
yet, or the recognition that this piece of information or this
bibliography was worth this amount of money. We were a
little bit ahead of our time, I think.

I had always wanted to get into a newspaper or a
magazine. I heard about an opening at the *Miami Herald*,
interviewed and got the job. That was 1979, and I was
there for 12 years, until I went to the Poynter.

What kind of searching do you do there?

We do several kinds of searching. We support the research activities of the faculty, who are all very active in writing and speaking, and who have their own research projects going on various journalism-type topics. We also do a lot of research for the seminar participants, a good number of whom are reporters and editors. I always do a presentation on databases and what's available. Even people who come from news organizations with very good libraries find this an opportunity to play with things that they don't get a chance to back in their shops, when they're under pressure. This is one of the perks of being here, getting to really play with some of the databases. I get my news research fix pretty regularly.

We also serve as sort of the journalism librarians of the world. The Institute library is a very special collection of journalism-related material. It's an excellent small library. The literature of journalism is not very widely available yet in terms of online access. Lots of journals are indexed only 20 percent-worth, I'd estimate.

Coming from a news library where everything I needed was available online, it was frustrating to confront old clippings files—the articles had been clipped out of journalism magazines and put in subject files. I'd really like to scan them and make them available as a database. But we don't own this data, so I'd have to deal with the whole copyright thing. I'm thinking of starting with some of the more esoteric newsletters and special interest journals, talking to them individually and asking if I can put their publications in a database.

Frankly, unless I can get the source easily, bibliographies drive me crazy. For the most part, the research we did at the newspaper had to be full text. Giving somebody a citation list just wasn't going to cut it, because they had to read the article by three o'clock and have the story written by five. So I'm doing more esoteric kinds of journal searching than I have in the past. We're working on questions like whether serif type or sans-serif type is more easily readable. We're hitting a lot of weird references that we can take the time to track down because they're not needed for a story today. A lot of people here are working on research papers, not newspaper stories, and if they get it three weeks from now, that's fine.

What is your search environment like?

We're networked, which is wonderful. We're building a lot of personal databases that everybody will be able to get at. We all use PCs, although I do most of my demonstrations on a Mac. What's especially exciting for me here—I feel like a kid in a candy store—is that, since we're an educational institution, we've been able to get instructional rates on all the major database services. It's an embarrassment of riches.

That's the good news. The bad news is that I've become sort of a decadent searcher. I don't want to lose sight of what real people have to deal with. I have to stay sensible about what's realistic. As it is, I do a NEXIS search, and say, "Let me start a new search, I don't care. I'll do it in OMNI," that sort of thing. So I do have to watch that.

What do you typically ask in a reference interview?

The first question is usually "What are you working on? Tell me what the story is." That starts a conversation about what they're really trying to get at. It's usually an educational process for the person you're talking to. If they come in and say, "I need a search on Cuban refugees," you know that isn't true. They need something very specific about Cuban refugees, and they might not even know what it is yet. You have to talk them through it, and give them ideas about the angles you can take.

For example, we did a practicum here on breast implant issues. For background, I started by searching on breast implants. Everywhere I looked there was stuff about breast implants. I panicked. I started searching and didn't know when to stop, because I didn't have a question that needed to be answered. I had no idea what I was trying to accomplish.

That's often the first thing that people ask at seminars. "There's all this stuff. How do you know when you're done?" You know you're done when your question has been answered satisfactorily. I realized on the implant search that I was breaking my own rule, which is that you can't go in without a very specific question. If you're not focused, the databases are useless.

So, instead of thinking in terms of sources, we sat down in the seminar and started talking about how to approach the research. We asked ourselves, first, who are the players in this area? We got a list of 22 different groups that have an interest in breast implant issues; several categories of patients, plus the doctors, the medical clinics, the manufacturers, the employees of the manufacturers who are getting laid off because of the controversy over implants, the legislators, and the lawyers who are jumping up and down over this. Next we started talking in terms of the particular concerns of each of those groups. What kind of information would you need to do a story on them? What would you need for background? Where would you have to go to find sources? How would you try to locate somebody? How could you put what they've just told you into a perspective based on something other than simply what they said? It ended up being an excellent exercise for all of us.

Once you break a topic into components, you can put together a shopping list of places to check. But you've got to know, first of all, what it is you want to find out, and why you want to find out about it. The basic reasons for doing news research are to background the story broadly, to find somebody who can speak about the issue, to verify a fact, or get statistics. Often, too, news research is done just to see if something has already been covered. If someone's already done it, let's not bother.

The first place I heard the phrase "news research" was on the Journalism Forum on CompuServe. Then I noticed that you were active there.

I've been participating in the Journalism Forum for a long time. I'm fascinated by electronic bulletin boards and the incredibly supportive community that's out there. People are generous there in a way that they're not face-to-face or over the phone. Even with their own librarians, journalists sometimes are not very open about what they're working on or how they've done things. You can go into a group of journalists in the newsroom and ask "Who knows about so-and-so?" and nobody will look up from their desks. On the Journalism Forum, they really open up. You end up getting lots of responses from all over.

Do you have any formal way of keeping track of the requests that come in to you at Poynter?

I've always been bad at that kind of housekeeping and record-keeping. I like it in theory, but I'm the worst offender. I love designing the form and figuring out the procedure, but then I'm the last one to follow it. We do have a reference form that we use with a database software package called Q&A. Now that we're networked, we can pull it up on the screen when we're talking to somebody and fill out the search template as we go along. Then we can keep track of how many searches we've done a month and for whom, and whether it was an inside or an outside request. We can generate all kinds of reports.

Given all the low-cost educational accounts you have with the online services, are you still conscious of budget when you go online? Do you think in terms of going all out for a search versus just doing a "quick-and-dirty"?

One of the key questions is always "How much do you want?" Giving someone too much is often worse than not giving them enough. I ask, "Do you want a couple of good articles, or do you want me to search the world for this?" That's my main determination. It has more to do with the requester's approach or need than with my time. That's one of the luxuries of this place—there isn't some huge project that has to get done every day or else you're in trouble. We can flow in whatever direction they want to go. Frankly, I don't get in big trouble going over budget like I would have at the newspaper. We're pretty well funded. I still can't believe it. I feel like Pygmalion or something.

How does it generally work in newspaper libraries? Is there a per-request or per-project budget cap? Or is there just a total operating budget for the newspaper library or for online costs within the library?

There are lots of different models. Some people have a monthly budget for online, and they control all that money. At the *Miami Herald* we began charging back to the department that asked for the search, and making the individual desks responsible for budgeting online services. That was very liberating. It was a headache to track the charges, but in terms of feeling responsible for budget control, we were much freer with fulfilling requests. We didn't have to juggle priorities. The desks were the ones that had to deal with the budget problems. In fact, they went over budget all the time, but nobody ever came and asked, "Hey, what the hell's going on; why are you doing all this?" People understand the value of research.

I could go on for hours about how I think about pricing and what's got to change. For most newspapers, budgeting and staying within budget are so critical. I think that until services move to some sort of subscription pricing option, there's going to be a lot of resistance in news libraries to most of the database services.

DIALOG is probably one of the least-used services in news libraries, partly because people resent getting hit so many times. You've got the online time, the telecommunications time, the display, and then the printing. It goes on and on. You have to have your calculator next to your terminal to figure out where you are.

NEXIS has been in the forefront of subscription pricing, but their approach to it sits badly with a lot of people. It feels so unthought-through that you can often work a better deal with them if you're a strong negotiator. It should be more equitable. Sometimes you don't even realize that you had room to negotiate. It's done under such a cloak of secrecy when it should just be a company policy. As it is, it's like air fares. "Are you staying over a Saturday night?" They've got to simplify things.

Let's get back to the search process itself. How do you plan your search strategies?

I do most of it in my head. I didn't use DIALOG as much in the past as I do now, and I'm learning a lot about individual files. I'm enjoying the process of doing a little research on the sources, looking at the bluesheets, before I go in. Again, I have the luxury of time to do that. Before, it was "get in and get out, because there's another search coming up fast." I'm also using the online "helps" a lot more, the online indexes and file descriptions. That's another function of my decadence here. I know most people's attitude is, "Why should I spend money to consult documentation online?"

Part of why I was interested in coming to the Poynter is that, after so long at the newspaper, a lot of what I did there felt like knee-jerk reaction stuff. They ask for that, I do this. I wanted a chance to stop and think about *what* I've been doing for so long. Now, I have the luxury of being able to do searches the way they should be done. Sure, you can get a little bit anal-retentive about over-constructing a search, but if you don't get the chance to construct one properly, you can miss a lot.

For example, a faculty member wanted some census material on a couple of cities on which she was doing circulation studies. One of the librarians was going into CENDATA. She figured out the zip codes for the cities and the surrounding areas. Then she discovered all these other geographic options and how to specify the level of the data you wanted to retrieve. She charted out the whole strategy. I was getting a little impatient. I knew that at the *Herald*, if somebody asked, "Whaddya got for this city?" we would have just gone in by city name, gotten out and handed them something. It was definitely quick-and-dirty, but it would have gotten them what I thought they needed, very quickly.

The approach I take here is luxurious. But it's the way it should be done, and few people get the opportunity to do it that way. It's still difficult for me to get over thinking that I have to just do the search and get on to the next thing. It's hard to realize that you don't have to work that way.

Do you use controlled vocabulary lists, thesauri and that sort of thing?

I'm learning to play with the controlled vocabulary in the DIALOG files. I do a broad search first and find one or two articles that are right-on. I see what terms are used to index them, then go back and do another search with those terms and get more. I've always been skeptical of "controlled vocabulary" because it's the most human part of building any database. Humans, of course, are prone to error and bias.

It's very hard to say that something is truly "controlled," and to agree on the exact interpretation of a given term. I never rely on controlled vocabulary. I'm sure it's a useful technique in the scientific databases where "this thing" means "that thing" and that's all it means. There, it's concrete. But in most of the social studies and humanities, it's difficult to make those clearcut equations. It's a lot more subjective, for sure.

In the news databases, you can't rely on controlled vocabulary at all. Papers like the *Los Angeles Times,* the *New York Times* and the *Washington Post* have pretty detailed keyword lists. But there's so little standardization. A group of newspaper librarians decided some time ago to come up with an added-terms list that we would all agree on. It was an incredible process. We all agreed finally that we'd use singular, not plural, and things like that. We put "murder" on stories that were about somebody killing somebody else. "History," "biography," and some of those "material"-type terms, were not hard to agree on. But when we started talking about content, it was very hard to get a consensus.

For example, in Detroit they had a list of 15 or 20 terms that they used specifically for the auto industry. One was "incentive." They put the keyword "incentive" on any story about price rebates, or giving you a toaster oven with every new Ford you buy. I said, "Well, I'm not going to use 'incentive' that way at the *Miami Herald*." But I had these long lists for drug smuggling and stuff like that, and the Detroit librarian said, "I'm not going to use those terms. We don't have enough of those stories."

I've had newspaper librarians tell me that they don't use keywords at all when they search.

I absolutely don't. There are maybe three or four that I try. If I want biographical information on somebody, I'll throw in "biography."

Why do you assign them in the first place, then? Why did the news librarians go through that exercise of trying to achieve some degree of standardization?

Frankly, we were leaping over a void. We were concerned about searching for information in an electronic environment, rather than just pulling out the clip file on Cuban refugees. Our thinking about subject headings reflected a mimicking of the old clip file. At the *Herald*, we started with a list of about 200 terms that we swore we would use. It eventually got down to about 15 that we used all the time. As our confidence level grew, along with our ability to select articles out of the news database, we relied less and less on the added terms. We found as we went along that they were unreliable, anyway, in doing any kind of cross-newspaper searching.

Some people are still very committed to assigning the added terms, and some don't do it at all. Some do it when times are good, there's nobody out on maternity leave, and they're fully staffed. Then, when a bunch of people are on vacation, it doesn't get done. So you don't have consistency over time, either.

Do you ever take the approach of searching National Newspaper Index or Newspaper & Periodical Abstracts, taking advantage of their more detailed and consistent keywords, and then going into the full-text newspaper files to pull the actual stories?

I haven't tried that, but it's an interesting idea. The newspaper index databases aren't as comprehensive, though, and I'm so used to using the full-text files. I wouldn't be confident saying, "No, this guy hasn't appeared in newspapers" if I had just done a National Newspaper Index search instead of a full-text one.

What's your general approach to a search? When you do you start broad? When do you try to be as narrowly focused as possible?

If it's something as specific as, "I need articles about John Smith of so-and-so company and the perjury trial he just went through," and I've found 15 articles that mention perjury and this guy's name, I'd probably just print those off, and that would be the end of that.

If the question is, "What do you have about corporate officers being involved in perjury?" that's a much broader topic. Then you have to ask "Do you want news stories about it, or do you want management theory? What are you trying to do with this story?" Then, if there's a lot, we give them citations or headlines and have them tell us what they're interested in. People really have no idea how much is out there. Librarians sometimes get exasperated about reporters coming and asking, "What do you have on breast implants?" "We've got so much stuff; you can't imagine all the stuff we have." Well, of course they can't. That's where we have to direct them. "Do you want it from the manufacturing angle, from the theoretical angle or the news angle?" Once the possibilities start to dawn on them, it's "Oh, wow, I can get all this! Now let me think about it." Or "Let's talk about it."

You often find yourself embarking on a search and coming up with a lot. Then you loop back to the reference interview saying, "Now it turns out that we have all these possibilities." Sometimes there are angles you might not have been aware of, going in. Something that sounded completely innocent or simple because it was new to you might have been the topic of tremendous debate someplace else. You thought you would pull just ten or 15 articles, but you find a huge amount, because the whole northeastern United States has been grappling with it for years.

So, sometimes you get a lot more than you'd expected, and that in itself is significant. What happens when you get too little?

Sometimes, getting too little is exactly what they want to hear. That goes back to the reference-interview again. Why do they want this research? Are they thinking about working on a story, and doing a reconnaissance mission just to see what's out there? If it's already been done by the *Washington Post* and the *New York Times*, they don't want to do it again. So, a negative answer might be exactly what they want. Often, I've gone back and said, "Wow, man, I've looked everywhere, and there was nothing," and they've said, "Oh, that's great!" Had I known their intention going in, I might not have spent as much time going through all the different convolutions.

I've had the same experience. I say, "Geez, why didn't you tell me?" They say, "Well, I wanted you to do a good job."

You mentioned global searching, which I'm sure you use in regional newspaper searching. Do you use it in the non-newspaper files at all?

In DIALOG, sure. I'm in love with those OneSearch categories. To be able to cover the humanities, education or marketing in a single search is wonderful. We do a lot of issues-type searches in those file groupings, on subjects like privacy or ethics. For example, some TV news directors, in one of our seminars, were saying "It's really hard to manage all these wonderful, creative people. How do you deal with creative people?" Going into DIALOG very broadly was a wonderful thing to be able to do. I got relevant information from subject areas and magazines that you wouldn't have imagined, like a journal for insurance actuaries.

I suppose that creativity might be a problem in the insurance industry. As you explore the capabilities of OneSearch, are you experimenting with duplicate detection as well?

I've started to use duplicate detection more. It doesn't really work with the newspaper files, though, because it depends partly on matching titles. The same AP story, for example, will run in 15 different newspapers with 15 different headlines. Then too, portions of wire stories are sometimes incorporated into something that's locally written, and that runs under the local reporter's byline. Even the style of attribution is different from paper to paper. One will say "From Herald wire services," another one will say "AP," another will say "From Tribune wire services," and another will just say "Compiled from wire services." There's just no way the system can recognize these as duplicates.

One of the things that seems to characterize newspaper libraries is fast turnaround and banging out those searches. Do you still have that newspaper librarian mindset?

Even though I'm not in a classic newspaper environment any more, when a request comes in, I still tend to drop everything else and do the search. I am still operating on the newspaper model, I guess. When they ask for it, that's when they need it. I have to get better about prioritizing. If that one doesn't get done until Friday, it's okay because the guy's out of town anyway. So it's usually same-day service, if not within a couple of hours.

We do work on some bigger projects, for example, a bibliography on ethics for a book that one of our faculty is helping to write. Also, Poynter publishes something called *Best Newspaper Writing*, which consists of the winning entries from the American Society of Newspaper Editors' annual awards, with background on each story. It includes a bibliography of articles that have appeared in the previous year specific to writing, editing and things like that. Projects like those might be worked on in stages for several weeks.

When you deliver search results, do you clean up the records at all?

I usually clean up the printout to exclude things that won't mean anything to the client—document ID numbers and all that good stuff. I like to print it out and, with a highlighter, highlight the titles. That gives me a chance to read through it a little more slowly. I still like paper, to a certain extent. You've got to read it like the reader's going to read it.

Is it important, in your setting, to document what you did in a search and to tell the requester what search terms you used and what sources you covered?

Absolutely. I consider qualifying what was done to be one of the searcher's primary responsibilities. For the most part, people lack so much understanding, that they can easily get the false impression that you've searched everything in existence and that this is the ultimate answer. I always tell them where I looked and what approach I took. That also lets them know that there is more there if they want it. You don't have to give them all the details about who published the databases and so on, but you have to let them know, conversationally, that this is not a totally comprehensive search. They do come back.

Do you keep any archive of search results after you've run them?

Yes. I'm hoping, now that we're networked, that our request template will include a section for the search strategy. Then when someone says, "You did this for me three weeks ago and I want to see if there's been anything since," if the person who did the search originally isn't here, we just recreate it.

Another thing I should mention is that we're experimenting with some of the bibliographic citation software, like Pro-Cite. We hope it will help capture and organize research results, and also track the literature that is not online. We're going to start building citations, at least, to some key articles. It will help with output, too, since faculty members often write for magazines that have different bibliographic styles, and Pro-Cite will flip it around any way you want it to.

Do you have any kind of formal feedback mechanism in place to make sure that the search was okay?

This is a pretty small and informal place, so for the most part it's a matter of hallway conversations. "How did that work out?" "Oh, it was just right."

At the newspaper, we tried to imprint on the reporters that we did have a role and that we were a player in this. When a story we'd worked on appeared in print, we said, "Hey, that was really good. That stuff we got helped, didn't it?" Often, our research involved trying to locate somebody that the reporter could talk to, so we asked, "Were you ever able to find that guy?" That kind of feedback also gives you good hints about what is effective and what isn't.

Now and then somebody wins a Pulitzer, and it's wonderful because news librarians are starting to get some of the credit. That happened not long ago at the *Sacramento Bee*. Also, one of the American Society of Newspaper Editors winners was interviewed and said, "One of the keys to being able to do good writing is having a good librarian and maintaining a good relationship. We're lucky to have one of the best, Linda Henderson." It's really neat when that happens.

I'll bet it is. Do you see any trends or issues, in particular regarding newspaper databases and newspaper searching, that you want to comment on?

One of the things that I'm starting to look at is CD-ROM and the role that's going to play in newspaper searching. We have NewsBank and a couple of other CD-ROMs, but we haven't really gotten into it much. I think news libraries will be getting more involved with CD-ROM as the prices go down. As it is now, you'd have to do ten searches a day on one CD to justify the cost. Some libraries can do that, but the only thing we would be using that heavily, the newspaper files, aren't current enough on CD-ROM.

The thing that I'm really concerned about is that the golden age of incredible access to a wide range of sources might be ending. I'm afraid that newspapers will start economizing by making their databases available on CD-ROM exclusively. Then instead of being able to search 78 different newspapers at once, each going back five or ten years, we might end up having to go pocket-by-pocket, little-newspaper-by-little-newspaper, shuffling disks. I could see that happening with the VU/TEXT newspapers that DIALOG is not interested in mounting. I could see those smaller papers going to commercial CD-ROMs or in-house systems. I'd hate to think about going back to the days of having to call around the country to see what people have in their clip files, even if those clip files are on CD-ROM, but I think there's a danger of that happening.

That's an interesting issue. Sound the alarm. Let's talk about something more positive now. What really turns you on about searching?

In terms of searching *per se*, what I'm really excited about now are the bulletin board services. I'm fascinated by the information that's uploaded that's not available in commercial databases. When we were doing that breast implant project, for example, I went into the CompuServe Health Forum and did a simple keyword search in the Library area, where they archive various files of interest. I found a 20-page survey about breast implants that had been done by the American College of Reconstructive Surgeons. It was a demographic survey that looked at reconstructive patients versus cosmetic patients, and it covered everything from how old they were when they had it done, to how much support they got from family members, to how happy they were with the results. It was a wonderful, detailed document, and it wasn't online anywhere else.

You know how it is in a newspaper library? Between nine o'clock and noon you will have done legal research, business research and public records research, plus tried to find an expert who could talk to you about the nature of happiness! It's very strange and a lot of fun. But, as more and more sources, especially those odd little standalone databases and esoteric bulletin boards, become available, you sometimes start panicking, feeling that you don't have any sense at all of what is really out there. I'd like to see a network where newspaper librarians could coordinate their expertise.

"Okay, I'll be the one that knows everything and stays up-to-date about legal stuff. You be the one that knows everything and will stay up-to-date about business research. I can tap into you, and you can tap into me."

As far as my present situation goes, as I've said before, I'm in nirvana right now in terms of having the time to chew on things. I can actually work on a research project instead of just pushing it through. I've been enjoying exploring the documentation and really seeing what a file consists of. So much of the job at the newspaper—I loved this part and miss it—was detective work. It was exciting; there was an urgency that doesn't exist here. Frankly, if you only find ten good articles on readability, you know, it's just not that crucial. It's not as fiery here as in the newspaper environment.

It was sort of a missionary thing for me. It was a challenge getting reporters to start including the researcher on their story, letting them know that we're as interested as they are, and that we have a lot to contribute. It was always fun to overcome a reporter's resistance and see that we made a real change, from being seen as just a service organization to an actual partner in building the story. That's why I'm glad I'm here. I have a soapbox again. The people who are here are here because they are receptive to new ideas and new ways of looking at things.

I'm sort of straddling the line, now, between being a journalism librarian and a news research person. Talking with someone about where they could go to check things out is a fun exercise for both of us. I miss that aspect of the job. It's interesting to be sitting on the sidelines a little bit, still watching my brothers and sisters in the news libraries having to deal with very real time and money problems. I hope I don't become irrelevant because I'm fat and sassy now. I don't think I will. I'm still tuned into that Solidarity Forever kind of mentality. I'm pretty sure I always will be.

SUPER SEARCH SECRETS

On the reference interview...

The first question is usually "What are you working on? Tell me what the story is."....It's usually an educational process for the person....They need something very specific...and they might not even know what it is yet. You have to talk them through it, and give them ideas about the angles you can take.

On news research...

The basic reasons for doing news research are to background the story broadly, to find somebody who can speak about the issue, to verify a fact, or get statistics. Often, too, news research is done just to see if something has already been covered. If someone's already done it, let's not bother.

On logging search requests...

We do have a reference form that we use with a database software package called Q&A....we can pull it up on the screen when we're talking to somebody and fill out the search template as we go along. Then we can keep track of how many searches we've done a month and for whom, and whether it was an inside or an outside request. We can generate all kinds of reports.

On controlled vocabulary...

I've always been skeptical of "controlled vocabulary" because it's the most human part of building any database. Humans, of course, are prone to error and bias....I never rely on controlled vocabulary....It's a lot more subjective....In the news databases, you can't rely on controlled vocabulary at all.

On OneSearch...

I'm in love with those OneSearch categories. To be able to cover the humanities, education or marketing in a single search is wonderful.

On deduping search results...

It doesn't really work with the newspaper files, though, because it depends partly on matching titles. The same AP story, for example, will run in 15 different newspapers with 15 different headlines. Then too, portions of wire stories are sometimes incorporated into something that's locally written, and that runs under the local reporter's byline....There's just no way the system can recognize these as duplicates.

On post-processing...

I usually clean up the printout to exclude things that won't mean anything to the client....I like to print it out and, with a highlighter, highlight the titles. That gives me a chance to read through it a little more slowly. I still like paper...

On CD-ROM...

I'm afraid that newspapers will start economizing by making their databases available on CD-ROM exclusively. Then instead of being able to search 78 different newspapers at once, each going back five or ten years, we might end up having to go pocket-by-pocket, little-newspaper-by-little-newspaper, shuffling disks.

CHAPTER 16

BARBARA QUINT: GRASSHOPPER SEARCHER

Barbara Quint is president of Quint and Associates, a consulting firm in Santa Monica, California. She is editor of *Searcher: The Magazine For Database Professionals*, a prolific writer and speaker on information issues, and a well-known online industry gadfly. Quint was head of reference at Rand Corporation for 20 years, where she searched 30 online services, and has been a searcher since 1973.

How do you tackle the reference interview?

I ask name, rank, serial number and who's going to pay for it. When we get into the subject itself, I start by listening aggressively. "What are you going to do with it? What is it for? What does that mean? Tell me about it; tell me a story." "Tell me a story," is a good approach. Really get interested in what they're saying. Don't be thinking about it as a search topic. Think about the role it's going to play. Get them talking in their own terms, as though they are talking to a colleague, not talking to you as if you were a different order of being. Your client may be an expert and you may be a layperson, but be an *intelligent* layperson. Be someone interested in a wide range of topics and who can understand just about anything if carefully explained.

How do you negotiate a search budget?

I listen to the question and make mental notes on what kinds of sources I will need to use. I have rough rules of thumb about how pricey certain databases might be and how long certain kinds of searches might take. Then I estimate by guess and by golly. Quite frankly, at the end I probably kick it up by $100 in case I figured wrong. Since it's only a cap figure, if my guess was right, the client will spend less than predicted. I occasionally have taken a bath when a search cost more than the estimated maximum. I almost never have eaten actual search costs, but about once every three or four months, I see my fee eaten by my machine. One out of 15 or 20 searches gets darn close to being done for free. It's not a good business practice.

If I did as much searching as I used to, I'd probably pick up a better feel for pricing. I'm still shocked by how high online costs have gone. Occasionally I still find myself drifting into what it was like in 1985, when I left full-time searching. Suddenly it's "Cowabunga! What on earth is this bill about?" Then I start to add it up, rounding up to the minute, hit charges higher than I remembered, online displays the same price as offline prints, etc., etc. I take a bath on missed estimates every now and then for sure.

What kinds of topics do you typically search?

I search any issue having to do with public policy—national, international, defense, business, private sector, anything. I have two absolute rules of thumb, however, two exclusions. I will not do chemical searching and I will not do patent searching. No way, José. Outside of that, I'm an old country searcher, I'll try anything once.

Do you use anything like a search intake form?

No, and I hate them. I find them restrictive. They're crutches—*glass* crutches; if you put any weight on them, they crumble. They're mostly used in environments in which people are passing searches on to third parties, which in itself is a very, very bad idea. It's easy enough to make a mistake when you're the searcher who's talked to a client. Making mistakes with clients you *haven't* spoken to is almost a foregone conclusion. I think that search request forms inhibit conversation, and the essence of my reference interview approach is conversational. If the client is present and sees you filling in a form, the process immediately becomes formal. You find yourself trying to get people to stop talking about those !@#$%@#$% keywords and start talking about their real information needs.

Always take rough notes while you're talking to the client. If necessary, you can fill in a search form afterwards. Even then they sometimes work perniciously if they lure you into feeling that filling out a perfect form means you have accomplished a major portion of the search assignment when, of course, you haven't even started. For example, some forms designed for internal reporting have sections for "databases selected"—as though an initial selection could possibly reflect all the databases a good searcher will use as the search blossoms. You could change your mind walking to the terminal. The machines talk to you as you search and *tell you* where else to go. "Now try this, now try that, and now try the other." How can you limit yourself with an arbitrary form numbering database selections from one to ten? How do I know before I start if I'm going to need ten databases or 200? Let's see how it goes. I'm a grasshopper searcher, and I like it. I don't like those darn forms.

However, I do think that searchers should log search requests for purposes of managing the search operation. I also agree that the forms may be a necessary evil in cases where you have staff gathering questions in off-hours for professional searchers working regular shifts or whatever.

If the same file is up on more than one system, what determines where you search it?

Generally speaking, ease of use and retrieval power are the main factors. If there's a marked price difference, then of course I would switch. If, for example, I thought that full text was a little bit cheaper on DIALOG—and I know DIALOG better—but Mead had the ability to do certain things to manipulate text output, and a particular search really needed certain system features, I'd be on Mead in a New York minute. So, in a sense, it's the ease with which I can get to the right information. If that means I have to pull out an old piece of documentation or take a quick look at a system's cheat sheet or whatever, to refresh my memory, that's fine.

Do you plan your search strategy on paper?

It may be a little absolutist to say I never write down strategies. I do make notes to myself of certain key elements to follow up on. You know, there are some files that you could search in your sleep. Occasionally there are files you don't use often enough to avoid researching, or ones that require special slanting to cover a particular angle of a search, or ones you may or may not need to search at all if you find enough. So just as a reminder, I write down the key information—file names or numbers, field tags, special codes, key descriptors, and so forth—to avoid scrambling around looking for documentation while I'm online. Beyond that, I don't plan a strategy in advance except in my head.

Once you're online, how do you build the search itself?

It depends on the question. The first decision you have to make is your basic tactical assessment of what kind of question you're involved with, what kind of terrain you're in, and what factor ultimately drives the search? By what "drives" it, I mean, what is the most critical factor in the search process—the quality of the information, the price or maybe the turnaround? Does cost control dominate, or a need for *totally* comprehensive information? The searcher makes that assessment first, and it will usually dictate the approach. If you're going for cost control, for example, you've got to shoot for the bull's eye, grab whatever you can, and then run like a bunny to get out of there.

What about full text; do you have any tips or techniques to share?

First, stay away from the AND connector. Full-text searching is phrase-making—word proximity, word order, etc. The N or NEAR, or WITH operator (on Mead), which picks up terms in any order, works much better than word-order adjacency if you're not quite sure of the terminology. And never, ever use a NOT. You have no way of knowing what you might be knocking out. In fact, in most searching, don't use NOT.

Use KWIC (key-word-in-context) for display, and on Mead use the FOCUS command. You can use KWIC to educate yourself on terminology. Full-text searching gets so tricky because you're searching natural language text. Any writer can express a concept in a multitude of ways. Someone's first name in a biographical dictionary may be William, but their first name in a full-text article may be Bill or Senator or CEO. I spoke with a guy who's a mystery novelist. He used to work for the CIA but now he writes spy books. He told me that after a while, in reading stories on himself, he started thinking "ex-CIA" was part of his name. Actually, those tags can be good shortcuts for a searcher aware that they're being used. Looking at records in KWIC format can show you what words are usually associated with the term that drove your interest in the article in the first place.

Do you do a lot of multifile searching?

I do in certain areas, as long as I know it's controlled and that I'm looking at all apples. I don't want any oranges, peaches or vegetables mixed in there. I don't want mixtures in format or files with widely different levels of indexing. For example, I don't want one big pack of databases that all use Library of Congress subject headings mixed with three others that use a completely different thesaurus or none at all.

Indexing in most newspaper files, for instance, is very superficial and weighted toward one area's interests, as one might expect. Some don't have any descriptors at all. Normally you use descriptors to narrow search strategies that pull too many results. When you reach the point where the search switches from relevance to precision focus, where you are willing to throw out an occasional baby to get rid of too much bath water, you can usually use indexing terms to filter for major stories the indexers caught. Even then you must remember about the mummy's curse, accidentally date-limiting search results to after the date a descriptor was introduced. Then, of course, there's the issue of indexer inconsistency. In any case, you can't rely on descriptors in multifile newspaper searches.

Do you use controlled vocabulary more in the sci-tech field than in news and business?

Of course. In the sci-tech databases, you can use a thesaurus to identify correct scientific terminology, not to mention spelling. The exception to the sci-tech-only rule has always been Predicasts. The only documentation that grasshopper Quint has ever kept right with the system manuals was the Predicasts code book. The product and event codes are useful and targeted. The cascaded geographic codes are a great idea.

How do you refine a search? What thought process do you go through when you've gotten too much? How do you generalize when you've gotten too little?

Well, some of it is just on automatic pilot—descriptors, current material only, and English language only. After that you start getting cute. You might make a format judgment. If we've got to get the document and we're cutting it pretty close on time, let's take whatever's in full text. Or we might take whatever has an abstract over whatever doesn't.

After you've made those broad cuts, you should look at what you've found. Decide whether you need to make little searches out of a big one. Consider whether you should take it apart, regroup, and figure out which elements of your initial search goal have been met and which are still missing. You may not have covered key factors like a European angle, the technical side versus the business side, or the private sector aspect of a public policy decision. After this assessment, I tend to target some key files for the missing elements and revise search strategies for specific angles. Basically, I start plugging gaps. I take that responsibility on myself, because clients often don't *see* the gaps. I don't want to give clients search results with whole chunks missing.

What I really prefer to do, but rarely can, is go back to the client and say "Okay, here's my bag full of goodies. Now let's figure out what the missing piece is." I tell clients over and over, "Online is a well that always has water in it. You can always go back. Let's not spend all your money on Day One. Let's hold some back and use it slower but longer." Unfortunately, clients get swamped or run out of money, and just take what they get the first time.

Are there ever times when you feel that you have to force the issue, that you *must* consult with the client in the middle of a search?

Yes, when I find nothing. Or when I find so much stuff and can't figure out why. Then I may back off and go back to the client and tell him, "Okay, here's a sample of titles, just titles, look at how much stuff there is! You told me there wouldn't be that much." Once a client gave me a topic, "iatrogenics," and told me it was a brand-new field with nothing written on it. Even though the client was a medical researcher, a physician, married to another M.D., with a double Ph.D., I still argued. "Come on, this is MEDLINE we're talking about. There's no medical topic so new that MEDLINE wouldn't catch it, no way." The challenge got me the search assignment, but he stood behind me watching with a slight sneer while I entered "iatrogenics." Up to the screen jumps over 1000 hits for the last three years alone. When we narrowed it to descriptors it dropped to 800. Major descriptor status dropped it to 240. "Well now," I said to him, "Can you think of any way to cut it further?" He regrouped and got back to me later.

That would be an example of when you would have to go to the client to get more parameters to refine or expand a search. Sometimes, a client has focused so much on one aspect that they didn't realize a topic has applications in other areas. When you point it out, they may have no interest in the new angle at all. Conversely, they may be very excited and even want to increase the search budget to chase the new data. In fact, some people, when they find out you can get peripheral material, only want that. "Now that I think about it, I've got a lot of the mainline stuff already, but this work that's coming from Outer Mongolia is great."

Is it usually obvious to you when a search is done?

The first criterion is: I've just run out of money. Ninety percent of the time you stop a search because you have run out of money. You hardly ever run out of data. But in the days when I had more unlimited budgets, I would stop a search when it looped back on itself, when I started reading references I had seen already.

The criterion of diminishing returns has value, but it is a dangerous rule to apply rigidly. Often the reason you come back on yourself is not because your strategy has elicited everything there is out there, but because all the sources you're using are covering the same material. What you actually should be doing is regrouping and thinking, "Okay, now, let's take another look at this. Let's look for a whole new category of sources—new subjects, different formats, different geographic areas, and so forth. Let's pick up those areas that *aren't* covered in the files we've been checking."

If I do a sci-tech search and start to loop, I may take the same subjects through some business files. If I still find I'm looping, *then* I figure the subject has tapped out. If you can go into different files with a different focus and still not come up with any original information, then stop.

How do you deliver search results to clients?

My favorite is fax, especially e-mail with a fax delivery option. It's fast, and it allows me to upload results electronically. I can send my bill right along with it. Also, it forces me to make some critical judgments. I hate throwing stuff away, especially something that's been paid for. But the fax forces you to be more discriminating and to pick out what's good, because you can't send 40 pages of fax. What I often do is mail the remainder. If I really think there's good stuff being left on the ground, I mail it with pleasure.

How about the output itself? How much cleanup do you do? Do you strip out codes or do any editing on that level?

I do it all the time. I assess it on an individual client basis. I figure if there's nothing the client can do with the information, all I'm doing is piling up paper. Standard cleanup for me is stripping out CODENs and ISSNs. I usually strip out descriptors unless there's something meaty in them. Often I strip record number positioning, the number-1-out-of-5 kind of stuff. I only give the client what he can *do* something with. For example, if he wants to read the article, he needs the name of the journal.

There are certain bibliographic rules of the road that even I obey. I do like to give the source. I like the person to know where the stuff came from. It didn't come from God. They should know who carries the copyright. Outside of that, I go straight for the information they're paying for.

The cover letter is critical, especially in an information brokering situation. You have to reinforce what the client asked you to do and confirm what you did. If you want to, you can go into detail about which files you searched. But there are two things you've got to include in that cover letter. First, is a pointer to what, in your opinion, is important—you have to indicate why you put asterisks next to certain items. You have to tell them to look at the material from this particular database, because that's the hot stuff. You might even give them a brief synopsis of what you think you found. The second element you have to include is any critical limitations of the search. "This search did *not* cover...We did *not* get a chance to look at...We have *not* done such-and-such...This material only updates annually, therefore it does *not* have materials later than..." All the critical elements have to go in that cover letter.

The cover letter is also your chance to indicate the value you've added. "Value-added" does not just mean that you've got a password and know how to use the search language. It also means that you've got a certain amount of CPU between your ears and that you have applied it on your client's behalf. You have used your judgment to provide a quality job. Whether you work in a library or as an information broker, all searchers have a professional mission and a duty in an ethical sense. We're professional informationists. Our business is information. We must keep clients from hurting themselves by attributing more reliability to key information than it actually has.

Tell me what you love about searching. Then tell me about your nightmares.

Sometimes when I've been away from searching for a while, I physically want to touch the keyboard. I hunger for a search. My fingers start to twitch. Then when I sit down to do a search and really get rolling, there is a sense of being a pianist, of being somebody whose fingers twiddle over the keys and magically information is summoned. Occasionally, this leads to the nightmare part. It's like the sorcerer's apprentice sequence from *Fantasia*. On a good day, you wave an arm and the violins soar, and you wave again and the brass comes in. In the next sequence, the waves wash over you and sweep you to disaster, leaving you praying to make it safely to the offline state.

The best time is when you feel really clever. When a client gives you an impossible task, even one they don't think you can answer, and you pull it off with a smirk...that's sublime. It's like an open challenge to the world, "There's nothing you can't ask that my machines and I can't answer." I just love it. That's the zen of it.

The purest zen experience I ever had happened at Rand when a gang of researchers dropped in with what they clearly thought was an impossible search. They had a project under an National Institutes of Health research grant that operated under NIH's rigorous rules for medical research. One of the rules forbade discarding materials or substances used in the research until the project was over. Researchers had to retain research material for the duration of the project, I assume so that the work could be replicated or verified. The specific project involved studying the impact of drug education programs on drug usage among teenagers in New York and Connecticut. To verify whether or not drugs were used after a drug education program, the researchers analyzed samples of spit.

So, according to the NIH grant rules, they had to retain all the spit. Now, these guys usually did paper research; they never worked in a laboratory environment. Suddenly, out of the blue, they had all these vials of spit all over the place. I can just imagine them sitting around their offices trying to figure out what to do, and then remembering the library tour where we regularly challenged all comers to give us any problem to solve. Ha, ha! Anyway down they came and asked me, "Okay, you say you can do anything. What do we do with this spit?"

I looked at them and said, "Well, let's just walk down to the computer." While I wracked my brains, we walked to the terminal where I realized I had *no* idea of how to solve this problem. My mind was blank. So I thought, "Let's see what we can do. Let's look at this as a problem of pure logic. All I have is this structure of facts and goals. Out of this structure must come strategy, so let's think through the logic. First, they are asking for a service to be performed. Services are performed by institutions that sell services. Therefore it's a commercial services directory problem. But what directory? Well, storing spit can't be too big a business, let's try the broadest directory, the Electronic Yellow Pages (now known as D&B's Electronic Business Directory)."

"Okay, I've got my database selection, now what do I do? Well, what do I know? I know it must be in a specific geographic area. Okay, we'll put in geographic descriptors—city name, zip code, and whatever. That's one building block. The third thing I know is that they want something stored. So I entered all the terms I could think of for that concept—storing, storage, inventory, warehousing, and whatever. The last thing I know is what they want to store—spit. What does spit mean to the database? Well, break it down to its components. What is the nature of spit? A little voice came back and said, 'Spit is organic; spit spoils.' So how do you deal with something that's organic and spoils? You have to keep it from spoiling. And how do you do this? By making it cold."

I entered all the terms I could think of for cold—refrigerated, ice, chilled, etc.—I put the whole strategy in. Out jumped three addresses and phone numbers for refrigerated warehouses in the New York/Connecticut area. "Any other questions?" I asked. They didn't reply, but they did cross themselves before they left...I had done a little praying myself.

Nightmare searches are the ones that make me wish I hadn't taken up this business. The worst searches are the ones where you know you are going too far and you pass the point of no return. You have desperately tried everything you can come up with. You are now into the second or third tier of ever-less-likely databases, and you still haven't found anything. By now you have spent so much money on trying to find *something* that you're too scared to go home and tell your client. You're out there in the middle of the night. You know that the longer you stay, the worse it's going to get. It's like being a kid scared to go home and tell mama about losing something, so he stays out looking until he adds the sin of staying out late to his list of crimes. After a while you start thinking, maybe you should just change your name and never go home again. Everything goes from bad to worse just like a nightmare. You know you should have stopped after the first two or three stabs didn't work. Now you've spent so much that you're scared to stop spending and you're scared to go on spending, so you're trapped.

I had one search early on at Rand, though, that I think burned the ultimate fear out of me. We had to search on this grim, cruddy, offline batch-processing system that shall remain nameless. The client wanted something on processing intelligence data, not the details of the automation but the theoretical, analytical and intellectual principles. We couched the strategy very, very carefully in our request. We used lots of caveats since it was a batch-processing job where you got no feedback, just the output. If we were lucky, we thought we might get half a dozen references of which one or two might prove relevant. Instead, back came this search weighing 35 pounds on a *cart*.

The search service had just put in the word "intelligence" and let 'er rip. We had monkeys, we had goats, we had dolphins, we had intelligent life on other planets, we had quality of instruction depending on the intelligence of military trainers, and we had every listing of the word "intelligence" in the entire database. But get this—fatal error—we actually hauled this horror up to the poor client. Obviously we should have gone through it ourselves, or just thrown it out. But we were embarrassed, and it went up to him, and this client—new on the staff—must have thought that he was getting charged for library services by the pound. He went through the whole thing, all 35 pounds, and found three pertinent hits, none of which he wanted. I felt like going on bended knee to him. "Please, mister, you weren't really supposed to *use* that."

What I should have had the courage to do, even then, and what I *have* had the courage to do ever after, was to say, "I don't care if we ordered it for him. Destroy it." The incident made me realize how alien clients may consider "library" material and how they will trudge through reference material with more patience than they should. I've come to realize that it's my responsibility to make sure that nothing we do compounds the problem by wasting the client's time as well as his money. It's like the Hippocratic oath says, "First, do no harm."

What has always bothered me about information systems is that you occasionally *do* see them do harm. That's one reason why I'm so vociferous about the issue of quality control. There are cases when somebody can actually come out with less information than they walked in with. Or they can come out distrusting the information they walked in with, even though it's perfectly valid. For whatever reason, if something doesn't show up in a database, the client may think the references they have in their hand are false. Sometimes they are, but more often it's the database or the search strategy that is at fault. You have to use good judgment in dealing with databases and clients. One thing I've learned as a searcher is to use your own best judgment. It's all you've got, so you're going to have to go with it. And, relying on your judgment in situations where you have something at risk is the only way to develop better judgment.

SUPER SEARCH SECRETS

On the reference interview...
    ...I start by listening aggressively...."Tell me a story," is a good approach. Really get interested in what they're saying....Be someone interested in a wide range of topics and who can understand just about anything if carefully explained.

On search request forms...
    ...I hate them. I find them restrictive....I think that search request forms inhibit conversation, and the essence of my reference interview approach is conversational. If the client is present and sees you filling in a form, the process immediately becomes formal.

On database selection...
    The machines talk to you as you search and tell you where else to go.

On selecting a system for a search...
    ...ease of use and retrieval power are the main factors. If there's a marked price difference, then of course I would switch....it's the ease with which I can get to the right information.

On full-text searching...

...stay away from the AND connector....The N or NEAR, or WITH operator (on Mead), which picks up terms in any order, works much better than word-order adjacency....And never, ever use a NOT. You have no way of knowing what you might be knocking out....Use KWIC (key-word-in-context) for display, and on Mead use the FOCUS command.

On documentation...

The only documentation that grasshopper Quint has ever kept right with the system manuals was the Predicasts code book. The product and event codes are useful and targeted. The cascaded geographic codes are a great idea.

On delivery of search results...

My favorite is fax, especially e-mail with a fax delivery option. It's fast, and it allows me to upload results electronically....it forces me to make some critical judgments....the fax forces you to be more discriminating and to pick out what's good, because you can't send 40 pages of fax.

On the cover letter...

The cover letter is critical, especially in an information brokering situation. You have to reinforce what the client asked you to do and confirm what you did....The cover letter is also your chance to indicate the value you've added.

On searching...

...I physically want to touch the keyboard. I hunger for a search. My fingers start to twitch....when I sit down to do a search and really get rolling, there is a sense of being a pianist, of being somebody whose fingers twiddle over the keys and magically information is summoned.

CHAPTER 17

ELLEN REINHEIMER: SEARCHING AS INSTINCT

At the time of this interview, Ellen Reinheimer was Director of Research at Research on Demand in Berkeley, California. Research on Demand was formerly the research department of Information On Demand, the pioneering independent research and document delivery company founded by Sue Rugge. Reinheimer is currently Director of Research at Information First, an independent research firm in Alameda, California.

What did you do before you arrived at Research on Demand, and where along the way did you learn how to search?

Before Research on Demand, I was at a large law firm in San Francisco for about three years, and then in the central library at Bechtel Corporation, an international engineering construction firm. I did a lot of searching before I came to Research on Demand, which was then known as IOD, Information On Demand. But I don't think I *really* learned how to search until I came to Information On Demand.

What's your search environment like in terms of hardware and communications software?

The searchers each have their own PC. We do a lot of our own word processing, too. We use PROCOMM Plus for telecommunications. We don't have any dedicated packages like DIALOGLINK, although we're looking into that. We're considering buying Trademarkscan on CD-ROM, and if we did there would be some applications for DIALOGLINK.

What kind of clients do you serve?

There's an incredible range. There are some very large companies and many individuals, also. We work with a lot of small business people, and people writing business plans for start-up companies. We do a lot with marketing types in large corporations. We occasionally do overflow searching for corporate libraries. We work for people in corporations in other countries who don't know how to get the information they need and don't have an established in-house information center. We have clients who do have a good corporate information center but who come to us with a project that is outside the expertise of that group. Sometimes they want an independent audit of information that they've gotten through that unit.

Do most of your clients contact you by phone?

Yes, although we do get quite a bit by fax, especially from established clients, or as the initial contact by a new client. Sometimes, after a 15- or 20-minute phone call, we'll ask them to summarize what they're looking for and to write it up and fax it to us. We find that that's a pretty good discipline for a lot of people. It forces them to think about what they're asking.

What do you ask in that 20-minute phone conversation? What goes on between you and the client?

The first pass with a new client is to find out how much they know about online searching. Sometimes people think they know quite a bit, but they have some erroneous assumptions that can get in the way. We tell them a little bit about what's available that would address their subject area. That sometimes stimulates the conversation. We try to find out what their end purpose is without making them feel that we're being too nosy. It's critical to know as much as you can about what they're hoping to accomplish.

When I was at Information On Demand, about 80 percent of all projects involved at least some online searching, if only as a point of departure. Does that statistic still hold?

I'd say it's higher than that now. It's the rare project that has no online component. That's probably a function of the new sources that have come online in the last few years. There's also a geographic factor. We used to feel that we had to be right next to the University of California campus because we'd go there all the time. That was a guiding principle whenever we looked for new office space. That's no longer the case, especially now that we're no longer doing document delivery from this office. We've moved about four or five miles from campus, and we only have to go there once a month or so. But it does mean that we look things up online that we might have gone to campus for in the past.

How do you keep track of projects?

We use a search request form that captures all the background information on the topic, what sources they've already checked, any language or date limitations, deadline, budget, that sort of thing. That form is usually filled out by me or by the person who's going to do the project. We also have a service inquiry form, a pre-search form, that is often filled out by an administrative assistant or marketing person. That form might contain preliminary notes about the project that we attach to the actual search form for backup and verification.

We also keep a manual search log, where we record projects as they come in. It's often helpful to compare that with our client database. For that, we use a project management package called MasterBuilder, which comes from the construction sector. It works pretty well for us. We can record descriptions of what we did, as well as costs and billing and payment information.

How do you estimate costs and negotiate a budget for a search?

We used to break out labor and costs, but we don't quote a labor rate any longer. We just quote a flat fee for the search. We don't itemize anything on the invoice. We find that gives us a little more flexibility in terms of how we attack the search.

Some of the obvious things that go through my mind when I'm trying to come up with an overall estimate are: What company are they looking at? Is it IBM or some tiny company I've never heard of? Is it a very heavily-discussed subject, or is it something where we're going to have to dig a little bit, or a lot? If it involves getting company names and addresses only, some kind of a mailing list search, we have to go in and get the number of hits before we can give a reasonable quote. That's something we do on spec. In fact, we do more searching on spec under this type of pricing structure than we used to. With many projects, especially for new clients, I will do a tiny bit of looking around to get some idea of the size of the beast. If it's something simple, a company name search or something like that, where I just want to get a feel for the number of hits, I use DIALINDEX.

How do you track online costs? Do you compare your records of what you've spent to the search service invoices when they come in?

We used to keep a log at the terminal, with a section for each online service. We'd record the project, the client, the files we searched and the total cost for each session. Now, each researcher has an individual log, and they track the costs for all the systems they use. We typically list the system, the date, and the total cost. I look over the DIALOG bill to see if anything looks vastly out of whack, but that's all I do. I do check the other system invoices more closely, especially the ones that don't give you an exact cost total when you log off, to make sure that we've calculated it correctly.

What are some typical projects?

I like to look back through the search log. It blows my mind what one page will show; it's all over the place. The market for rubber gloves; the market for fill-in-the-blank. We do a lot of that kind of search. We run a current awareness search, an SDI, with regular updates, on extremely low-frequency radiation. That's an interesting one because it ranges across all kinds of literature, and we run it in a huge number of databases. We did a search on the outer continental shelf. The client wanted *anything* having to do with the outer continental shelf. It was incredibly cross-disciplinary; we went into dozens of databases. The classic one was on canine hip dysplasia. That was our longest-running SDI. Eventually, I got a lovely note from the owner of the dog saying, "Thank you for all the help over the years. Gypsy lived a long and wonderful life." And she enclosed a picture of the dog.

We run all of our SDIs in-house rather than storing them on DIALOG and having the service run them for us when the files are updated. Our experience has been that a lot of the strategies change from month to month. Either the client wants to add or delete something, or the terminology in the databases changes. We save the search strategies online, especially if they are long, but we have to modify them fairly often. I do one on forklifts for a company in Japan. I run it every two weeks, and it changes every two weeks. Very few of our SDIs are like the canine hip dysplasia one, where it's a relatively simple search. It's stored, and you just run it that way forever. We still bill for SDIs at a lower rate than we do for custom searches. It means that we might not make as much money on them, but it's also nice to know that you have that steady business. A major current awareness search every two weeks is a nice piece of business. It builds good client relations, too.

What online services and databases do you use the most?

We use DIALOG and LEXIS/NEXIS heavily. We also use STN and DataTimes. The databases we use depend on the subject matter, of course, but PROMT is an excellent source for a lot of what we do. It seems to fill the bill most of the time. I really like using the PAPERS file on DIALOG, too. It gives you a broad-brush perspective, and you can post-qualify, if you get too much, to just the major papers or just a certain region. That's really helpful.

How do you plan your search strategies?

I make notes, but I don't write out the whole strategy *per se*. I really do like having access to printed documentation, and I make a point of annotating it and keeping it up-to-date. I almost always look at the database documentation before I do a search. I check just to see what sources address the subject area that I might have forgotten about, what the coverage is, what the searchable fields are, that sort of thing. I write down little oddities or features that I think I might use, like the available LIMIT options in DIALOG, for instance. I might write down the terms or codes I'll start with.

I like the building blocks metaphor, but I don't start out by building a structure in my mind. I might have building blocks—whether they're search terms or date limits or language limits—but I might not know exactly how they're going to fit together. I've got a pile of those components that I might use, but they're off to the side until I need them. I have a picture in my head of how a search is likely to unfold, but I don't know how it's going to fit together until I'm actually doing it. It's an intuitive approach, more than a highly-structured one. It's like biofeedback.

I gather that you do a lot of full-text searching. How does your approach there differ from your approach to bibliographic searching?

I don't use controlled vocabulary, especially in newspapers, because the terms are so unevenly applied. If you were in the PAPERS collection, for instance, on DIALOG, and you wanted to search all of them at once, there's no way to smooth out those differences in keywords. It's more important, I think, to know your output options, so you can check what's going on. Look at the lead paragraph, or the paragraphs where your terms appear. The KWIC format is indispensable.

My searching behavior has really changed since the advent of full text. I download a lot more, and I do a lot more browsing of large quantities of records than I used to. With downloading as opposed to direct printing or ordering offline prints, there's a much higher tolerance for retrieving irrelevant material. You can always edit out the bad stuff. Of course, the way pricing trends are going, with the online systems charging more for each item you retrieve, downloading vast quantities may be something that you won't want to do too much of in the future.

What do you do if you've done a search and nothing turns up?

It depends on the subject matter, whether I believe it or not. There have been times when I have simply accepted that there's nothing there. Clients occasionally ask us to perform searches where they are virtually certain in advance that there's nothing there. Sometimes they tell us that when they give us the search, sometimes not. I've had people react ecstatically when I've gotten back to them with nothing. When I worked for a law firm, that was the *modus operandi* for a lot of searches. That's what they wanted. As for not finding anything when I expect something, I check the obvious things, like spelling. That's sometimes a problem, especially with regular clients, where you may not spend as much time dotting the i's and crossing the t's, and—lo and behold—they have something spelled wrong, or you heard it wrong. There is potential for miscommunication.

I have two cautionary tales in that area, myself:

A client left a message on my answering machine asking for a search on Gatorade. I'd actually begun planning the search in my mind when it occurred to me to wonder why an electronics manufacturer wanted to know about beverages. It turned out that they were looking for information on "gate arrays."

Don Ray, who's an investigative reporter in Los Angeles, told about another one, where a journalist was invited to talk about breast feeding in South Africa. "Well," he thought, there are all kinds of problems involving malnutrition and so on; I can address that, though it's not really my area. So he went, and was on the podium starting his talk, and the moderator began tugging on his jacket and whispering "Not *breast feeding—press freedom!*"

Considering that you no longer itemize your labor costs, how do you decide how much time to spend on a search? When are you finished?

That's individual to the researcher, but personally, I try to be conscious of that point where I'm not getting very much in the way of new results. As Director of Research, I have to look over the researchers' shoulders sometimes, because they tend to want to continue with what they're doing longer than they should from a cost-effectiveness standpoint. But you also know that you're not going to be able to realize the same profit on every search, so you can't make a hard-and-fast rule. Every project is different. It's partly a matter of budget and partly a matter of the individual client. Sometimes you'll do more for an existing good client than you will for someone who is going to use you once, has an extremely limited budget, or is going to be a pain to deal with.

It's amazing how often those three factors occur in combination. How quickly do you turn projects around?

Sometimes the same day. Some clients use us regularly for a certain type of search. They'll call it in in the morning and expect the results by three or four in the afternoon. But our standard line is still seven to ten days from start to finish. Depending on the project, that's usually a fair amount of time to get it into the queue and get someone working on it.

Do you order offline prints? What kind of post-processing do you do?

Almost never. We download directly, or occasionally order prints by electronic mail. Every two or three months, we might order paper prints offline. We did that not long ago on a very large search. It was an academic subject, and the client wanted absolutely everything. It was a true "dump" of three or four databases, and we did have it printed out for them. The post-processing on something of that size would have been hideous. We knew that we wouldn't be editing anything out or adding any analysis, so we just ordered offline prints.

Typically, though, we get the results in electronic form, and we do quite a bit of post-processing. We get rid of the records we don't want, bold the titles, and put in page breaks. Sometimes, if it's a collection of newspaper articles, say, we use WordPerfect to pull out the highlights and create an index or table of contents. If you highlight the title, for instance, as you create the document, the software assigns the correct page number and puts in the little header and that sort of thing. Some clients like to scan the titles of the articles, and they'll say, "Oh great, page 16, go right to that one; it looks perfect." That saves us from having to say something in the cover letter about "Note the article on page 16..."

Post-processing can be a really lengthy and time-consuming process. We've gone back and forth, trying to decide whether the researcher or an administrative assistant should be most heavily involved in it. We always come back to the conclusion that the researcher should be doing most of it because of the editorial function that goes along with it. They have to decide which records are relevant, and as long as they're stripping out irrelevant records, they might as well go ahead and do the rest of it. We often write an executive summary, and the more familiar you get with the material as you go along, the better that summary turns out.

Do you keep a record of the searches that you've done?

We keep a printout. We still call it "the flimsy," from the days when we used dumb terminals with that thermal paper. We toggle the capture buffer on and off during the search; everybody seems to do that differently. But we do keep a record of the cost information and the strategy, and print it out and file it with the search form. I think it's easiest to access the whole picture if you have it in print and it's attached to the search form. We refer back to old printouts fairly often, to update a search, or to answer a question from the client about what happened or didn't happen. The results themselves we keep about a month, just in case there are questions or the client says he never received them or something, before we get rid of them.

Do you ask for feedback from the client after you've sent the search out?

We used to make a follow-up call after every search. We haven't had time to do that routinely for quite a while. We certainly expect clients who have a question or a problem to get in touch with us. Sometimes a marketing person will take a batch of searches from a month or two ago, and call the clients and ask some general questions about whether they were satisfied, whether it was what they expected.

Do you send an invoice with the project?

No, but usually shortly thereafter. We try to do an invoice run every Friday. So it's often just a day or two behind the search, and never more than a week. Some clients do want the invoice with the search, in which case we just run a separate invoice for them.

Do you have any tips we haven't touched on yet for more efficient and cost-effective searching?

I know what works for me. I think everyone is going to have their own favorites. People discover things on their own and then remember them because it's of particular use. In terms of saving money, I feel it's really important to know the databases you're going to use before you get online. Especially if you've never used a certain one before, you should spend fifteen minutes looking at the documentation first. I don't necessarily have to know what I'm going to do and how the search is going to play itself out, but at least I'll know what I can and can't do. I like the online documentation and help files, too. I don't look at the DIALOG bluesheets online, but I definitely check "rates" online for different output formats and the costs associated with them. I think that's essential, especially since the format options haven't all been standardized—like Format 5 doesn't give you the fullest possible record, like you'd expect it to, in every database.

What kinds of quality and usability problems have you run into?

I think INVESTEXT still has some problems, not with quality, but in the way the data has to be manipulated and how it's costed out. They're getting better at allowing you to determine what specific part of a report you want before you pay that $5 or so a page for it.

In terms of quality, we have to explain to clients all the time about problems in the Dun & Bradstreet databases. Directory files, in general, are really problematic. It may be getting worse instead of better, as the database producers become more competitive and try to add not only more records, but more information to each record. I hear from clients who have done a mailing and had 20 percent returned because addresses are wrong. It's hard to make them understand that the database producers are the ones at fault. Of course, some of that is the nature of directories, in general; they're out-of-date even before they're published. We sort of hedge, routinely, on directory-type projects. We really try to tell people in advance that there's a high percentage of inaccuracy.

Database producers and online services, in general, are getting better at trying to let us know what's in the database and what it's lacking, but the actual quality of the data is something I don't think is getting better. That's true of directory databases particularly, but not exclusively. Some bibliographic databases have bad data. There are a lot of faulty citations. I know that from ordering documents that we turned up in a search, and having Information On Demand's document delivery department tell us that the volume, date or page number was wrong.

It's an interesting issue because we're starting to hold database producers much more accountable than we have print publishers for the quality of their data. People don't expect everything they read in books to be accurate. We expect to have to exercise a certain amount of critical judgment. But we expect databases to be perfect, I guess because of that aura of infallibility that computers had when they first came out.

What do you think makes a good searcher? Why are *you* still in this business?

I also do crossword puzzles. People think a certain way and enjoy a certain type of activity. For me, searching never loses its appeal; it's always interesting. There is a puzzle aspect to it, a working-out aspect. I enjoy it much more than I do the administrative part of my job. In my position, I get to say which searches I want to do, so the ones that look really terrible, really messy, I can give to someone else. Then I can stay a safe distance away and just give them the benefit of my advice.

I've seen some people try to approach searching from a very organized, lock-step, linear point of view. Those people seldom understand the process, and ultimately don't do very well at it. You have to be willing to accept the branching kind of process that happens when you get involved in a search. It's not going to be linear. There is a kind of feedback loop involved. You have to base whatever you do next on what you've already seen. That presumes that you've got your eyes open, and your eyes are going to be *wider* open if you don't have a preconception about what's going to happen. That can be difficult to learn, if it doesn't come to you instinctively.

One of my classic examples is a terrible 200-set search I did for fighter aircraft parts in Commerce Business Daily. Just about all the terms were part numbers for fighter aircraft; we were looking for all the notices of someone wanting to buy those kinds of parts. I did some truncating because some were part number such-and-such-A and some were the same number such-and-such-B. So I put the whole search together and ran it, and I could not figure out why I got the results I did. I got lots of records having something to do with military aircraft, all from the same Air Force base in Kansas, but none of them had any of the parts numbers I was searching on. I finally made a paper printout and took it home and stared at it. It turned out that one of the part numbers was KS-67. What I'd pulled for those records was part of the address: "Kansas" and the start of the zip code. It was close enough, subject-wise, that I couldn't analyze it with clear eyes; it was so "almost right" that it threw me off.

That points up that you have to really look at what you're getting back, and why. It can get even more complicated than that aircraft parts example. If the statement that's causing the problem is part of a more complex search, the results from it will be mushed in with everything else. You get a few hits that are less precise and less targeted, but you can't quite figure out why. So, perhaps being able to decide what to do next, based on what you've already seen, is the most important thing about being a good searcher. The other important thing about searching is enjoying it while you're doing it.

SUPER SEARCH SECRETS

On search software...

We use PROCOMM Plus for telecommunications. We don't have any dedicated packages like DIALOGLINK...

On quoting prices and billing...

We used to break out labor and costs, but we don't quote a labor rate any longer. We just quote a flat fee for the search. We don't itemize anything on the invoice. We find that gives us a little more flexibility in terms of how we attack the search.

On favorite files and systems...

We use DIALOG and LEXIS/NEXIS heavily. We also use STN and DataTimes....PROMT is an excellent source for a lot of what we do. It seems to fill the bill most of the time. I really like using the PAPERS file on DIALOG, too.

On search strategies...

I like the building blocks metaphor, but I don't start out by building a structure in my mind. I might have building blocks...but I might not know exactly how they're going to fit together....I have a picture in my head of how a search is likely to unfold, but I don't know how it's going to fit together until I'm actually doing it. It's an intuitive approach, more than a highly structured one. It's like biofeedback.

On getting search results...

We download directly, or occasionally order prints by electronic mail. Every two or three months, we might order paper prints offline.

On post-processing...

...we do quite a bit of post-processing. We get rid of the records we don't want, bold the titles, and put in page breaks. Sometimes, if it's a collection of newspaper articles, say, we use WordPerfect to pull out the highlights and create an index or table of contents. If you highlight the title, for instance, as you create the document, the software assigns the correct page number and puts in the little header and that sort of thing....Post-processing can be a really lengthy and time-consuming process.

On quality...

Database producers and online services in general are getting better at trying to let us know what's in the database and what it's lacking, but the actual quality of the data is something I don't think is getting better. That's true of directory databases particularly, but not exclusively. Some bibliographic databases have bad data. There are a lot of faulty citations.

On searching...

There is a puzzle aspect to it, a working-out aspect....You have to be willing to accept the branching kind of process that happens when you get involved in a search. It's not going to be linear. There is a kind of feedback loop involved. You have to base whatever you do next on what you've already seen...can be difficult to learn, if it doesn't come to you instinctively.

CHAPTER 18

LEE SAPIENZA: TURNING KIDS ON TO ONLINE

Lee Sapienza is the chief librarian and information specialist at Wayland High School in Wayland, Massachusetts. Sapienza and Wayland received Dialog Information Service's First Place Award in Excellence in Online Education in 1989. The word "sapienza" means "wisdom."

What is your high school like? How does the searching program fit in there?

Wayland is quite a school. *Boston Magazine* has picked it several years in a row as one of the top ten in the area, and *Redbook* picked it this year as one of the top 16 for student academic achievement. William Bennett, the former Secretary of Education, gave it a National Award for Excellence a few years back, and he used Wayland's curriculum as one of his five models of a perfect high school curriculum.

We started going online in 1986. This year, 1993, we joined a global network of schools called International Education Research Network. They've got bulletin boards of all kinds, and we can work on projects with other schools. One school in Israel wants to work on a virtual country. They have to choose where the country is going to be located and set up a border. Then they have to write the laws. They have to set up the legal system, the economic system, and the political system. Then they have to run the country and start solving both domestic and foreign problems. What better way could we get to raise our future leaders? Kids get into problems with this country and then solve them.

That's a classroom project that the kids and the teachers work on together. All of the actual online searching goes through me. We have CD-ROM, too, but I find that CD-ROMs have a great many drawbacks. The kids have found that, too. I'll hear, "I've been on the CD-ROM, but can I go online?" It has to do with the depth and the scope of information. No school library can afford enough CD-ROMs to get the subject coverage you need.

Do a lot of these kids have computers at home?

Yes. Halfway through their search, the question arises, "Can I get this at home?" And I say "You can, but you're going to pay an awful lot," and at that point I tell them about KNOWLEDGE INDEX. We use straight DIALOG, here, in command mode. We tried menu mode—in fact, we were a beta test site for it—but menus take too long. They're a waste of time, at least in a school setting, where you don't have the luxury of time. You've got a limit of one period to work with a kid. In that short span of time, you've got to get the search explained, you've got to show him how to choose a database, and you've got to make sure he knows what he's looking for, which is the hardest thing in the world to do, because *he doesn't* know. Online searching is the best thing to come down the line in years in the educational field, because it teaches kids how to think. For the first time they have to ask themselves what it is they're really looking for.

So in effect, they have to learn how to do a reference interview *on themselves*?

That's right. Say they've been studying world cultures all year, and for their final papers they've each chosen one country. Now, they have their background information, but the teacher wants them to go online to find out the current political situation. Here is where *recently* is uppermost; nothing older than three months is going to do. The problem is that they don't know what they're looking up about the country. Chances are they will get swamped—they will get 100,000 references. When that happens, I'm ready with the next limiting factor, a date range or a subject heading or whatever, so they can see how that works instantly. It's wonderful going online with kids. They don't believe it until they actually hear the dialing of the modem. And then there's that moment when they start getting the results, and they see 100,000 hits, 200,000...

Can you tell immediately that certain kids are going to take to this like ducks to water, while others just go through the motions?

Yes. Some of them will take off on their own. It's amazing. When they go online a second time they remember, they know what to expect. They might not feel quite secure yet in drawing up a command statement, but they're ready to go. These are the same kids who, if the teacher asks them to do a research paper using print indexes, will hang over the library desk, and the conversation will go like: "I gotta do a paper on pollution." "Pollution, what kind of pollution?" "You know, pollution!" "Well, do you mean air, water, noise...?" And they'll look at me and say to themselves, "Oh, she's going to be a b-i-t-c-h." And to me they'll say, "I don't know, but when you find it I'll know." They can't get away with that if they're going online. They have to pinpoint what it is they're after.

We teach these skills very deliberately, in a couple of different ways. We did a genetic engineering unit, in which every student selected a different paper from a bibliography printed in 1983, read the paper, formulated keywords and a search strategy, and then went online to find out what had happened with that particular issue since their paper was written. Each student had something very concrete, very specific, to work with. They didn't have to spend hours trying to figure out what it was they were trying to look up. They didn't have to make a decision. All they had to do was read that article and thoroughly understand it so they could start pulling it apart for concepts.

They showed a lot of ingenuity in individualizing their research. Most weren't content to just locate current sources dealing with the same general topic as the earlier article. They got very stringent in their search requirements; if the article mentioned certain scientists, they wanted to know what those same scientists had accomplished recently. If the original dealt with genetically-improved crops and mentioned alfalfa, wheat and corn specifically, then their search had to target up-to-date citations on alfalfa, wheat and corn, not just crops in general.

These kids were literally whooping with joy when some minuscule item of information that they were desperately seeking would appear on the screen. It's marvelous what you find online, and the kids get real hyped with it. When you put a bunch of high schoolers online, you're under a lot of pressure. You've really got two missions going: one, you have to make sure that, in the limited time available, the kid finds what he needs. But you also have to make sure that kid's experience is such that he wants to come back a second time. You have to convince him that this is the way to go. You don't get a second chance. You have to get those databases to *produce* something.

What databases do you find yourself going to over and over again?
We use the newspapers constantly, for anything and everything. They're so full of the unexpected. Their hidden resources aren't apparent when you're just reading them, but they really leap out at you online. We use all of the full-text databases, like Magazine Index ASAP and Trade & Industry ASAP. Those are beautiful files for high schoolers.

We've used CENDATA for the social science/urban studies group. A couple of years ago, the kids had to pick a city and analyze the census results. But this was early in the year, and the CENDATA figures hadn't been updated. But we did find the numbers in the newspapers, along with all the discussions of the different regional issues. So they got a lot more value and analysis by going the newspaper route.

We used Donnelley Demographics for that urban studies group, too. They loved it when they found they could look up any town and find out whether more people drove to work or took the train, or how many households had kids under five.

We have a crime and criminal justice course, and for that, of course, we use NCJRS, the National Criminal Justice Reference Service. That has terrific abstracts. The social science teacher used to go nuts trying to find up-to-date criminal statistics. You've got that solved online.

You've mentioned papers several times. I'm curious about how you approach searching them, because for me, papers are the epitome of what's difficult about full-text searching.
Exactly. Papers is the big world of "everything online" that we have all yearned for. But it is full-text searching at maximum throttle. It can be treacherous. Unless your search terms are very specific or delimited by fields, it can be an exercise in absolute futility. What I advise students and teachers alike is to scan their search results in KWIC format, so they can verify relevance before downloading the full text of any record. Once they've browsed and gotten some that sound good, I tell them to limit to *long* articles, so they get in-depth analysis instead of a lot of little 500-word stories all repeating the same thing.

I also tell them about using proximity operators instead of just AND, and about limiting by date and so on. I suggest limiting to selected newspapers like one of the regional categories, or major papers only. If the topic is one of highly localized interest in the area served by a major metropolitan daily, I advise them to conduct the search in a single newspaper, like the *Boston Globe*, or to limit the search to specific sections of the newspaper, like the Business section, or to the lead paragraph.

To what degree do you teach them about differences in structure and features among different databases?
I don't do that much; I just don't have time. They do understand that certain databases have features that others don't, and that these can be very powerful. I do make them

aware that the more they know about individual databases, the easier it's going to be to either maneuver on their own later on, or to be more helpful to the searcher who goes online for them in college or in a business setting. All I can do is plant the seed.

We did do an honors chemistry unit where the kids used MEDLINE's *MeSH* descriptor codes. The subject was the medical applications of nuclear isotopes. Each student was assigned a specific isotope, and needed to find detailed information including its pharmacology, half-life, diagnostic and therapeutic uses for a specific organ of the human body, dosage, toxicity, and so on. They used a combination of *MeSH* descriptor codes and free text, and just romped through that mammoth database with gusto. This was a unit that all of us—teacher, library staff, and most of all the kids—had come to dread, and yet being able to do it online cloaked it in an environment of *fun and games*.

Do they have any problems with concepts like Boolean logic?

They get it because I show it to them on the screen. I'll say, "Now we've got to connect *this* concept with *that* concept." I'll show them how a set number has been assigned to every word. "If we're going to find this AND this, we'll get this many. If we're looking for this OR this, we're going to get a lot more." When you've shown them enough examples, they start understanding the difference.

Do you use any online services besides DIALOG?

Well, my favorite reading every month is DIALOG's *CHRONOLOG*. But we also subscribe to Dow Jones and to NewsNet. What we use depends on what we're doing. There's that nice industry cross-indexing that you can get in NewsNet. Some of the kids were studying the background of the Pilgrim Nuclear Power Plant here, and they found wonderful information in the technology newsletters on NewsNet. But what really helped was that it gave them a direct reference to the government regulatory process, and that's where all the problems were coming out. So they were able to have a full and informed discussion of the pros and cons of reopening the Pilgrim power plant. I love to watch the kids work on this sort of thing. I always proceed on the assumption that everyone is going to find what they're looking for. And usually it happens.

Do you capture or print out the search session as you go so the students have a record of what they did?

The kids get the actual articles; they have to turn them in to their teachers along with the papers or whatever they write based on them. I save the strategies myself so I can refer back to them, but usually they get thrown out with the passage of time. The kids learn more about online from the experience itself than they would from reviewing what they did. It's so vivid, so startling, so different and so successful. It really sticks with them.

That's what you need for these kids; you've got to grab them or you've lost them. Their attention span is limited because of television, where everything happens in half an hour. I give them a whole period, which is about three-quarters of an hour. We spend ten to twelve minutes, maximum, online. Mostly, we talk about what's going to happen, *how* it's going to happen, and then, *after* it happens, *what* happened, and whether we got enough of what they need.

We do kind of a postmortem, so the experience means something to them. The other thing I do is to make sure the kids realize that we're on a special classroom program; I leave the actual cost display right there for them to look at. I tell them what the school is paying. Then I show them how much time they've spent online, and how much the database costs per minute, and how much it costs to get each article. Believe me, it makes an impression when a kid sees that the school's been charged $4.57 whereas he would have been faced, ordinarily, with a bill for $64. The other day we hit $112. I tell them, "Learn how to do it well while you're in high school, because soon enough you're going to be paying real money." But, you know, I think the kid who hit $112 the other day was very proud; it was kind of a macho thing.

You can have an awful lot of fun with the kids. It's really serious to them. Remember the stock market crash back in October 1987? We were using Media General on Dow Jones News/Retrieval. They have a beautiful setup where you can compare a company against an industry, or two companies against each other, side-by-side on the screen. Each kid adopted a company, and they went online in pairs, with one representing, say, IBM, and the other representing Apple. You could see the financial profiles side-by-side, and they'd print those out and take them back to discuss in class. Well, we couldn't get online to Dow Jones for days after the market collapsed. Those kids were going nuts. All the stockbrokers were on, of course, and even though Dow Jones put on lots of extra telephones, they still couldn't get through. But it was a wonderful teaching opportunity: "See, this information is used in the *real* world."

You should have seen what happened with the San Francisco earthquake in '89. The kids were lined up, and it was hit or miss whether they were going to get through. First, DIALOG was down for almost the whole day, so I threw them into VU/TEXT and Dow Jones. But they really needed the medical databases that we were using on DIALOG, so I had to do something. They were expecting to use DIALOG and they already had their searches written out, so on the fly I had to tell them "Well, you can't use that command in Dow Jones, you have to start with //TEXT, and then type dot-dot..." That was a little disconcerting to the poor kids. DIALOG came back up rather quickly, but my high schoolers were every bit as upset as a business person would be who needed a report in a hurry.

Online has really changed the curriculum. It's even been able to cure "senioritis," the disease that afflicts seniors from early March through June each year. We had a Computer Applications course that covered advanced database theory and design. The students had had several online experiences before May when they got to the unit on local hi-tech companies. This is similar to what I was just describing; they worked in groups of two, adopting and investigating local high-tech companies, like Wang, Digital, Raytheon, Prime Computer, Kurzweil, Data General, and so on. They collected information online, saved, edited, and printed the files, found and photocopied the articles that were available in the local collection, and created notebooks from the information. They used Readers' Guide on WILSONLINE to identify magazine articles that were available in our collection. A file of our holdings was stored online on that service so the kids could AND it to their search criteria. The teacher wanted them to start with popular nonspecialist information.

The students then switched to DIALOG and searched one of the company directory databases to find addresses, ticker symbol, number of employees, sales and so on. Next, they searched Standard & Poor's Corporate Descriptions either by the ticker symbol they had already located, or by company name, for information on its history and description, its economic health, officers, founders and subsidiaries, and to determine if the company would be a good investment. The final part of the assignment was on Dow Jones

News/Retrieval, where they located daily news summaries on their specific companies and officers through the //DJNEWS service, using only the ticker symbol for access.

Each student group was responsible for both oral and written reports. The class as a whole created a database of the companies to hold all of the information they'd retrieved, each group being responsible for the entries on its particular company. Each team of students used this information to produce a spreadsheet giving a financial picture of the company, and a graphed version. Finally, they transferred the report, the spreadsheet, and the graph into a word processor and produced their own "company reports" to be sent, theoretically, to the stockholders.

The kids had to access the services of three different vendors. Since the class was composed mostly of seniors, the teacher offered an additional incentive to avoid the hazard of "senioritis." The group that did all the online searches the fastest and most efficiently would be exempt from the final written report. Boy, did that work! Some of them came in with "crib sheets" with step-by-step procedures written out in full, so they could move from one service to another with a minimum loss of time. They were really in earnest. The winning search time, including downloading, was 16 minutes; the slowest was 28 minutes, which isn't too shabby, either.

What do you find most fulfilling about working with kids the way you do?

The best part is seeing them put in one search term and come up with a dozen absolutely perfect articles, and seeing how they whoop and holler when that happens. I bounce out of that computer room time after time after time. My staff sees me. I'll be way up on cloud nine even though I'm in there hour after hour, going through one search after another. It's always as much of a thrill as it was the first time. The whole answer, in one word, is *discovery*.

SUPER SEARCH SECRETS

On teaching kids about online...

You've got a limit of one period to work with a kid....you've got to get the search explained, you've got to show him how to choose a database, and you've got to make sure he knows what he's looking for, which is the hardest thing in the world to do, because *he doesn't* know. Online searching is the best thing to come down the line in years in the educational field, because it teaches kids how to think.

On teaching search strategies...

...every student selected a different paper from a bibliography printed in 1983, read the paper, formulated keywords and a search strategy, and then went online to find out what had happened with that particular issue since their paper was written.

On favorite databases...

We use the newspapers constantly, for anything and everything. They're so full of the unexpected. Their hidden resources aren't apparent when you're just reading them, but they really leap out at you online. We use all of the full-text databases, like Magazine Index ASAP and Trade & Industry ASAP. Those are beautiful files for high schoolers.

On searching newspapers...

Papers is the big world of "everything online" that we have all yearned for. But it is full-text searching at maximum throttle. It can be treacherous. Unless your search terms are very specific or delimited by fields, it can be an exercise in absolute futility. I advise students and teachers alike to scan their search results in KWIC format, so they can verify relevance before downloading the full text of any record. Once they've browsed and gotten some that sound good, I tell them to limit to *long* articles, so they get in-depth analysis...

On teaching Boolean logic...

...I'll say, "Now we've got to connect *this* concept with *that* concept." I'll show them how a set number has been assigned to every word. "If we're going to find this AND this, we'll get this many." If we're looking for this OR this, we're going to get a lot more.

On search costs...

I leave the actual cost display right there...I tell them what the school is paying. Then I show them how much time they've spent online, and how much the database costs per minute, and how much it costs to get each article....a kid sees that the school's been charged $4.57 whereas he would have been faced, ordinarily, with a bill for $64. The other day we hit $112. I tell them, "Learn how to do it well while you're in high school, because soon enough you're going to be paying real money."

CHAPTER 19

BONNIE SNOW: ONLINE IDEALIST

Bonnie Snow is Director of the MidAtlantic District for Dialog Information Services. She is a medical search specialist and co-editor of CADUCEUS, the column on medical and healthcare searching that appears in *ONLINE* and *DATABASE* magazines.

How long have you been with Dialog? What does your job involve?

I've worked for Dialog since 1980. Prior to that, I was at the Philadelphia College of Pharmacy and Science, where I was the head of reference services and search analyst in charge of the drug information center. I'm now responsible for the customer service, training and sales arm of Dialog in Pennsylvania, Delaware and southern New Jersey. I also teach continuing education courses for the Medical Library Association. Recently, I developed and taught a course for the Special Libraries Association Pharmaceutical Division on competitive intelligence in the pharmaceutical industry.

Much of my searching is done in the course of developing training materials, and for my CADUCEUS column. We do specialty workshops, especially in the chemical and pharmaceutical areas, and a lot of the ideas for the column come from customers who say, "I'd like to hear more about this," or "Have you thought about writing about this?" They mention that they need more information about how hospitals advertise, on getting health statistics, or on all the alternatives to animal testing. I get so intrigued in helping them on a one-on-one basis. It's like a protracted customer service relationship, and if it's a big project, it can go on for a couple of weeks. Other field office representatives funnel requests to me, too, because of my specialty. People call who took a class from me ages ago or who read the column, hoping that I might be able to help them.

In working with customers, I learn what's going on in their industries and what they're going to need down the road. I trust my own instinct. If it interests me, it's probably going to interest someone else. I've learned that some library school professors assign CADUCEUS as part of their required reading. Since there aren't many medical bibliography courses, there are no textbooks on the subject, so the column serves as a resource.

I feel extremely fortunate that I don't have to make up excuses to do searches. I do business and news searches, too, to keep up-to-date on what's happening in my own region and with my major customers. Until recently, I still taught the introductory DIALOG seminar which attracts all kinds of users. That keeps you on your toes. You see what business people need, what an academic librarian might need, and so on. When you do training, you are learning as much as you are teaching. As I give examples of applications, people tell me, "Oh, I also use it for this." Then I revise my presentation a little, try what they suggested and work it in.

How do you approach the reference interview? How do you teach people to structure a search in their own minds before they go online?

First, I try to get the real story. What people initially ask is not necessarily what they really need. I get them to talk about how the information is going to be used. Once we have the question established, I ask them to identify keywords and to prioritize among them. I try to get them to tell me what the lowest occurrence term is. In other words, if you had therapy of Disease X in children, then Disease X is going to be the lowest occurrence term, the most unique and defining concept. Therapy is going to be the highest occurrence, the least unique, and "children" as a concept will also be high. People often think they have to use all the concepts they've identified, when in fact they only need to use one or two.

I suggest starting with the low-occurrence term. Put in one or two terms and see how many references you get; then bring in the third or fourth terms. Also, be aware that your choice of database will sometimes take care of some concepts. Be constantly alert that if you're in a medical file, you don't need to state the obvious. Some things will be implied; you're getting the concept of "therapy" already. Or, if you're in the Smoking and Health database, you don't need to use words like "smoking."

Especially with all the cross-file searching we do now, people tend to forget that they may be over-specifying for some files. You often need to adjust your strategy from file to file. You have to juggle controlled vocabulary with natural language. If you have a specific file with lots of bells and whistles, look up the controlled vocabulary. If it doesn't have the keywords you need, prepare to pull out all the stops.

If MEDLINE has a term for something, you can rely on it pretty religiously. You won't miss a lot if you use the *MeSH* terms. Then there are files like BIOSIS that have very broad concept codes, which are not always going to fill the bill for specific searches. You have to completely change your strategy depending on the database. What works in one file doesn't always work in another.

Is it difficult to reconcile the real power of coverage you get in a OneSearch with the need to focus on what various files do and do not have to offer?

It is. Experienced searchers can grasp that you can use a command to display records from specific files to hone your search strategy. They can overlook messages that tell you that a prefix is being ignored because it doesn't exist in all the files you're searching. You can plan a OneSearch that incorporates separate strategies for MEDLINE and BIOSIS and the other files you're searching. Then you can use FROM to display results selectively from different files. In effect, you're using OneSearch as a holding tank so you can ultimately use duplicate detection on the combined results from the separate strategies.

It depends on how far you need to go with a question. In the health/science area, you often need to go as far as you can get. You never give up, because what you find is going to affect the quality of someone's life or the business of improving the quality of someone's life. I usually work with people who have to go to the nth degree when they're searching, which means they plan for the big picture, not the quick-and-dirty approach.

When you're doing an exhaustive search, how do you decide which files to search in what order? Are there certain ones you start with, regardless?

I usually look at MEDLINE first. You can often use your MEDLINE results to beef up the natural language terms you have to use in other databases. It's cheap, it has excellent controlled vocabulary, you're bound to get something, and it's safe. You can logoff, evaluate the results, and use what you've found to build a strategy to use in other files. It depends on the kind of question, of course, but the MEDLINE thesaurus alone can help, even when you're approaching other files, just to give you ideas. The way it classifies chemicals, for instance, or diseases, might often suggest words you might not have thought of on your own, even if you're a medical practitioner.

So I usually start with MEDLINE, unless it's clear that another file is key for that particular question. On the other hand, sometimes a specialty file just fills the bill, like the Occupational Safety and Health Database. But if it's a generic medical or pharmaceutical topic, I usually go with the cheapest, and the tried and true, then build on that.

Excerpta Medica (EMBASE) tends to be stronger than MEDLINE in the pharmaceutical area. That's partly because its journal list includes more basic science journals and partly because of the way it is indexed. Many of the same references are in MEDLINE, but Excerpta has added more access points for the pharmaceutical searcher, including trade names, manufacturer names, and things like that.

I tend to go to certain files for certain kinds of questions when I know they have just the kind of indexing I need. Since they may be more expensive and less familiar, files like Excerpta Medica and SciSearch aren't always the starting point for a search, but they're always included. You can't afford to overlook them, because they often contain unique references that you can't find elsewhere. If I plan ahead, I can do a SciSearch search just as cheaply as a MEDLINE search. I search the other databases first, I'm really prepared, and I know that I'm going to go in, grab what I'm missing and get out. The connect time rate is high, but I'm not spending very much time. It's a fast process, especially if you upload your strategy, download, logoff/hold, look at your results, and then log back on to finish.

I encourage people also to use aids like DIALINDEX. I use it religiously, even when I think I know exactly where to go. We all fall into ruts; we tend to have our favorite groups of files. I always run a DIALINDEX search just to see where else I might look. I'm a big user of the supercategories, like the ALLSCIENCE category. It's so quick, and so powerful. Sometimes you get a hit in a file you hadn't thought about. Maybe it's a false drop, but even then, it alerts me to the possibility that, "Oh, this word is ambiguous, so when we go into this file we need to add something, to modify it somehow." I'm never overconfident about my file selection. DIALINDEX has taught me a lot.

I'm finding that as more and more full text comes online, you really have to change your searching habits. Medicine has fewer sources than other areas, but I've found more than 225 sources on DIALOG alone. There are eleven key journals in the MEDTEXT collection. The Health Periodicals Database is a gold mine. It has well over 100 sources, both professional and consumer-oriented. The Predicasts Newsletter Database comes in second in sheer numbers. Then there are the single source full-text files, like FDC Reports. Some of these databases have one foot in business and one in the healthcare world, but that's where a lot of people are searching today.

Pockets of medical and healthcare information are in other places, too, like Trade & Industry ASAP and the other IAC files. McGraw-Hill Publications Online has some,

ABI/INFORM has been adding more. Then, I haven't even counted the major reference books online, like the Merck Index or Martindale Online.

Full text is becoming more of a factor in medical searching, and I'm finding it a big adjustment. For one thing, the indexing is often absent. Even when it's there, like in the IAC files, it's a whole different flavor of indexing than you find in the traditional health science files. It's more natural language-oriented and, therefore, more prone to false drops.

So you have to develop a different search technique. You have to think more about degrees of proximity. The AND operator is a disaster in a full-text situation. I use SAME to group keywords in the same paragraph, at least in full-text files. Sometimes you have to go even narrower. If you're getting a lot of false drops, go for "within 10" or even "within 5" words to try to stay in the same sentence. You also need a high degree of tolerance. Just realize that you will get more false drops. There's nothing to prevent all of them; it's just the nature of the beast.

One change I've noticed in my own full-text searching behavior is that I scan titles a lot more. I download 500 titles, logoff/hold, scan them, and then print selectively. It seems impossible to refine a full-text search beyond a certain point without looking at the records themselves.

I do the same. I use a combination of title and KWIC formats. Both are, fortunately, still free formats in most databases I use. But sometimes even 50 titles is too many for end-users to look at. I have to tell them, "Look how much time you're spending. Don't try to evaluate online; use logoff/hold, and go back and get what looks good to you. It's going to pay off in the long run. It's cheaper and ultimately takes less time than printing full records and finding you've got reams and reams of garbage."

Do you recommend that searchers browse thesauri online if that's possible?

If they search MEDLINE regularly, I recommend using the printed thesaurus. It is very good and, since it's a government document, relatively cheap. I don't feel that it's cost-effective to look at online thesauri if you're a frequent searcher, although it's very elegant. If you're doing just a few medical searches, the online thesauri are great. When it's a file you don't use very often or that doesn't really have the equivalent of a hard copy thesaurus, then look at it online.

Often, I tell people to just go in using natural language, and look at selected records to see how they're indexed. Even if you plan your search thoroughly, using print thesauri before you go online, you still need to look at the actual indexing of the records because it's easy to miss some possibilities. I'm always prepared to modify my strategy once I'm online. The iterative approach is something I really stress. I've seen a lot of people go directly for a print or display of the record without the index terms. I tell them to always look at the keywords in a decent sample of their ultimate results, or what they think are their ultimate results, before they go for the final product. Maybe the most appropriate term was added to the database in the last six months, and isn't in the print thesaurus. Maybe there's another aspect to the subject that you didn't think about.

What happens when you've simply gotten too much? Do you refine the subject angle, or cut results by language or time period instead?

Sometimes you don't really know what you want until you see it. That's especially true of end-users; they want to find out what's out there. In that case, I limit things that are not subjective, where you're not relying on what keywords, concepts or codes an indexer chose to assign. I limit by year, language, and human, if that's an issue and if it's an option in the database. If we still get too many hits, sometimes I say, "Hey, don't assume that it's not precise just because there's a lot. There could be a lot. It may just be that you have to pick from what's there, maybe just the first 100. Just accept as a given that there's a lot more out there. Let's not limit arbitrarily."

If we get a lot of false drops, then we take more of a subject approach. We look for a term in the title or descriptor field. In a full-text file, you can sometimes restrict to title and abstract along with descriptors. You're going to miss some things, that's the nature of indexing. But in practice, that doesn't always matter; it depends on the purpose of the search.

How about the opposite situation, when you've gotten very little or nothing at all?

I usually figure that happens because I haven't picked up all the synonyms I should have, or I chose the wrong databases. That's a time to really go into DIALINDEX. I drop some of the keywords to make it less restrictive; if I've used three, I try two, and so on. I seldom stop if there are zero results, since then I suspect we've got a wrong spelling or something.

Sometimes you get a question where, even before you start, you wonder if anyone's ever written about it. Someone wanted articles about the likelihood of nurses and other healthcare workers getting AIDS. They wanted to know what nurses themselves thought about it, they wanted statistics, and they wanted public opinion. They had already searched the CINAHL (Nursing and Allied Health) database, and had come up with zip. It occurred to me that maybe no one had written about the subject. Think about it. First you have to design the study, then you have to poll the opinion, write it up and distribute it, and so on. Maybe the literature was just lagging, or maybe a study was in progress but not in print yet.

We did go into places like the POLL database, the newspaper files, Health Periodicals Database, and Magazine Index. We found the best stuff in POLL. We didn't find anything that was exactly on target, which didn't surprise me, but we found some things that were close. We eliminated some keywords that we had originally used to refine our search, and broadened the number of databases and the number of items we would look at. We looked at 150 or 200 titles, and found some things that we thought might suit. It was a case of, "This is as close as we're going to get."

Now that I think back on it, I would have used a couple of other files if the customer hadn't had the requester breathing down her neck. I might have checked things like the EBIS database, which covers employee benefits issues, or some of the other human resources literature. Maybe LABORLAW might have had something. Who knows?

You mentioned doing an exhaustive search and going after every last bit of information. What is realistic? How do you counsel people in terms of putting a reasonable limit on how far they take a search?

In the corporate environment, someone may check literally everything they've found in DIALINDEX. They may even redo the DIALINDEX search at some point, because as they look at some of the output they realize they should have used other keywords. If it's for an FDA filing or something like that, you really have to be as exhaustive as possible. In other situations, a "comprehensive" search just means "within reason" in terms of cost, time and search results.

I always caution people that they'll never know that they've gotten it all. For one thing, online doesn't have "everything." Something will be missed, either because of your strategy, because the database doesn't cover it, it was indexed strangely, or there was some glitch.

How important is it to issue a disclaimer, to say, "Here are the files we searched, and this is what we were able to do for you within the time and budget available"?

I am really concerned with quality and ethical issues, especially in the health sciences. Most experienced searchers know how to present those limitations, to say, "I can get you more if you need it," or "We may not have gotten it all, but here's what I've searched." There are malpractice issues, of course, so they need to clearly state where they've looked and why, and to have that information in their records. I think we need to go even further than our requesters would expect of us, just to protect the practitioner. It's not really a disclaimer. It's simply a statement of the facts as far as I'm concerned; you never know that you've gotten it all.

You don't deliver search results to clients in the traditional sense, but do you use any special formatting or post-processing tricks that you might want to share?

I use NOHEADER a lot in asking for DIALOG records, for browsing lists of titles and that kind of thing. You just add the word "noheader" to the end of your type command. It leaves out the record counter, the set/format/item number display, and the spaces between records. I often use it in combination with tagged output, because the field tags, AU, TI and so on, set off the individual records. I use NOHEADER most when I've requested a user-defined format, like just titles, manufacturer names or corporate sources. It produces a nice, compact list.

User-defined formats (UDF) are another neat feature. Often, I only want to look at certain parts of a record, or I want to rearrange them. If you use a UDF and ask for tagged output, you get the elements in the order in which you specified them. In effect, you get DIALOG to do a little word processing for you.

I don't have favorite formats, although I tend to go for long or very short. By very short, I mean citations only, or even just titles. I always browse titles first, then do a lot of selecting and resequencing. I also use the REPORT format when it's appropriate, like with the Finder files. The Journal Name, Product Name and Company Name Finders are like a front end, almost, to DIALINDEX. They have additional features that DIALINDEX doesn't offer. They have rotated indexing, if you EXPAND on a keyword that might be embedded in a phrase. That's something you don't normally get with an EXPAND command. Then they give the database location where a name appears, and you have the ability to MAP names in the correct format into the databases themselves, and execute the search.

If I've found some typical nomenclature in PharmaProjects, then I can MAP those synonyms, bring them over, and execute them in Product Name Finder to locate some additional references. (I can't execute a saved search in DIALINDEX itself.) I still go to DIALINDEX, too, because not every file has a product name field, and the Finder files only index databases where the field has been defined.

You can create some nice user aids for yourself using the REPORT feature and the Finder files. You can create lists of databases that cover certain journals, and lists for your clients of additional files that have information on their company or product. It's a neat way to get a cross-section and to see where the information actually is. I do a lot of that for myself.

I look forward to the addition of more Finder files. I'm seeing more and more creative applications. People are using them for in-service training. A reference librarian might say, "I just took this example of a company name. Here are all the different files we can look in for this kind of thing in the future." They print in REPORT format and use the list for future reference material. The Journal Name Finder is used a lot in selection decisions. Serials budgets are being cut. People are finding that Ulrich's does not always list all the databases in which a publication is available. If they can find it online when they need it, they might be able to cut their print subscriptions.

We touched on database quality and reliability a bit earlier. Any further thoughts on that subject?

When I think of quality issues, I think of them from the searcher's perspective. As information providers, whether it's hard copy or online, it is our responsibility to ensure the highest quality we can. That holds whether we're educating people or doing the searches ourselves. We can't just fall back on disclaimers. We have to have our own quality control.

Sometimes organizations work at quality control internally, but it's very difficult to set up real evaluative mechanisms. User feedback is not enough, because the user is often satisfied with far less than the best. User satisfaction is not an indicator at all of the quality that we need to aim for. This is a huge issue, particularly in the health sciences—realizing that the customer isn't always right.

Then there's the related matter of end-user searching. Part of educating end-users, especially in the medical area, is making them realize that they should not rely totally on the results of their own search. If it's important, and especially if it has to do with the quality of patient care, they should have someone more experienced check it out. They shouldn't just rely on what they've done themselves, because they're too easily satisfied.

One of the quality issues in medical searching is that, because MEDLINE is so good and so cheap, many health science searchers don't go any further. I have serious concerns about how this could ultimately affect the quality of medical care in the United States. I'm a MEDLINE lover myself. I can see why, as peoples' budgets are being cut, they go for the cheapest and most familiar file. But they just don't realize how much more there is out there. So often, I've found the single crucial report on how to handle a particular adverse reaction in a database other than MEDLINE—a more expensive database, but worth it, especially for that person's life.

The advent of CD-ROM is part of the picture, as is the fact that MEDLINE is available from many different sources. Lots of people are just going to go for MEDLINE on CD-ROM. I know that economics have to be part of the picture, but I try to teach people that our souls are not wrapped in dollars. Cost-effective searching is one thing, but we also want high-quality results, and the reality is that no single file has it all. That's why there are so many databases available, especially in the healthcare area. That's why they survive.

Do you think that searching multiple files diminishes, somewhat, the shortcomings—the gaps and the dirty data—that people are concerned about?

You don't really see a lot of dirty data in the sciences. When you're dealing with the whole biomedical business, yes, you do see some, in the news files, particularly. As with any kind of research, though, you try to check your facts in more than one source.

What I do see as a major quality issue is standardization for basic things like the way fields are constructed. Not every database producer can do things the same way, and I'd never expect them to. Competition is what keeps things fresh, when somebody comes up with a new idea, develops and markets it. I'd hate to gain standardization at the expense of creativity and competitiveness. But at the same time, I'd like a little bit more standardization in terms of our asking ourselves, as information providers, "What does the customer really need?" and saying, "Let's plan our products this way to try to make life easier for them."

What is it that you like about searching?

I often think about why I love it so much and what makes it so wonderful. Part of it is what made me go into the information field in the first place, the fact that information truly is power. It turns me on to be able to help people find the information they need. There's nothing like having a physician exclaim out loud in his very first hour of searching, "I have been looking for this for ages, and I was able to find it after being online for only five minutes." It gives them the power to help themselves. That's one of the reasons I like teaching. Online is such a powerful tool, and it's so easy to help people help themselves with it.

You really have to enjoy information for information's sake, even if it's a disgusting topic or one you're not personally interested in. There's so much serendipity. I learn so much along the way. It seems like everything that I have ever read, heard about or learned in the humanities, where my background lies, I have ultimately used in searching and information work. The weirdest little facts have paid off, so that years later I say, "Oh yeah, it's a vocabulary thing," or whatever.

Good searching requires a lot of skill in language and a love of puzzles and whodunits. I'm a mystery fan. I love language, reading and vocabulary. It's not just having a good vocabulary, although that's a real bonus, but noticing the way language works and all the funny stuff about it. You have to have a sense of humor, especially on a bad day when you're getting all these false drops out of the newspaper files, those wonderful false drops.

I did a search on hospitals advertising their plastic surgery programs, and found some hilarious false drops where "plastic" was used to refer to credit cards. You run into that in the IAC files, too, because they've got such a broad spectrum of sources, the popular literature mixed with the serious professional journals. In newspapers, there's a lot more colloquial usage. It teaches you so much about your language and how to use metaphors in the best possible way. You can get a lot of giggles along the way.

You also have to enjoy software *per se*. I like delving around into files, seeing what they can do, and also seeing what DIALOG can and cannot do. I know that searchers are often under stress and don't always have the opportunity to explore those things, so I like customers asking me to help them. That gives me a chance to go in and maybe screen some of the things to watch out for.

The final thing I love about searching has to do with being one of those flaming idealists from the Kennedy era. I've always wanted to do something with my life where I'll be able to feel, when I die, that I've done something for society. It sounds awfully idealistic, but there it is. I am an idealist. I think people who work in searching, in information work, are doing something for society. I feel very fortunate that I happen to have stumbled into a position in the healthcare field. I know of patients who have benefited from the help I have given behind the scenes, and it gives me a sort of inner glow. There aren't many jobs where you can say that you've made a real contribution that way. It's not something you're going to get a Pulitzer Prize for, but then you're not relying on outside praise. You can see that you've done a good job.

SUPER SEARCH SECRETS

On the reference interview...
    First, I try to get the real story. What people initially ask is not necessarily what they really need. I get them to talk about how the information is going to be used. Once we have the question established, I ask them to identify keywords and to prioritize among them.

On OneSearch...
    Experienced searchers...can overlook messages that tell you that a prefix is being ignored because it doesn't exist in all the files you're searching. You can plan a OneSearch that incorporates separate strategies for MEDLINE and BIOSIS and the other files you're searching. Then you can use FROM to display results selectively from different files. In effect, you're using OneSearch as a holding tank so you can ultimately use duplicate detection on the combined results from the separate strategies.

On MEDLINE...
    I usually look at MEDLINE first. You can often use your MEDLINE results to beef up the natural language terms you have to use in other databases. It's cheap, it has excellent controlled vocabulary, you're bound to get something, and it's safe.

On searching full text...
    ...the indexing is often absent....You have to develop a different search technique. You have to think more about degrees of proximity. The AND operator is a disaster in a full-text situation. I use SAME to group keywords in the same paragraph, at least in full-text files. Sometimes you have to go even narrower. If you're getting a lot of false drops, go for "within 10" or even "within 5" words to try to stay in the same sentence.

On using documentation and online thesauri...
    I tell people to just go in using natural language, and look at selected records to see how they're indexed. Even if you plan your search thoroughly, using print thesauri before you go online, you still need to look at the actual indexing of the records because it's easy to miss some possibilities.

On getting zero hits...
    I usually figure that happens because I haven't picked up all the synonyms I should have, or I chose the wrong databases. That's a time to really go into DIALINDEX. I drop some of the keywords to make it less restrictive; if I've used three, I try two, and so on. I seldom stop if there are zero results, since then I suspect we've got a wrong spelling or something.

On output formats...

I use NOHEADER a lot in asking for DIALOG records, for browsing lists of titles and that kind of thing. You just add the word "noheader" to the end of your type command. It leaves out the record counter, the set/format/item number display, and the spaces between records. I often use it in combination with tagged output, because the field tags, AU, TI and so on, set off the individual records. I use NOHEADER most when I've requested a user-defined format, like just titles, manufacturer names or corporate sources. It produces a nice, compact list.

On being a good searcher...

Good searching requires a lot of skill in language and a love of puzzles and whodunits. I'm a mystery fan. I love language, reading and vocabulary. It's not just having a good vocabulary...but noticing the way language works and all the funny stuff about it.

CHAPTER 20

N. J. THOMPSON:
EXPLORING INTELLECTUAL PROPERTY

N. J. Thompson is a law librarian at Limbach & Limbach, an intellectual property law firm in San Francisco, California. She has a law degree and has practiced law.

Tell me about your search operation, and where you learned to search?

I'm self-taught as a searcher. I had not touched a computer before I came to this firm. I have a 386 PC, an HP LaserJet printer at my desk which I've had for years, and a Hayes 9600 Smartmodem. LEXIS supports 9600bps, so we search at 9600. We use LEXIS' own session software. We find that it works best because of the many different machines we run it on, and because of its editing features. We use WestMate for WESTLAW. I use DIALOGLINK, too, because DIALOG is the primary non-legal databank we use, and because it supports image capture for trademarks.

The firm also has an office in San Jose and a branch in Palo Alto. A typical scenario is that I receive, via the network, an e-mail message requesting a search. I perform the search and print it in hard copy at this location. Or, if it's for one of the satellite offices, I put it onto a network drive and inform the requester via e-mail that their results are waiting for them.

We have several attorneys who, because of our remote ability, now work outside the office one day a week or so. They do patent applications at home, and can either call or e-mail me for information. I can, in turn, put it on their network drive, and they can get it at home. So the library has been able to offer quite a bit of support to people outside the office, including people who are on trips to Japan, and that kind of thing.

My immediate clients are attorneys. Most search requests come from them rather than their clients, partly for reasons of liability and malpractice. I do not bill myself here or to the outside world as a practicing attorney, so I mostly deal indirectly with the firm's clients. Occasionally I deal directly, but it's just a lot cleaner if it goes through the attorney at the liability level. Our clients tend to be high-tech Silicon Valley companies, or Japanese companies who are into high technology. Our firm's strength lies in the electrical engineering area, but we have people who do mechanical and biotechnology work, and we have a lot of people in the food industry.

Do your search requests tend to fall into certain categories, or is there a lot of give-and-take in your reference interviews?

Both. For people whom I've worked with a long time, with something like a trademark scan, it's very simple. It may just be, "Please do an availability search for this mark." This a very direct request for me, and there's little need for interaction. But sometimes people say, "Find me this mark," and in fact they just want to know if it's out there in exactly that form. They're not concerned about what's available. I need to know that, so I try to interact with people before I do a search to confirm what they really are after. Sometimes people will say, "Please do a D&B search on X company." They may be right or they may be wrong about needing a D&B. I might be able to get them better information in a different location if I know their ultimate goal, so I tend not to blindly get a D&B. People tend to use "D&B" generically. I usually ask "What information do you really want?"

I spend more time with someone who might be new to the firm, with some of the law clerks or associates, even a partner who might just be getting used to it. Each individual I work for expects something different from me. One thing I've had to learn is what does *this* person want when I give them back material? Even if it's just a trademark scan, one person may want something focused very narrowly, someone else may want a much broader search. So it can depend on personal style as well as the particular case.

The other thing it can depend on significantly is the client's budget. Do they want something quick-and-dirty, or do they want a "scorched earth" policy? My searches range from one extreme to the other, but it's something that I need to find out from each person. A typical question is, "Find out if this patent has been litigated." The cost of that can range incredibly, because no single source can be relied upon to have that information. So the question is, "Do you want to check a couple of basic sources, or is it really important?" In that case, we will go to the ends of the world to find the answer. We're talking about a difference of several hundred dollars.

Do you keep budget discussions within a relative range like that, or do you actually negotiate a "not-to-exceed" figure?

Most of the time it's more generalized, but sometimes we get an actual dollar limit. The requester might say, "I told the client this would not exceed x dollars," so that helps me know what they're thinking about. I can frame my search better, and my limitations are enforced. We often work with the client to arrive at a budget, too. We say, "Okay, let's start with a budget of this, which will give you this kind of information. From there you can see where you want to go."

We bill back our computer time with a very small markup. We also bill the time of the person who is doing the search—that may be me, or my assistant, a law clerk. We keep track of the online costs manually. I find that that's the easiest way for me to do it. I have a log right at my computer, which lets me write down what I did right away. The immediacy of the log lets me keep track of how I spend my day. It also helps me monitor other searchers and find out who might not be using the system properly. We also have a time-billing program on my computer.

How many people do you have searching there?

Basically all the attorneys and law clerks have IDs for LEXIS and WESTLAW; that would encompass 35 or 36 people. Only about half of them really do any searching. There's just one searcher besides myself on the library staff.

You specialize in intellectual property searching. What does that involve?

In the patent area, I search for products invented by certain people or patented by certain companies. I do some patentability work, where you're given a particular technology and you want to see what else has been patented in this area. Particularly in litigation, you're often looking for prior art, which can be either a prior patent or prior publication in the science and technology literature.

I do a lot of "who's on first," as I call it. What company introduced this new flavor of bottled water, or whatever, and when did they introduce it? That may take me into PROMT and the other Predicasts databases, and into all the company news databases. Now that copyright filings are online, I use them to check names for software, for instance, or to look for information that's been copyrighted by a particular company or individual.

We also use Information America for secretary of state and other public records information. We use DataTimes occasionally, for its newspaper coverage. We use several Dun & Bradstreet products, including the credit report service, which we use for internal purposes. It is a part of our client intake process and our conflict searching, finding out whether we can represent somebody or not.

We do lots of trademark searching, which can range from finding if X company owns a particular mark, to determining whether mark XYZ is available for use by a client, to finding marks owned by a particular company. For that, I use Trademarkscan on DIALOG and a Swiss system called IMSMARQ, that we access through DunsNet. IMSMARQ has the most international databases and trademarks. We can search trademarks in Germany, Denmark, Finland, Great Britain, Italy, Norway, Sweden, and the U.S. It is also an incredible source of international pharmaceutical trademarks. One thing about IMSMARQ is that the data varies extremely, depending upon what the source office does to provide that data. The United States Patent and Trademark Office provides the most information, and Great Britain is probably next. For Norway and Finland, even Germany, all you get is the mark itself and the class it's in. But at least there's some kind of coverage.

We don't always search international sources for U.S. clients; it depends on the project. There's a constant tradeoff about how much money to spend in-house. The other option is to do something preliminary and then send it out to a full trademark search firm like Thomson & Thomson or CorSearch that owns the data or buys it at a wholesale price, where we have to pay absolute retail. We do not have a policy about where searches go. Individual attorneys decide who they like. Most people start with us, at least for a preliminary search or, if they have ten or twenty marks, to knock out a bunch of them right away. One of the things I have to cope with is deciding when I should shut down a search. Sometimes I have to say, "There are so many marks here, so many potential conflicts, or what's called 'likelihood of confusion,' that it's more economical now for you to just take this out to a full search firm." The client is going to get better information for less money. I think that's an important part of my knowledge, deciding when to blow the whistle.

In the computer area, people often come up with marks very similar to others, something like MicroTech. There's a ton of stuff out there with both the words "micro" and "tech," and there are also a number that are Microtech. It's very easy if you get Microtech right on, and you can say, "I'm sorry, that's out." But often they want something that has an S in it or a slight variation, and then you have to see if somebody has a family of marks that has part of those words. An illustration, not in the computer area, is Ocean Spray with its CranApple, CranZip and CranSnack marks. It's important to know, if you ever deal with "cran," how strong their whole family is; it's not just one isolated mark. If there are a large number of hits in a particular class, even if you narrow it with the description of goods and services, and the client is still serious, then it's time to shut it down and say, "Let's go pay elsewhere." It's going to be more economical for the client, and that's something that I, as a searcher, think is important, to provide our clients with the best information by the most economical means.

That may mean not doing it internally. Okay, we started here, now maybe it's time to take it to a searcher in Washington. We go outside with a lot of our patent searching, too. We have someone go to the U.S. Patent and Trademark Office for us. We work a lot in the electrical area. It's quite different from chemical searching in that there are so many online products for chemistry now that give you structures in graphic form. That doesn't exist so much in the electrical area, and having the drawings is sometimes more important to people searching than the actual written language.

We've looked at the patent image products on CD-ROM. So far they seem to me to be bulky, and they don't cover a long enough time period. I don't need all the patents that came out of the patent office in a given year. We tend to work more in a particular area of technology and we need that area covered for a longer period of time. So the imaging products so far haven't met our needs. I think they're more geared toward someone working in a big chemical company or something like that, where you are restricted to a very small number of classes, so you can monitor by class and get everything. We work in such a diverse area and over such a great period of time that the CD-ROM image products don't have the coverage we want.

When you've done a search and you haven't found a conflict in the trademark files themselves, do you go into directory databases and the trade literature and look for common law usage?

We do, but it depends. Once we undertake the process of going beyond the trademark file and we turn something up, we have a duty to investigate it. So a question arises there out of an area of the law called nonfeasance and malfeasance. Nonfeasance means you don't have a duty so you can't be liable for not doing it. In the real world, if you don't stop and try to help somebody who's been in an automobile accident, nothing can happen to you. If you do stop and try to take care of this person and you do it improperly, you've assumed kind of a duty, and you're going to be liable if you do it improperly. The same general principle applies to the trademark area, where if we do common law searching and we turn up something, we have a duty to go ahead and investigate whether this company is still in business or not. We do it a lot, but it is a limitation, something to consider.

But if someone is out there using a name, isn't that information that your client needs to know, regardless?

It depends. If they haven't registered it and we've done a registration search and submitted the application, and the Trademark Office says they don't find a problem, then the mark itself is published in the *Official Gazette*. After that, there's a 30-day period when anybody can object to the registration based upon the fact that they have a mark that they think is likely to confuse. There's always the possibility that somebody beat you to it. You want to know that, but that's the kind of case where we'll have someone else do the common law stuff because economically it makes the most sense.

The computer field, though, is great for common law searching because it's so well covered. You've got the software files on DIALOG, the trade name directory, Thomas

Register, and the Product Name field in some of the business and company news databases. There's a lot of inconsistency, though, in how the Product Name field is used. Legally, a trade name refers to the name of a company or a business, and a trademark refers to the name of a product or a service. But you'll often find both in the Product Name field.

If the same database, or the equivalent information, is available on more than one system, what determines where you go for it? Is it system features, cost or habit?

All of the above. I think that as a searcher I have to choose what systems I'm going to be really good on, what systems I'm going to be adequate on, and what systems I'm going to have to look at the documentation for. I think I'm a very good DIALOG, WESTLAW and LEXIS searcher. So habit enters into it. Even if something is a little more expensive on DIALOG than it is on ORBIT, as is the case for some of the patent databases, my ability to execute the search is so much better on DIALOG that I may go ahead and do it there because it will actually be cheaper for the client. I am better at it, and I am more efficient. I know I'm not as good a searcher on ORBIT, but when there's information there and I'm already in it, I will stay and work in it instead of switching back to DIALOG. If there's really a big cost difference, then I switch around. An example is when we're looking for a patent that has been cited in subsequent patents. The cost of doing that on DIALOG is expensive, but on ORBIT it's really cheap, so there's no way I'm going to pull that information on DIALOG.

It's always a goal to minimize costs, but system features figure in, too. For instance, IMSMARQ has U.S. trademarks online and so does DIALOG. For awhile, the IMSMARQ databases had the best status information, but the system doesn't have any of the search features. All you can search by is your mark and the classes. You can't find out ownership. There's nothing that's really an availability search tool. So often I'm not going to use it even though their records are cheaper to print than on DIALOG. It's not nearly as searchable.

Speaking of searchability, how do you map out your search strategy?

If it's straightforward, I do it on the fly. I think part of being a good searcher is to be creative based on your search results, to realize, "Oh, wow, look, this company may be involved in *this*." You can't plot that out beforehand, you go with the flow of what you get. I think it's important, especially for searchers who don't search a lot, to sit down beforehand and at least figure out how you're going to create your search. With DIALOGLINK and some other communication programs, you can type in part of your search before you even get online. I do that a lot to minimize the costs. If I'm searching for a particular technology, I type in several lines of information before I go online. I sit there and map it out, plot it out in my type-ahead buffer.

That's a good approach, too, when you're working with a lot of codes and technical terminology, where there's a major potential for typos. It's also good just to *see* it written down. I start writing something and then say, "Let's put this in one set of parentheses." Then I go back and slap in another set of parentheses, that kind of thing.

I tend to keep the paper that has the search request on it in front of me. I use it for two purposes. One is to formulate the search before I do it, and the second is, as I'm going through the search, I make notes on that piece of paper. If I have a number of classes in a trademark, I set it up so that each class is a separate set with the keywords at the end in a set of their own. That way, if I get too many hits using all of the classes, I can just go back and take the "beverage" set and combine it with some of the classes, without having to rekey anything. I try to plan beforehand an approach that allows flexibility when I'm in there.

I think in terms of a building-block approach. This gives me the option of delivering one set that is obviously the most relevant for the client to look at, another set that's broader and might be of interest, and then a third set of, "Well, these came out and you might want to look at them anyway." The way it works is, I might get a request to find a patent assigned to this company relating to this technology. I may find that the company has *no* patents relating to that technology. Next, I might focus a little bit more on the technology itself, print out a list of patent titles, and go back and say, "This company didn't have anything in this area, but here is a set of patents with this information. Do you want me to stop, or do you want to see the patents in the field even though that wasn't part of your original search request?" More often than not, they ask me to go ahead and print some of those records, even though that wasn't what they originally asked for.

There's a lot of back-and-forth with the client, particularly in technology searches, because I'm not a chemist or an engineer so I don't understand the terminology. What is important for me is to understand the relationship between terms. I always ask about that in my reference interview. Is this a term of art that's always going to be expressed in a phrase like this? Do you think we should truncate this word? In what relationship in the database are these terms going to appear? That kind of definition is the most important thing that I can do for someone.

What kinds of documentation do you find indispensable?

I have a chart of the trademark classes. We buy a product put out by CompuMark, which is now owned by Thomson & Thomson. Every year they send out a little card with the U.S. classifications on one side and the international classifications and conversions on the other. That is absolutely near and dear to my heart, as are a number of laminated products from other vendors with basic commands and quick tips about their systems. The patent classification manual isn't that important; rarely do I search through that huge volume before I start. There's always a point in the search itself where you start to see the classification you want come up in the records.

Do you tend to start broad when you're searching, to try to be really comprehensive? Is that necessary for intellectual property searching, when you have to be sure not to miss anything?

No, I actually start really narrow. If I'm searching Trademarkscan, the first thing I do is use the ET field to look for an exact trademark, because if I can knock it out on an exact hit I've just saved somebody a lot of money. My very next step is to go to the TR level, the permuted index, which is the broadest level. I'll combine what I find there with goods and services classifications to narrow it down. Even then, the categories are so broad that you may still have to look at a lot of marks.

In patents, too, I usually go for the narrowest search possible. At the same time I try to set it up so that it's quite easy to broaden it. I do the same thing with legal searches. I find that the trainers who teach my law clerks how to search always start broad to get the most comprehensive results. Their attitude is, "We don't want to get sued because you missed something." But in practice I've found that I don't need to know everything that's out there. I don't want to spend time online. What I need is to find a way to get into the cases, to find a case and use it as a source, and move back and forth from that. The more searching I do, the more focused I am initially. Partly, it's a function of growing confidence. It's going from, "I hope I don't miss anything," to being reasonably confident that if you structure the search properly from the beginning you can go right to what you need without missing anything crucial.

I've also learned the cost of going really broad, and realized over time how much money and time I've wasted by taking that approach. The alternative is being more narrow and going back and communicating with the person I'm doing it for. Usually, they *don't* want the world; they want an answer. After a preliminary search, they might say, "Now, let's go get the world," but rarely do we start off with that.

What about controlled vocabulary versus free-text searching?

Since I started out with LEXIS, I feel like I grew up doing free-text searching in full-text files. I think it's important to know when I should use controlled vocabulary. Because so much of my searching is legal, it's second nature to try to think of every way a certain judge or law clerk might have expressed something. Consider the word "attorney" itself; you have attorney, counsel, lawyer, prosecutor… One thing I've done on this job is increase my awareness of synonyms. And my spelling of British terms is better than it ever was.

Do you do a lot of multifile or global searching?

Absolutely. LEXIS and WESTLAW are constructed as broad multifile systems. I really like OneSearch in DIALOG, too. I try to go for the narrowest file selection that has everything I need. You have to know the limitations of multifile searching, though, like making sure your fields match. A great example is DIALOG's software group, which contains only something like three databases, but if you're looking for a product name you have to do it differently in each one: Maybe there's a PN field, or maybe you have to use the ID field, or maybe you can only search it by title.

What's the driving factor in deciding how far you take a search?

It varies depending on whether we're involved in litigation, or whether someone just wants to know whether a certain competitor has produced anything in the field. Lots of forces come into play, but I often take a preliminary approach and say, "Here it is, but there's a ton of other stuff." Then the attorney says, "I'll get in touch with the client and see if that's enough." If budget is not an issue and it's important to have the information, I tell them, "I have searched here, here, here and here, and this is what I've found. I don't think I can do anything more." If budget *is* an issue and they want more information, I say, "Here are our options, and this is how much time and money it's going to cost."

How do you present the search results to your client?

I pretty much give them the search as it was done, including the files listed and the strategy, without chopping it out. I put in page breaks, clean up really cruddy typos, and delete false hits. I find it frustrating when we get searches that were done by other law firms or organizations, and there's nothing but a group of records with very little search strategy. If somebody asks me, "How do you think this was done?" or "Do you think this was a good search? Do you think we should do anything more?" I can't say. I can't tell anything from what they've given me. So I've found that it's better to try to preserve the integrity of the search as it was originally done.

When I deliver a search, I try to summarize what I did and point out what looks really important. It doesn't take more than a couple of minutes to say, "This is how I approached this. Are you satisfied with this? Why don't you look at it and get back to me if you want to go over it?" I think the communication between the person who gets the information and the searcher is incredibly important. It's important that the firm's clients are happy, but my immediate clients are the 30 or 35 people here who use me repeatedly. Building a collaborative relationship like that is one way that you market yourself.

What do you like least about online searching?
The most frustrating thing is running up against the limitations that the producers don't tell you about that affect the integrity and quality of the data. That's something that I've learned about the hard way. A database will claim to cover electronics when in fact it doesn't cover it comprehensively. They don't tell you what criteria they use to determine what they do and don't include. I also find typos annoying; they make me question the quality of the product, and attorneys look at me like, "What are we getting here?"

One of the rewards of doing what I do is being able to participate in the development of online products. It's fun helping the information providers get it right in the first place, being able to say, "This is great, but why don't you do x?" I also find myself acting like a consumer watchdog, calling them up and saying, "This information is *wrong*, and it's easy to change it, so do it."

Overall, I think the quality of databases has improved over the years. The fields have improved, the search systems have improved, and that's because searchers have said, "Wait, this isn't good enough." That's not the only reason, of course, but I know that we, as consumers who vocalize our opinions, do have an impact.

Tell me what you enjoy most about searching.
From an intellectual property point of view, I love driving down the freeway, seeing a big billboard and realizing that I searched that product and helped give it an identity. It's very gratifying to feel part of something that's much larger than you and now has a life of its own.

Another thing I really enjoy is the teaching aspect of my job. I train law clerks and associates in using computer technology. It's very satisfying to see people learn how to use the tools and then actually use them.

I feel very lucky to have stumbled into all this. I didn't set out to do it; I don't have a degree in library science. But when I was in law school I worked at the City Hall law library, which was a great training ground in reference work. I got questions ranging from homeless people who felt that their civil rights had been infringed, to world-famous trial lawyers with a major trial coming up. Fortunately for me, this profession has been a lot of fun. It has come of age; when I started doing it at the end of 1984, information technology was still the land of the nerds. Now it's the hottest thing going.

My undergraduate degree is in geography, and I sort of regret that I was born in the wrong century to be an explorer. I was always intrigued by people who went off into uncharted lands. What searching does for me, in this very boxed-in modern-day world, is let me go out into uncharted lands every time I go online. It's quite amazing to be sitting in San Francisco looking at a screen and, in a minute, be in Germany looking at information. Whenever I go online, I'm going exploring, going spelunking.

When I go to work in the morning, I have no idea what I'm going to be doing that day. It depends on what's out there and on my ability to take people's desires to know things and give them back something tangible. And that "something" doesn't particularly come from me; I'm the medium for finding it. That's the fun part, the unknown and the ability to find it. It's like the ability to create something.

I do think searching is creative. For a good searcher, it's a creative process to begin something and know how to weave it as you go, until you've produced something that they need. Certainly not all searches do that, but I love it when someone comes in and says, "We need to know everything you can find about such-and-such." Yeah! No budget constraints! That's enough to bring a smile to my face.

SUPER SEARCH SECRETS

On online search costs...
We keep track of the online costs manually....I have a log right at my computer, which lets me write down what I did right away. The immediacy of the log lets me keep track of how I spend my day. It also helps me monitor other searchers and find out who might not be using the system properly. We also have a time-billing program on my computer.

On CD-ROMs for patents...
We've looked at the patent image products on CD-ROM. So far they seem to me to be bulky, and they don't cover a long enough time period....We work in such a diverse area and over such a great period of time that the CD-ROM image products don't have the coverage we want.

On deciding which system to search...
I think that as a searcher I have to choose what systems I'm going to be really good on, what systems I'm going to be adequate on, and what systems I'm going to have to look at the documentation for....habit enters into it....If there's really a big cost difference, then I switch around.

On using a type-ahead buffer...
I do that a lot to minimize the costs. If I'm searching for a particular technology, I type in several lines' worth of information before I go online. I sit there and map it out, plot it out in my type-ahead buffer.

On planning search strategies...
I actually start really narrow. If I'm searching Trademarkscan, the first thing I do is use the ET field to look for an exact trademark, because if I can knock it out on an exact hit I've just saved somebody a lot of money....In patents, too, I usually go for the narrowest search possible. At the same time I try to set it up so that it's quite easy to broaden it. I do the same thing with legal searches.

On being a good searcher...
I think part of being a good searcher is to be creative based on your search results, to realize, "Oh, wow, look, this company may be involved in this." You can't plot that out beforehand, you go with the flow of what you get....For a good searcher, it's a creative process to begin something and know how to weave it as you go, until you've produced something that they need.

CHAPTER 21

ANN VAN CAMP: ANT SEARCHER AND PROUD OF IT

Ann Van Camp operates Van Camp Information Associates in Westfield, Indiana. She has a background in chemistry and specializes in medical information. Ann is a regular columnist for *ONLINE* and *DATABASE*.

How did you come to be an online searcher?

I've been doing online searching since 1970. I've always been in the medical area, so I primarily search MEDLINE and the biomedical databases. Currently, I do backup searching for several large drug companies and I do training for the EMBASE database. I also do BRS training for INCOLSA, the Indiana Cooperative Library Services Authority. I also write documentation for database producers and online services.

For many years when I was searching for faculty and students at the medical school at Indiana University, I had no help at all—I know for a fact that I have done over 55,000 searches. I don't even count the number I do these days; I don't keep track of that kind of stuff any more—except for the IRS. I do keep a folder on each client. I know exactly what I've done and I retain the searches for a while. Most of the time I use the client's password, so they get the bill. I don't even know how much it costs. I just bill them for my time.

How do you approach the reference interview?

I try to get as many details as possible. The people that I'm working for are usually scientists or physicians or, during my medical school experience, health science students. In general students don't know what they want. But when you're talking to researchers and physicians, they know what's out there and they know exactly what they want. Since I have a chemistry background and a lot of experience as a searcher, I know that if I don't understand what the question is, then I have to ask them enough to find out. I think that there are a lot of people working in hospital and medical libraries who don't even know how to find out what the question really is, so they don't know whether they're getting the right thing or not.

If someone has to give a little speech or write a short paper, they don't need the world's supply of literature on the subject. Maybe they only want a few relevant articles and they don't care if I get everything. Maybe they just want review articles. So I try to find out what they're going to *do* with the information.

Typically, what subjects do you search?

One search I get frequently these days is "everything on a specific drug in a specific time period." If they want a comprehensive search, I routinely search EMBASE, MEDLINE and BIOSIS. That's a good combination because not everything is in MEDLINE. The overlap between EMBASE and MEDLINE is only about 35 percent, so you get a lot of stuff that you don't get out of MEDLINE when you add EMBASE. Most of the unique material is pharmacological. I like to search these databases together using Data-Star's StarSearch.

You've anticipated my next question. What systems do you use?

I prefer BRS or Data-Star. There are some significant differences between the two. I use NLM, too. NLM is probably cheaper for MEDLINE than any other system, but it's not as flexible. BRS, DIALOG and Data-Star all allow the searcher to make something the main point of the article after the fact. They let you add the subheadings later in the search. And, of course, MEDLINE has that wonderful controlled vocabulary with main headings and subheadings. When you know how to manipulate the system, you can do marvelous things.

Data-Star has StarSearch, and new KEEP and ORDER features for ordering records, and PARK and GO for when your search is interrupted or you need to stop to look something up. It does not have a couple of things that BRS has that are very handy. BRS has MEDSPELL, which automatically looks for both British and American spellings. It also has automatic pluralization. Both features you can set for each online session if you want to, or have them set permanently on. I certainly think that any user who's familiar with one system could use the other because they both use the same fundamental BRS search software.

If the same database is up on more than one system, what determines where you go to search it?

The number one factor is client preference, since I'm often working with their passwords. Right now I've got a bunch of searches that have to be done as DIALOG Alerts because the client wants them done on that system. Normally I go to BRS first because I'm most familiar with it. If I'm trying to save a client money, and for most of the searches for my drug companies, I use BRS. If I want to use multifile capability and remove the duplicates, I go for StarSearch on Data-Star.

Do you plan your search strategy in advance?

I sure as hell do. I'm an ant. I'm not Barbara Quint's grasshopper searcher. Sometimes, if I don't know what I'm looking for and I want to see if it's indexed, I'll be a grasshopper. I'll print out some titles and indexing terms and go from there. But in general, when you work with a database like MEDLINE that has a controlled vocabulary, then you tend to look at the search guide; at least I do.

I plot out my search strategy, more or less, before I go online. I use codes and controlled vocabulary wherever they're available. Then I might supplement them with free text in the title field. I really rely on the print thesauri.

I'm also very much aware of how differently you search on different online systems. Anytime I go to a training session, I find myself thinking, "Oh, well, you can do it this way, and then you can do it that way on another system." I sort of think ambidextrously.

How do you approach the average search? What files do you search and in what order?

This is the way I teach it: Go into the cheap database, which is MEDLINE. Do MEDLINE, EMBASE and BIOSIS. Now, BIOSIS has all kinds of things that are not journal literature. It covers meetings and technical reports and books and that sort of thing. All of that is going to be unique, because MEDLINE and EMBASE don't cover that kind of literature. So the three make a good combination. If you search MEDLINE first, it knocks out the duplicates from the other two. The thing I like about StarSearch on Data-Star is that, if you're running those three databases, it automatically integrates the output. It's so much easier.

When you're online and you're looking at preliminary results, how do you evaluate them?

I browse titles and then I look at selected descriptors for the titles that look good, and refine the search from there. I'll make descriptors "major," or add subheadings, or put in another parameter—or sometimes go back to the drawing board completely.

Another thing I do is ask the person how much they think was written on this topic. Students hardly ever have a sense of that, but researchers tend to. They'll usually be able to say "very little" or "a lot" or something like that. If they say "lots" and I get zero hits, I go back to the drawing board. Maybe I've misspelled something, or not heard the terms correctly. But I have enough tools around here to look up spellings and stuff like that, so I try to verify before I go online.

I think the worst kind of searches are when someone asks for something very general and you can't pin them down to anything less than that. You can't get them to focus.

I've found that an effective technique is to say, "I've found 8,742 references to what you told me to search, and this would cost you so much to retrieve. What shall we do now?" Then they ask you to read a few sample titles and they say, "Oh, no, I'm not interested in that aspect at all." You've caught their attention, at least. Sometimes people don't realize the granularity of the databases, that they can get a fairly fine-grained cut in terms of specifying what they want.

I think that if you're looking for very specific things, that's the time to use full-text databases, like BRS's Comprehensive Core Medical Library file, which has the full text of a whole bunch of journals. If you don't find anything in MEDLINE and the usual places, then search for it free text in a full-text file. You may only find two or three relevant paragraphs in a ten-page article, but at least you found something.

Do you ever search the popular literature, magazines and newspapers and so on, for more popular treatments of a medical subject?

I did a big project with the Indiana Regional Cancer Center. Their nurses in charge of patient education wanted articles about people who had specific kinds of cancer, personal narrative kinds of stuff. So I searched the popular literature to find references for their bibliographies: WILSONLINE's Readers' Guide to Periodicals, and Health Periodicals Database and Magazine Index.

How do you decide when a search is finished? Is it a matter of diminishing returns, or when you run out of money, or just run out of places to look?

It's a combination of those things. If the search is for an individual instead of a company and I don't really want to charge them a lot of money, I probably won't be as thorough as I might be if somebody says they really want a comprehensive search. It goes back to the reference interview and what they want to accomplish and what their situation is, whether you'll go to the ends of the earth for them.

How quickly do you usually turn projects around? Is time a real factor for you?

If I'm not involved in a writing assignment, I usually do a search the same day it comes in. If it's only one question, I do it and send it out the same day. Some of the searches I do on clients' passwords I order printed offline—they're sent to the client directly so I never know when they get it or if they don't. I assume that if they haven't gotten it when they're supposed to, they will call.

What about feedback? Do you check to make sure that everything was okay?

No, I don't do that. I probably should. But I'll tell you—I feel confident that I've done a damn good job. That's the truth! I have done so many searches and I have had so many compliments from people. I understand the questions and I know a hell of a lot about medicine because I search in so many different areas. I know what's out there and when I'm getting it and when I'm not. I have a lot of confidence in what I've done.

I've done most of my searching in situations where I haven't had to think about charging back costs. You have a different attitude when you don't think about money. I think people who have to think about the money are "jack rabbit searchers." They get in, they don't think about what they're doing and they download 300 citations of which maybe 25 are relevant. I never felt that I did that kind of thing. I've learned to do a workman-like search, as targeted and relevant on the final cut as possible, partly because there wasn't the pressure of the ticking meter.

Some searches are fairly complicated to begin with. I can usually tell from the question that it's a very complicated kind of search, that it has a lot of parameters to it. When I do an excellent search on those kinds of searches, I really feel great. I really love searching. I think it's a great job to have.

SUPER SEARCH SECRETS

On tracking search requests and costs...

I do keep a folder on each client. I know exactly what I've done and I retain the searches for a while. Most of the time I use the client's password, so they get the bill. I don't even know how much it costs. I just bill them for my time.

On medical databases...

...I routinely search EMBASE, MEDLINE and BIOSIS. That's a good combination because not everything is in MEDLINE. The overlap between EMBASE and MEDLINE is only about 35 percent, so you get a lot of stuff that you don't get out of MEDLINE when you add EMBASE. Most of the unique material is pharmacological.

On favorite systems...

I prefer BRS or Data-Star. There are some significant differences between the two. I use NLM, too. NLM is probably cheaper for MEDLINE than any other system, but it's not as flexible. BRS, DIALOG and Data-Star all allow the searcher to make something the main point of the article after the fact. They let you add the subheadings later in the search.

On searching style...

I'm an ant. I'm not Barbara Quint's grasshopper searcher. Sometimes, if I don't know what I'm looking for and I want to see if it's indexed, I'll be a grasshopper. I'll print out some titles and indexing terms and go from there. But in general, when you work with a database like MEDLINE that has a controlled vocabulary, then you tend to look at the search guide; at least I do.

On planning search strategy...

I plot out my search strategy, more or less, before I go online. I use codes and controlled vocabulary wherever they're available. Then I might supplement them with free text in the title field. I really rely on the print thesauri.

On multifile searching...

Go into the cheap database, which is MEDLINE. Do MEDLINE, EMBASE and BIOSIS. Now, BIOSIS has all kinds of things that are not journal literature. It covers meetings and technical reports and books and that sort of thing. All of that is going to be unique, because MEDLINE and EMBASE don't cover that kind of literature. So the three make a good combination. If you search MEDLINE first, it knocks out the duplicates from the other two.

On getting zero hits...

If you don't find anything in MEDLINE and the usual places, then search for it free text in a full-text file. You may only find two or three relevant paragraphs in a ten-page article, but at least you found something.

CHAPTER 22

WENDY WARR: THE JOY OF STRUCTURES

Wendy Warr is the principal in Wendy Warr & Associates, which provides consulting services to users and vendors of scientific, technical and medical information services in Europe and the U.S. She has published several books and dozens of articles in the areas of chemistry and chemical information, and is Associate Editor of the American Chemical Society *Journal of Chemical Information and Computer Sciences.* She is based in Cheshire, England.

Tell me something about your background. How did you get into the "information" side of the chemical field?

I've been in it for more than 24 years, actually. Until recently, I was Manager of Information Services for ICI Pharmaceuticals. I ran three libraries there, plus the Technical Information Unit, which handled online searching and records management, and the Research Information Services Unit, which supported end-users of both internal and external information systems. Before that, I was a Senior Systems Analyst and Project Team Leader in the Information Systems Department of ICI Pharmaceuticals. Right now, however, I'm really more of a consultant than I am a searcher.

What online services are most important to you in terms of chemical information?

The systems I know most about are the chemical structure searching ones. Basically they are the CA Registry files on STN and on Télésystèmes, and Beilstein Online, which is on three hosts, STN, DIALOG and ORBIT.

For Beilstein I prefer STN to DIALOG because DIALOG isn't quite as nice an implementation. On DIALOG, you have to use a less attractive front end for drawing a structure, and the system isn't as fluid. Also, DIALOG sends character strings down the line that aren't error-checked. They claim it's much cheaper and more effective to send just text, while STN claims that its way of working is both more sophisticated and better because they've put in error-checking.

The STN Express environment is so much friendlier for the ICI end-users, and for me for that matter, that I wouldn't be tempted to use Beilstein on DIALOG. We certainly wouldn't use Beilstein on ORBIT because the structure drawing isn't very nice and the system is what I would call esoteric. It doesn't really link into anything else, and it really isn't similar to anything else. I think it would be a backward move to put a whole lot of users on that because it's not really a standard product.

STN Express, however, is a fairly standard system. It may not be the best way of drawing chemical structures.

However, the rest of the package has such important features that people have accepted it readily, and it's compatible with other systems, too. It will be even better when Molecular Design's ISIS (Integrated Scientific Information System) is linked to STN Express. They're planning to link their drawing package, ISIS Draw, so you'll be able to draw your chemical structure in ISIS, and convert it into STN Express. Then you'll have the best of both worlds. You'll have the chemical drawing you're familiar with if you're using MACCS and Molecular Design systems in-house, plus the telecommunications, error-checking and scrolling graphic output that STN Express provides. This ISIS/STN Express link could be, I won't say the best thing since sliced bread, but a definite advance.

Unfortunately, it doesn't allow true downloading. You can't take the structure out of CAS ONLINE and bring it into your in-house system. It's still only a picture. What chemists would like is to be able to manipulate and search those structures in-house. Of course, Chemical Abstracts doesn't want you to be able to download large numbers of structures for fear of losing online revenue and control of the database.

STN is still not giving Molecular Design a free hand in the ISIS development, and they are really compromising the usefulness of their data. I don't particularly want to attack them, since for years I've been asking, publicly, "Why won't they work together?" Now they are doing so, and one must applaud that. However, both parties are still very wary in the areas in which they are competitive. Besides downloading, users would like some other things as well. They would like to be able to put a Registry number in and get that picture from the CAS file, and then change the structure and send it back up as a search query. It takes quite a while, even in a really slick system, to draw a chemical structure. So they think, instead of having to draw it with a mouse, why not simply say, "Give me 1, 2, 3, 5, hyphen-whatever," and then have the structure come up. That's a whole lot faster. For technical reasons, you can't do that in Chemical Abstracts at the moment. That's one of the features we lack in Express. So it isn't absolutely perfect, but we're getting there. They do listen to user suggestions.

Is there a formal instruction program at ICI for training end-users?
When ICI first started with online in the early '80s, CAS sent over some of their best trainers. This was in the early days of CAS ONLINE, just before they had the menu option for drawing structures online. This was just about pre-mouse, too, so the first chemists were actually taught text-structure input. That meant that in order to get a sort of honeycomb onto the screen, you had to use a set of commands to explain how to build it. They didn't find that terribly satisfactory. Shortly after that, CAS enhanced the system so you could draw lines with a mouse, and that's what they called graphic-structure input. End-user training took off much more rapidly at that point.

For the first couple of years or so, ICI always used Chemical Abstracts training. They came over from Columbus, usually in conjunction with a European online meeting, and trained a new bunch of chemists each time. Eventually they did a train-the-trainer program, so several people within ICI could take over the training. Over the years, that function has grown into a 14-person department. They've become an all-purpose port of call for all kinds of hardware, software and firmware problems, not just with online, but for a lot of in-house systems, too, whatever the users need help with.

Even with that support, end-users at ICI tend to fall into three groups. First are the heavy searchers who get trained and who keep on doing it, searching almost as much as the information scientists. Then there are middling people who search enough to keep them in practice, but they only use it when they really want to. Finally, there are some who, despite all the training and all the efforts, are virtually non-users. Quite often, it's not because they're computer-illiterate, but because they don't have a great need for it. At ICI, we found about one-third in each category.

Even the more sophisticated end-users don't really know where their databases are. They might be in Columbus or sitting on their VAX or on some ICI network. In fact, when we first got PCs in-house, some of them thought that the Chemical Abstracts database was sitting right there in their PC. When you think about it, why *should* it matter to them? It's just a keyboard and a screen. In fact, they might not even know what you and I mean by "online."

Does that mean they're oblivious to the cost factor when they're hooked up to a commercial system?

In the pharmaceutical division they are, a little bit. Some of the managers are fairly cost-sensitive, but chemists who are very keen on the system certainly don't have a taxi-meter feeling at all. Management is told what it's costing at monthly intervals. They're told that Hiram Q. Potts of Section 10 searched £2000 worth of Chemical Abstracts this month, or whatever. But they wouldn't normally intervene unless they saw that somebody who's not of very significant status in the company seems to be spending a lot of money. Then they might question it. But if it's one of the prime research workers, it's unlikely the section manager would criticize how much he spent last month. It's really a monitoring thing.

Other ICI businesses handle search costs differently. ICI Agrochemicals had a cutoff figure beyond which they said, "No more searching money for this section." The pharmaceutical industry has always spent much more on research than others. They tend to regard it as part of the research process, and they're a bit freer about costs. They realize that it costs an awful lot more to make a compound unnecessarily than it does to discover that it's already known, published, patented, or whatever. So it may *look* expensive to spend a lot on CAS ONLINE, when in fact it could save an awful lot of money.

Chemistry is very information-intensive. The concept of the chemical structure has always given chemists a nice way into databases. I found that biologists at ICI were different animals from the chemists. Bioscientists need quite a lot of databases. They need TOXLine, BIOSIS, and so on, and often on different hosts. They have to do keyword searching, use Boolean logic, and deal with the fact that all sorts of terms may be handled differently on different databases and different hosts. Doing end-user searches in bioscience is much more complicated than for the chemist who's got a nice little chemical structure to fool around with.

So online information has had chemistry end-users playing with it much longer than some other fields. Still, end-users are never going to be as expert as information scientists, even in structure searching. There are fairly strict guidelines within ICI, and even stricter ones in some other companies, about the kinds of searches that chemists are allowed to do. In some places, they're only allowed to do single-compound lookups to make sure they don't synthesize something unnecessarily. They're not allowed to do generic searches, and certainly not full-blown substructure searching, which is quite expensive. ICI never restricted its chemists that much, but they do have a set of guidelines. Informally, they say, "Thou shalt not search if a big financial decision depends on it, if a patent depends on it, if it involves a regulatory decision, if it's at all tricky, or if you really want 100 percent recall. Anything along those lines must be referred to an information scientist."

So there is an assumption that an information scientist will formulate a better search than an end-user. I don't know that chemists would even want to go through the bother of making sure they've got 100 percent recall. If it's that sort of job, they probably would prefer to have an information scientist do it. But they sometimes prefer to do it themselves for the immediacy and the browsability.

ICI didn't notice any decrease in the number of information scientists after they put all these end-users online. End-users haven't put information scientists out of a job. It's given them a different sort of job, perhaps. It's created a whole new section of the end-user support people.

Do full-text databases play much of a role in the environment you've been describing?

Now, that is a whole new ballgame. No chemists at ICI are doing full-text searching. The full-text database that would probably interest them would be Chemical Journals Online on STN. Some Wiley and Elsevier journals are online, too, along with some others. In actual fact, those journals haven't really sold very well online for a lot of reasons. Even most information scientists, let alone chemists, don't want to search databases when you've only got about four years backlog online.

Also, the database is text-only, no graphics, tables, chemical structures or anything like that. Scientific publications without tables, graphs, diagrams and so on are pretty poor. For business searchers, that may be a relatively minor consideration, but anything scientific is going to be packed with pictures, diagrams, tables, numbers and chemical structures.

On the other hand, I think that scholarly journals on the Internet will impact the online industry tremendously. Many have developed completely outside the commercial publishing structure. It's too soon to tell how successful they will be, but it's certainly something to keep an eye on.

Let's talk a bit about search technique. In your field, a search that retrieves zero hits is often, I imagine, a pretty significant search.

It's in the patents area that no hits is most interesting, because no hits might be exactly what you want. The greatest thing you can be told, if you think you've created a new drug, is "no hits." That's wonderful, valuable information and ironically, if you're being charged per record output, it's almost free. From the patent searcher's point of view, of course, the problem is, "Do I go on?" It's so absolutely vital to be comprehensive on a patent search that when you get no hits, you really do get worried.

The no-hit search is one of life's big problems. "Have I done it wrong?" Then, if you do what searchers typically do, which is to broaden it out, to make certain you haven't missed anything, you start losing relevance. This is related, in a way, to something that's coming up in chemical structure searching. Similarity searching has become quite a buzzword lately. The idea is that you don't simply say, "Give me molecules that literally match my search," but "Give me everything that's even similar to what I've asked for, then rank the output." The interesting question is, how do you define similarity? It's a whole new science.

It's also becoming important for two other reasons. One is that databases in chemistry are getting bigger; you've got these huge chemical reaction databases and so on. When you start putting the structures up, the data related to them, and all the graphical information, the whole thing becomes vastly bigger and the problem of retrieval that much more complicated. But if you can rank them and say that, for one reason or another, these ten are more similar than the others, that helps you compare large quantities of output in terms of their structures.

The other reason similarity is important is, for the pharmaceutical industry, in terms of finding new drug leads. If you've got six compounds that you know are active cardiovascular drugs, finding the ones that are most similar to those is important.

The point I'm trying to make is that searching isn't just a matter of *exact* searching, like "Give me Bloggs' latest paper," or "Find me aspirin." It's "Find me aspirin, but where this atom is either nitrogen or something else," which is what you call substructure searching. There's also the whole, much more vague, question of similarity searching, which applies not only in chemistry, but in textual searching as well.

Once similarity searching becomes more commonplace, it will be one of your answers to the question of when you know you have 100 percent recall or sufficient recall. Similarity searching would do the job for you; you look at the first ten and if you're satisfied with what you see, that's your answer right there. If you want to do a bit more, you know that the next ten will be your next best answer.

It sounds like there's an experimental mechanism at work in similarity searching. "Let's try this. Now let's try tweaking *that* a little bit and see what that does." Do you think there's something in the nature of research itself that makes the kind of end-user searching you're describing such an iterative process?

That's exactly what appeals to the end-user, that and the browsability factor. When he sees the output himself, he's inspired, and it gives him an idea of what to do next. Some people have said that the best combination would be to have the scientific expert, the chemist or whatever, sit alongside the search expert, and for them to do the search together. That's not practical in a big company because there are so many people doing so many searches, so few information scientists, and so little time. You just couldn't do that for every search. So end-user searching, I guess, is a compromise.

The intermediary searcher tends to fill in a form, have a go, go back to the scientist if there's too much output, and so on. It's not truly interactive, and yet it probably will produce the best search from an information science point of view. But it may not produce exactly what the end-user wants; there's always the danger that you may have looked at something that is absolutely what he wants and thought, "That's a load of rubbish," and he never knows that you found it.

That's always the danger of intermediary searching, which is why a lot of people tend to err on the side on inclusion rather than exclusion.

Another approach to this problem of too much output is that people could just think about making databases that aren't so big. That sounds like a daft idea, doesn't it? But, in fact, in chemical reactions especially, selective databases used in-house are preferred by most end-users to huge online ones.

The in-house systems—and Molecular Design is the leader here—not only have slightly smaller databases, but also ways of ranking output if you do get too many search hits. The selective databases will give you reactions in certain areas like organo-metallic chemistry, or they'll give you the current literature only or novel reactions. Chemical Abstracts, on the other hand, takes the warehouse approach. Their attitude is, "This is in the literature and so we must index it."

In a field like this, I imagine that end-users accumulate personal databases to a considerable extent?

Oh, absolutely. We discovered at ICI that users were building up little card indexes of their favorite literature references. Once PCs came in, they started building their own personal databases of favorite references. There are arguments pro and con about doing this sort of thing. Some people think it's dangerous to build a little literature database of your own, because after a couple of years, the thing gets pretty unmanageable. Since they are personal, they can't share them with other people as they please. If you leave the company, that's a loss of information to the company. Also, if you've been building the thing from a current awareness search done a couple of years ago, your needs will have changed somewhat, even in ways of which you're not consciously aware. That means that the concepts you use in your search profile may not be keeping up with the literature you really are interested in.

The result is that your personal database has become something very different from what you'd get if an information scientist did that search today. So there are some dangers in end-users taking the literature function offline like this, but realistically speaking, nobody's been able to stop them. They like doing it, so it's been accepted. It was decided that it was better to help them do the system properly rather than stop them from doing it at all. So the computing department took a standard package with a menuing system and built an application for these chemists. Now, when they've got a reference they want to keep, they can key it in very nicely on a forms-design screen. It also links into a system whereby searches that are run for them can be transferred electronically to their PCs, and then added to their journal reference database. They can also receive the search results on a floppy and transfer them to their database. Current awareness searches can be added automatically.

It seems to me that CD-ROM would be an appropriate technology for much of the chemical searching we've been talking about.

From my point of view in the chemical structure world, there are only two CD-ROM products. One is Current Facts in Chemistry on CD-ROM, which is a Springer-Beilstein product, and the other one is the Chapman-Hall Natural Products database, which is just coming out. Some of the reasons are purely marketing, of course. Chemical Abstracts doesn't want to put its database on CD-ROM in case it kills the online sales, although they are doing a CD-ROM of the next Collective Index.

It's actually quite difficult, technically, to do chemical structure searching on CD-ROM. I think that's been a major part of the holdup. Disk access is slow and input-output is slow, so you've got to set up your search to go in once and grab a lot of information which can then be read serially. That is not a technique that's normally been used for substructure searching; some of the methods that have been traditionally used have to be modified a bit to make it fast enough on CD-ROM.

Another factor is that CD-ROM, by its nature, is for big databases, and as we've discussed, doing big databases with graphical content is quite difficult. So you've got a double problem with CD-ROM: the need to search a big database quickly, and to do so with a rather different technology, one that minimizes I/O and uses more CPU processing.

Some people feel that CD-ROM might be an interim technology, anyway. There's a lot of interest right now, of course, in CD-ROM networking. It's not so much that people want CD-ROMs, but that they want the data in-house, on a network, so they can use it lots of times cheaply. It doesn't have to be CD-ROM; there could well be some different way, eventually, of holding the database on your network. CD-ROM as a technology doesn't interest me as much as the concept of in-house against online. I think there will be a move toward getting data in-house, but not necessarily on CD-ROM.

It's all fascinating, isn't it? I look back at some of the prognostications I made in 1987 or so, and a fair amount of them have come to pass. There are always surprises in this field. It keeps life interesting, don't you think?

SUPER SEARCH SECRETS

On favorite databases...

For Beilstein I prefer STN to DIALOG because DIALOG isn't quite as nice an implementation. On DIALOG, you have to use a less attractive front end for drawing a structure, and the system isn't as fluid.

On STN Express...

...is a fairly standard system...has such important features that people have accepted it readily....It will be even better when Molecular Design's ISIS (Integrated Scientific Information System) is linked to STN Express. They're planning to link their drawing package, ISIS Draw, so you'll be able to draw your chemical structure in ISIS, and convert it into STN Express. Then you'll have the best of both worlds.

On search costs...

The pharmaceutical industry has always spent much more on research than others. They tend to regard it as part of the research process, and they're a bit freer about costs. They realize that it costs an awful lot more to make a compound unnecessarily than it does to discover that it's already known, published, patented, or whatever. So it may look expensive to spend a lot on CAS ONLINE, when in fact it could save an awful lot of money.

On getting zero hits...

It's in the patents area that no hits is most interesting, because no hits might be exactly what you want. The greatest thing you can be told, if you think you've created a new drug, is "no hits." That's wonderful, valuable information and ironically, if you're being charged per record output, it's almost free.

On CD-ROM...

It's actually quite difficult, technically, to do chemical structure searching on CD-ROM. I think that's been a major part of the holdup. Disk access is slow and input-output is slow, so you've got to set up your search to go in once and grab a lot of information which can then be read serially.

CHAPTER 23

SHERRY WILLHITE: ONLINE DETECTIVE

Sherry Willhite was an information services librarian and chemistry specialist in the Science and Engineering Library at the University of California, San Diego (UCSD) at the time of this interview. She is currently with the MELVYL User Services Group at the University of California Division of Library Automation in Oakland.

What brought you to where you are today, and where along the way did you learn to search?

I had a degree in pharmacy and was a practicing pharmacist for nine years. Then I began looking for a career change. I wanted to do something that would be a bit different every day yet still have a strong public service component. Librarianship seemed like it might be a reasonable thing to do. I went to the UCLA library school and, while I was there, I took all the online searching courses they offered. As part of my internship, I worked with one of the faculty members in the chemistry department to learn how to search STN for chemical abstracts. When I got the job at UCSD, I took every online course that I could. It's always been a very strong interest.

Who are your clientele?

We serve the entire university community—UCSD faculty, students and staff members. We also have a Corporate Associates program, where companies can join for a fee ($2500, $10,000, or whatever) which entitles them to library privileges, including online searching.

Do most of your search requests tend to be routine, or do you conduct a detailed reference interview with each client?

It depends. Even if the request is straightforward—an author search, say, from 1985 to the present—I might go back and ask if they wanted abstracts, or what area the person works in, if it's not obvious from what I've been given. But we've been doing this long enough now, and I put notes in our newsletters about how the search process works, so my requesters usually anticipate what I need to know. With people I've never worked with before, their e-mail request usually turns into a phone call and a more complete interview.

Many people like to be here with me while I'm doing their search, especially the graduate students. I like that, because it helps them understand what I'm doing, and why I ask them the questions I do. They get an idea of how interactive the system is and that, for basic searches, at least, it's pretty simple. That encourages them to get their own account, so it's also a teaching tool. The more they know about the process, the more aware they are of the limitations of the databases, and of how to frame their questions to get a good response. It helps them realize why I sometimes have to tell them, "I know you want every pyridine derivative in the world, but the way Chemical Abstracts indexes them is by name. That means that we might get a few articles talking about them in general, but if you want all of them, I need the name of each one," and so on. It doesn't hit home with them until we go online and do it their way, then do it my way, and they see the difference.

Often, with the students, anything will do. They're just looking for a thread to pull to get started, a few good articles. They don't need to be really comprehensive. At the other extreme, though, are the people who are at the point in their dissertation research where they need to know that no one has published on this subject before. Those searches tend to be much more complicated, so there's a place on the request form that asks, "Do you want just a few good articles, or are you trying to be comprehensive?"

I also ask, "Do you expect to find information on your topic?" That's primarily for the chemists, because sometimes I'll search six ways from Sunday and not find anything. Then I call them and say, "I did this and this and then I called so-and-so, and then I did this and this and this and I still didn't find anything." And their response is "Good." Oh, I could kill them! Here I am, feeling so stupid. So I put that question on the form, too. Then, if they say, "I hope not," and I don't find anything, I feel good about it. I still search as hard, but when I keep getting empty sets I don't have to think, "Where am I going wrong?"

If they expect to find something and I'm not finding anything, I often call the help desk of whatever database I'm using and say, "Okay, we're trying to find out this, I've done XYZ, what else should I be doing, is there any other way to approach it?" I'm much more likely to ask someone else to second-guess me, or to second-guess myself, if I know that they're trying to prove that it hasn't been done yet. My users seem to have bought into the idea, finally, that I need to know what they're trying to accomplish, because it may change the way I have to approach the search. I may want to go much broader than they think necessary, just to be sure.

Do you work in a charge-back situation?

Yes. We do two types of searching here at UC San Diego. We do ready reference searching at the discretion of the reference librarian. If I decide that the most effective way to answer your question is by doing an online search, then I go online, do a focused search, get your answers or your citations, logoff and give them to you. That kind of searching is free because I decided to take that approach rather than go to a print source. We've cancelled some subscriptions to indexes that are available online, and we spend, maybe, $15 each time we look it up online rather than $3000 for an annual subscription.

Our other kind of searching is the mediated search, which we do on patron request. For that, we bill back on a cost-recovery basis. For the Corporate Associates program, we add a search fee on top.

How do you negotiate what to spend on a search, and how far to take it?

I try to give a client an idea of how much what they're asking for would actually cost. One of our faculty members works on a certain chemical, and once a year we print out anything that mentions that chemical. That's what he really needs; it fulfills his needs, so we do it. If a graduate student came to me with the same request, I would explain to him how big a search it would be, and how much it would cost. I would suggest that he talk to his advisor and make sure the budget can stand it. If he comes back to me and says, "My professor says I can spend $34 on a search. What can we get?" then we switch to "sweat equity" searching. This means that to keep the costs down, we just list out the part of the equivalent print index the answers are in. We can do that on the ready reference account, and the student has to do the work of getting the index volumes and looking up the citations.

In cases like that, we're using databases as direct indexes to the print volumes. For a few dollars, we can get articles very specific to the search term, even when the narrowest term used in the print index is still quite broad. Of course, some of the publishers have changed their numbering systems, so it's a bit more difficult, but we try to use tricks like that whenever the situation seems to demand it.

With the Corporate Associates program, setting a budget is very much a negotiation process. We sit down with the documentation and the price list, and figure the possible cost.

Do you keep some kind of search log?

We keep a simple handwritten log, with the person's name and affiliation, their department or company name, the date, what databases were used, and a description of the search. That description is very brief, like "three authors" or "substructure" or "phase diagram." It tends to be a pretty generic description simply because we try to protect patron confidentiality. We record enough so that, if they question the bill, we can check back and say, "Oh, we did three author searches for you that day." But it's not enough to be informative to a casual observer. We also write down how much online time we spent and the cost, plus any additional fees. We record which accounts we used, since that varies depending on the person and the reason for the search.

Typically what kinds of searches do you do?

We do a lot of author searching, both for people who want to see what their competitors are doing and for graduate students trying to decide where they want to do post-doc work. People also want to look at the makeup of the committees that are overseeing disposition of grants. They can say, "These guys have this kind of scientific background, so let's make sure that we focus our proposal in a way they'll understand." Some people are routinely very successful at getting grants. If they know who is going to be on the deciding committee, they'll research it that way.

It's sort of strategic academic searching?

Right. Speaking of author searching, STN now lets you do an EXPAND CONTINUOUS, so you're not limited to 50 terms in an EXPAND command. That can be a lifesaver. It means you can expand on Smith and then expand on Jones, and instead of starting all over at one, the list is consecutive, and you can go back to the earlier part. So if you've picked out the name with initials, and then with the full name spelled out, and then you think, "Oh no, did I remember to select the one that also said "editor?" you can go back and get it without having to do the whole EXPAND again.

Another common type of search we get is the "Find the physical property in the haystack" search, where the requester has been through all of the standard handbooks. Then there's, "I want to use this technique on something; has anybody used this technique on something similar?" That's probably the biggest category. There's also a lot of "Give me every paper that this very prolific person wrote." It's not unusual to get 300 abstracts. Of course, around promotion, review and tenure time, there is, "Who has cited my papers?" or "Who has cited this list of people's papers?" With those, the requester always tells me, "This is really, really, really confidential."

Much of what I get are "Go fish" searches. Graduate students and researchers often are not sure exactly what they're looking for. They like to get big search results and sift through them, looking for "Has anybody talked about this?" Those are the basic categories. The bulk of it, though, for me personally, is chemical structure searching.

In my business, when someone asks what kind of searching I do, I say, "Everything but chemical structures." So, you and I are occupying completely different universes. What *is* a structure search? What does a structure query look like?

In a structure search, what I'm doing is drawing a picture of the structure with keyboard commands. If you're going to draw a six-membered ring, you say "graph r 6." "Graph" tells it to draw something that is going to have bonds and elements in it; "r" says to put it into a ring format. So it will give you a six-membered ring for all of the elements that are carbons. What I might want to do next is say "turn node three into nitrogen instead of carbon." I have to tell it what kinds of bonds are supposed to be where.

It's kind of a programming language, really. It's a different sort of command language and a different way of searching. What you're doing is communicating with a structure connection table; that's your thesaurus. The structure connection table doesn't know what the whole thing looks like when it's put together. It only knows what the connections are. It knows that I have a carbon with three connections to it, or a carbon that has only two connections. You can have that because hydrogen doesn't count as a connection.

There are all kinds of weird rules that you have to learn, and I've learned them very painfully over the years. They all know me at the help desk at STN, especially now that some of my guys are getting into these polymers and metallic complexes that are really hard for the people at STN to do. It always makes me feel better when I call and they say, "We'll have to get back to you," and it takes them two or three days to get back to me. I think, "It's a really hard one for them, too; oh, good, so I'm not stupid."

What you do in a substructure search is build a query that the structure connection table can understand. You draw it so that it looks like the picture you have in your hand, but you characterize it in terms of the connections. It's just a learned thing; you could learn this. It does help to have a background in chemistry, but as I explain to my patrons, they know a lot more chemistry than I do or ever will, because I don't have time to go back and learn chemistry. My last structure class was a very long time ago. So they're responsible for knowing if what I'm giving them is accurate chemically. I'm responsible for knowing if it's accurate in terms of the search language.

That's something you can say about the information professional/end-user relationship regardless of field.

Exactly. I am the search specialist; you are the content specialist. They're supposed to know their field; I'm supposed to know how to get things out of the database. When it comes down to the thesaurus, it's their responsibility to pick the terms that most accurately represent their query. My responsibility is to enter them in the right way and to think of alternatives if the first approach doesn't work.

Let's talk about searching *per se*. When you're approaching a search, how do you plan out your strategy? Do you actually make notes on paper?

Yes, they look like chicken scratches. One reason I use a search request form is that it forces me to write down all of the boring, routine things that I don't really want to think about. Do you want abstracts, how many articles do you really want, and how much money do you want to spend? Those are the things that you need to know to do the search properly. They aren't the fun, intellectual-content part. For a structure search, we draw the structure, and we show all the bonds and all the hydrogens and list the variables. Some of the searches can look pretty bizarre on the computer in text mode. With some of the more complicated ring structures, it gets quite distorted. But that doesn't really matter because the end result is not pictures of other peoples' structures. People want to get the references and abstracts, and then go read the articles. So we display a few structures to make sure we're getting the right thing, but once they're satisfied we're on the right track, we just pull up the related citations and abstracts. We don't even bother displaying them. The answer is not the drawings. The answer is the journal articles.

What systems do you use?

Since my focus is chemistry, I primarily use STN and DIALOG. We have accounts with Data-Star, ORBIT, BRS and EPIC. On CD-ROM, we have COMPENDEX and MathSci, both of which are very heavily used by the patrons. The off-campus community, especially now that we have COMPENDEX, has discovered CD-ROM; they like it a lot. What we've been doing lately is have patrons do their search on the CD-ROM first, and we help them frame out their strategy. If they still need more, or if they want to go back further in time than what we have on CD, then we go online for them. The engineers in particular are generally more interested in the recent stuff, so having the last five years of COMPENDEX satisfies probably 80 percent of their information needs. Once they find they can do it themselves, they get bored with the menus and start looking at our cheat sheets for the command language. They do quite a bit of good searching on the CD-ROM.

We also have Bowker's Sci-Tech Reference Plus, which is American Men and Women of Science, on CD-ROM, the sci-tech sections of Ulrich's Periodical Directory and Books in Print, the CRC Composite Index, and the Information Handling Service Index to World Standards. We don't have the standards themselves on CD-ROM, but we do have the index. We also have the Sigma+Aldrich Materials Safety Data Sheets, which is quite popular.

If the same database, or equivalent information, is available on more than one system, what determines where you go for it?

The first factor has to be cost. We get academic discounts on quite a few files on STN, so if it's for a research project rather than a classroom situation, we go to STN after five o'clock. They discount the Chemical Abstract files, INSPEC, COMPENDEX, the core sources that one would use at a sci-tech library, by 80 percent in the evening, so we really have no choice but to use it.

We have classes, too, where part of the assignment is to understand what online searching is and to see how it works. For that, we use our DIALOG Classmate account, which we can use during the day at $15 an hour. If you've got four groups of students, you can give each an hour, which is plenty of time, and the maximum cost for the class is $60.

After cost, the main determinant is features. If it's during the day and we need abstracts from Chemical Abstracts, we have to go into STN. If we don't need the abstracts, we can do it on DIALOG. If we want to search something interdisciplinary, where we need to cover INSPEC, Chemical Abstracts, COMPENDEX and NTIS at the same time, then we'll probably do a DIALOG OneSearch.

If you're doing a OneSearch, how do you rank the files in terms of what you want to retrieve?

It depends a lot on what the person is doing. I often go to DIALINDEX first in the files I'm planning to use, to see how many hits we're going to get and whether it's going to pay to include them all in a OneSearch. I use DIALINDEX all the time, especially for weird stuff, when I have no idea where it's going to be. Then I do a OneSearch and usually remove the duplicates. I don't necessarily prefer a file with abstracts because we probably own the journal. If all someone wants is a few articles to get started and the subject is pretty well-defined, I just give them the citations and let them go.

Once you've mapped out your general approach and decided what systems you're going to use, how do you go about building a search strategy?

I try to enter it the first time exactly the way they asked for it. Then, depending on how many answers I get and what they look like, I know whether to go broader or narrower. Say you use a proximity connector and you get two articles, and you're not really comfortable with that, it doesn't seem right. You think, "What would happen if I broadened it a bit, just to make sure?" So you use AND instead of the proximity connector, and you get seven hits, and out of those seven, five are actually good.

It's a pretty standard technique, narrowing a search. Ask if they really want to see 472 things. Maybe yes, maybe no. If they don't, what types of things do they not want to see? If patents aren't useful, rule out the patents. If they only want review articles, we just look for review articles. I try not to limit to English except as a last resort, because a lot of very good research is published in other languages. If there are only seven things on your topic and six are in other languages, we can probably get you a translation. Language is never the first cut I make, because we might lose potentially good stuff.

Limiting by date doesn't always work, either. "I only want things published since 1987." Well, we expanded on this author's name and found 47 articles, but since 1987 he's only published one. Do you want to see the other 46 or not? In a case like that, they probably didn't realize that this person was nearing the end of his career and was not publishing very frequently any more. They were picturing the author as in their 30s or 40s, and really he's 80 and most of his work was done 15 years ago. If they're here with me, I try to do it in an interactive way. We look at some citations and see what they like and don't. We probably spend a little more money that way, but it's usually worth it. There are times when you just can't cut it down. I had one guy who was doing a literature review and we just ran out of ideas. We ended up with hundreds and hundreds of hits. I printed all the titles and asked him go through and make check marks.

You do what you can do. If all your searches go smoothly all the time, that's not the real world of searching. Searches have a way of turning on you and getting complicated when you least expect it. The people I deal with have been really responsive to this. I tell them, "Okay, this is our theory; this is what we tried. It didn't work the way we thought it would. We had to go back and rethink it." They're scientists; they go through that kind of thing all day. For the most part they're pretty understanding and willing to be actively involved. If it doesn't work the first time they don't say, "That's okay, I don't want it to be too much trouble." It's more like "How long can you stay tonight?"

They make you buy into it, don't they?

You really are part of a team. I've had clients mention at faculty meetings and at national meetings, "We couldn't have done any of this if the library hadn't been there to do the searches for us." We try very hard to provide Nordstrom-level service. What they get from ready reference is really more like K-Mart "blue light special" searching. These people live on information; that's what they do for a living. For our guys, the end product is usually not something marketable. In industry, they're trying to put something out by a certain date. They have a lot of constraints in terms of production and time spent on product development and that kind of stuff.

Here, we have a bit more luxury. "We'll just do it and see what happens," or "This is kind of neat chemistry. Let's play with it for a while." The process itself is the end product. They're always coming up with something new. At least once a month someone comes in and asks for something that gives me that feeling in the pit of my stomach. "Oh, no, why did they ask me that? Why was I here? Why wasn't someone else at the desk? I'm never going to be able to do that."

Then, of course, you just go ahead and do it, and it's hard, and that's when you learn. There's one guy I call my "learning experience." Fortunately he's got a sense of humor, because I call him that to his face. He walks in and I say, "Oh no, another search from hell!" And he says, "Oh, this won't be so bad." The point is that his searches are the hardest ones I do, but they're the ones that I learn the most from. They're the ones where I get all these nifty little weird techniques that I could have used in the past, if I had known them. They are things like finding out that they actually do index this concept three totally different ways—things that, in the normal course of events, you would never learn.

Every once in a while, you find a use for a command that you thought was stupid when they first announced it. Or you discover, after you've talked with the customer service people, that the reason you can't find what you want is that it's not indexed that way. The reason it's not indexed that way is because they hadn't thought of doing it, and they say, "My, that's an interesting concept!" Or they'll tell you, "It's sort of indexed this way but sometimes there's this other way." You can actually have brainstorming sessions with some of the people who are responsible for indexing that part of the file. That's invaluable. I tell them that they're my advanced-advanced training. I think of all the basics I learned, and all the advanced training classes I took, and now I'm doing my postgraduate work with these guys.

One thing I can say, especially for DIALOG and STN, is that people at the help desk are so helpful. Most of my questions are not the kind that the people who are actually answering the phones can answer. Instead of putting up barriers, they say, "You really should be talking to so-and-so." They go out of their way to put me in touch with the right person. I don't feel like I'm being sloughed off. Not all services are like that. Of course, there are times when I think they must have a picture of me on a dart board...

Controlled vocabulary, coding, and so on must be especially important in the kind of searching you do. Do you ever find it appropriate to do free-text searching?

For ready reference, we use free text a lot, especially in the field of computer science. That changes so fast that, very often, it's the only way you can find anything. They invent jargon for all these new concepts and developments, and the indexers can't keep up. They have to fit it into a broader construct or an older term that may not really be appropriate. Sometimes, they will put emerging terms, programming language names or software names in the identifier field. That can be a lifesaver if the name is the same as a common English word or phrase.

It's like searching on a company with a name like Computer Systems, Inc. If you don't have a company name field to restrict it to, you run into trouble with the generic nature of the phrase.

Exactly. But often you're looking for something that's not going to be in the controlled vocabulary but may be in the abstract, like a specific property in a chemical. Or it may be a very specific aspect for which you do have controlled vocabulary, but you're getting so much junk that you would rather have precision than recall. You're willing to miss a few nifty things as long as you get some good ones. We do a lot of creative proximity searching, using order-independent operators to look for interchangeable phrases like shale oil or oil shale. You have to ask yourself how many different ways you can say the same thing.

When I'm training end-users, I tell them not to use the NOT operator unless they're really willing to give up a lot of stuff. I try to convince them to save NOT for controlled vocabulary and other kinds of field limiting. If you're not careful, you can inadvertently lose the one thing you've been looking for.

Do you deliver search results electronically, for the most part?

Definitely. When DIALMAIL first came out, I fell in love with it, and I used it a lot. Now, because I have access to all the utilities on the campus network, I tend to use File Transfer Protocol. I download the search results to my hard drive and then use FTP to move it to the requester's account. It works like the DOS COPY command, where you just copy a filename from one drive to another. It saves a lot of time at my end because I can shift these sometimes humongous files as a packet instead of having to read them in. More than half my search results go out by FTP. We don't print much out anymore.

Do you do any post-processing? Do you look through your results for false drops and that kind of thing?

I do post-processing because I just turn "capture" on when I start searching and capture everything that goes across the screen. I take out all the interim search statements, postings, and the structure-building commands, and just leave the final answer set. If it's a structure search, I give them the structure as we built it, with all the connections and so on.

I also leave in the header flag you see when you log into each file because it gives the date, the time, and the update number. I tell them that they have to keep that forever because if they ever want to repeat the search, we can update it from that literal point in time. So it's the patron's responsibility to keep track of that information. They can take that search to any other searcher and that person should be able to look at it and see what databases we used, when we did the search, what our search strategy was, and what our results were. The graduate students, when they go off and do post-doc work somewhere, know that wherever they are, it should be easy for someone else to update a search for them.

Do you have any kind of formal feedback mechanism once a search has gone out?

I don't have a form. But I've had people roaring back in here to tell me it was a piece of garbage, they hated it, and I had to do it over. I've had others call and say, "That was really helpful. I really liked it." They usually follow that up with, "Now can we try it this other way?"

When I deliver a search, I do tell patrons to get back to me if they have any questions or problems. I make sure they have my phone number and my e-mail address. I encourage them to let me know if something doesn't make sense to them. It won't bother me, and I won't see it as punitive. If a search didn't work for some reason, I need to know it, too.

What haven't we touched on in terms of money-saving tips that you might want to share?

If you're really not sure where to look, go into DIALINDEX on DIALOG. That's always the first place I look if I'm not sure what database to use. I just round up the likely suspects and try it there, even if I don't end up running the actual search in DIALOG.

Another thing I do is compare the connect and display charges for the same file on different online systems. I'm thinking of one in particular that's incredibly cheap to search on STN but incredibly expensive to display the records. On DIALOG, the same file is incredibly expensive to search but incredibly cheap to display a full record. DIALOG charges more than four times as much per hour, and depending on what segments you choose, STN typically costs twice as much to display. Naturally, I search it on STN and display it on DIALOG.

What kinds of quality problems do you encounter in the databases you search?

Well, apparently I live in a town called "San Deigo." We really notice those transpositions. Often I have done searches on our faculty members who have common last names, like "Professor Lee," and I tried to limit the results to them and not the other guys by putting in the name of the university. I've learned to type it in as "Deigo" as well as "Diego." If I don't, I miss something every time. It's standard procedure. It's in almost every database that way.

Another pet peeve is that SciSearch still hasn't figured out that you can have over 9,999 pages in a journal. Some chemistry journals have over 10,000 pages; they number sequentially throughout the year. So you see a cite to page four, and you look at the volume number, and the date, and sure enough, it's the end of the year. You just know that it's page 10,004. They can really lead you down the garden path. Little things like that you just have to know.

And that comes with experience.

It comes from not knowing what's going on, and hitting your head against the wall. You keep trying to move forward, and there's a wall there, until you finally realize, "Wait a minute..."

Tell me what, in your mind, makes a good searcher. It's obvious that you love searching. Why?

I like being able to play with a computer and make it do things it wasn't designed to do. I use DIALOGLINK to search STN, Data-Star, EPIC, and basically anything I want to because there are some features, like type-ahead, that I adore. There are some things about DIALOGLINK that I hate with a passion, but I love type-ahead. I get some of my best ideas as a search is going along. There's only so much uploading you can do. You eventually get to the point where you need to OR this or AND that or limit it to this date. You need to do something but you don't want to do it until you see how many answers you get. If there are only three answers, why bother limiting it by anything? So I love type-ahead.

I especially love type-ahead because I can't type. I know that sounds bizarre for a person who made her living as a pharmacist and makes her living as a searcher. I never took typing in school, and several of my fingers don't touch the keyboard. As far as searching itself goes, I enjoy it because the questions are never the same. Even if you're sitting there doing three million boring author searches, they're all different. It's continually surprising. You never know where you're going to find something, and you never can be satisfied with taking "no" for an answer. If you don't find it here, you might to find it there. You can use your creativity: If I were a horse and I were lost, where would I be? Well, then go look and find that horse. You get immediate feedback and immediate gratification, unlike the delayed gratification that you get from most of the other parts of life.

It's like a puzzle. I'm a crossword puzzle junkie. I like playing with words and with language. The concept of indexing fascinates me. How do you build an index that will last? How long will it last? How do you find a mechanism to bring together a body of knowledge that will be useful ten or 20 or 100 years from now?

I've got to give Frederick Beilstein credit. That man came up with his indexing system for organic chemistry in the 1800s, and it still works. No matter how much chemistry has changed, it still works. The rules are still functional. They haven't had to change the system. I cannot think of any other indexing system where that is true and I have looked. I have tried to find one that hasn't gone through changes. The Library of Congress changes theirs all of the time, Dewey's changing all the time. With the whole computing explosion, there's not an index done in the 1960s that's useful now in anything other than the broadest sense. So the whole idea of having to index something and make it last a long time has always fascinated me. It was the thing I liked most in library school. Oh, what a cool puzzle! I have a pretty high frustration tolerance so I perceive a lot of the problems as challenges, not frustrations. "Oh, you don't want to show it to me? I'll make you show it to me!"

Woman against machine?

That's right. I know it's in that computer somewhere and I'm going to find it. You can't hide these things from me. I feel like the armchair detective taken to the nth degree.

SUPER SEARCH SECRETS

On the reference interview…

I also ask, "Do you expect to find information on your topic?"…sometimes I'll search six ways from Sunday and not find anything. Then I call them and say, "I did this and this and then I called so-and-so, and then I did this and this and this and I still didn't find anything." And their response is "Good." Oh, I could kill them!

On using databases as indexes to print sources…

…we're using databases as direct indexes to the print volumes. For a few dollars, we can get articles very specific to the search term, even when the narrowest term used in the print index is still quite broad. Of course, some of the publishers have changed their numbering systems, so it's a bit more difficult, but we try to use tricks like that whenever the situation seems to demand it.

On using EXPAND on STN...

STN now lets you do an EXPAND CONTINUOUS, so you're not limited to 50 terms in an EXPAND command. That can be a lifesaver. It means you can expand on Smith and then expand on Jones, and instead of starting all over at one, the list is consecutive, and you can go back to the earlier part.

On chemical structure searching...

In a structure search, what I'm doing is drawing a picture of the structure with keyboard commands....It's kind of a programming language, really. It's a different sort of command language and a different way of searching....There are all kinds of weird rules that you have to learn...

On the relationship between clients and professionals...

I am the search specialist; you are the content specialist. They're supposed to know their field; I'm supposed to know how to get things out of the database.

On the search request form...

...it forces me to write down all of the boring, routine things that I don't really want to think about...the things that you need to know to do the search properly. They aren't the fun, intellectual-content part.

On help desk personnel...

One thing I can say, especially for DIALOG and STN, is that people at the help desk are so helpful....Instead of putting up barriers, they say, "You really should be talking to so-and-so." They go out of their way to put me in touch with the right person.

On delivering search results...

...use FTP to move it to the requester's account. It works like the DOS COPY command...It saves a lot of time at my end, because I can shift these sometimes humongous files as a packet instead of having to read them in. More than half my search results go out by FTP. We don't print much out anymore.

On choosing which system to search...

...compare the connect and display charges for the same file on different online systems. I'm thinking of one in particular that's incredibly cheap to search on STN but incredibly expensive to display the records. On DIALOG, the same file is incredibly expensive to search but incredibly cheap to display a full record. DIALOG charges more than four times as much per hour, and depending on what segments you choose, STN typically costs twice as much to display. Naturally, I search it on STN and display it on DIALOG.

INDEX TO THE SUPER SEARCHERS:
THEIR SPECIALITIES AND THEIR WORK
ENVIRONMENTS

This brief listing is to enable readers to quickly find super searchers who search in subject areas and environments similar to their own. Many expert searchers search very broadly and defy easy categorization, so the groupings here are purely arbitrary. Others, especially searchers who are also entrepreneurs, are often information consultants as well as hands-on searchers.

Academic
Terry Hanson
Ruth Pagell
Nora Paul
Sherry Willhite

Business
Carol Ginsburg
Anne Mintz
Marydee Ojala
Ruth Pagell

Chemical
Nancy Lambert
Wendy Warr
Sherry Willhite

Corporate
Carol Ginsburg
Nancy Lambert
Anne Mintz
Wendy Warr

End-Users
Roger Karraker
Tom Koch

**Generalist
(Everything But...)**
Susanne Bjørner

Steve Coffman
Lucinda Conger
Linda Cooper
Anne Mintz
Barbara Quint
Ellen Reinheimer

Government
Lucinda Conger
Robert F. Jack

**Independent
Professionals**
Susanne Bjørner
Karen Blakeman
Linda Cooper
Marydee Ojala
Barbara Quint
Ellen Reinheimer

**Journalism/News
Research**
Roger Karraker
Tom Koch
Nora Paul

Legal
Nancy Lambert
N.J. Thompson

Medical
Tom Koch
Bonnie Snow
Ann Van Camp

Patent
Nancy Lambert
N.J. Thompson

Pharmaceutical
Karen Blakeman
Bonnie Snow
Ann Van Camp
Wendy Warr

Public
Steve Coffman

School
Lee Sapienza

Sci/Tech
Susanne Bjørner
Robert F. Jack

Social Sciences
Lucinda Conger
Terry Hanson
Anne Mintz